The Lemon Popsicle Book

by Roy Mitchell and Paul Sutton

Acknowledgements: We would like to thank the many contributors to the films, the fanzine and the book, particularly the members of the cast and crew who took time out to talk with us. The interviews were originally published in *Popsicle Fanzine*. The illustrations and promotional material featured in the book are from our personal collections and used in the spirit of education, celebration and preservation. A special thank you to Sara Rosenquist for doing the Japanese into English translations, and to the films' stills photographers whose work made assembling this book such a joy. Yoni Hamenachem was the stills photographer for the first four *Lemon Popsicle* films and *Summertime Blues*. *Baby Love*'s stills photographer was Amram Galmi. *The Last American Virgin* stills photographer was Tami Peri-Porath.

Contents

Lemon Popsicle, 8

Going Steady, 52

Hot Bubblegum, 80

Private Popsicle, 98

Baby Love, 126

Up Your Anchor, 156

Young Love, 168

Summertime Blues, 182

The Last American Virgin, 192

The Party Goes On, 218

Introduction, 6
Private Manoeuvres, 118
Popcorn und Himbeereis, 123
The Adventures of Guru Jakob, 124
The Ambassador, 125
British Reviewers, 222
A (mostly) German Scrapbook, 226

Home Movie Releases:
Super 8mm, 270
VHS, 271
TV, 276
DVD, 278
Blu-ray, 282

Introduction by Roy Mitchell

Eskimo Limon, Eis Am Stiel, Lemon Popsicle. Whatever name you remember it by, the film spawned seven sequels plus a spin-off film, *Private Manoeuvres*; an American remake, *The Last American Virgin*; and a reboot, *The Party Goes On.* The producers Yoram Globus and Menahem Golan filmed Hebrew and English versions of the first two films but, from *Hot Bubblegum* onwards, the series became a joint German/Israeli venture. Sam Waynberg, the German distributor, joined the producing team and brought in German and Austrian casts and crew members to ensure the series's continuing success across Europe. To this day the films are still shown on German TV.

The films first came to my attention when I rented *Lemon Popsicle* from one of the many local video shops which sprang up in the early 1980's. I enjoyed it so much that I went back looking for more. I wasn't disappointed because the sequel, *Going Steady*, was staring at me on the shelf when I went back! Due to the sudden explosion of the home video market, *Hot Bubblegum* was also available. With *Private Popsicle* and *Baby Love* following soon after, I lapped it all up and came back hungry for more.

The *Lemon Popsicle* films were without doubt sexist, crude and smutty. It's hard to imagine such films achieving success in the current climate of political correctness. But if you don't take them too seriously you won't get offended and you will find plenty to enjoy. The films are wonderfully funny and richly entertaining. They are so special because they remind us of our youth, either what we used to get up to or what we would have liked to get up to. They tell of three 17-year-old boys growing up in Tel Aviv in the 1950's. Bobby (Jonathan Sagall) is the good looking guy who has girls falling at his feet. Benji (Yftach Katzur) is the shy, sensitive one who is always falling in love. While Huey (Zachi Noy) is the fat guy who always seems to get the worst of things!

The guys hang out at the Montana, the local ice cream parlour, and their main aim is to get laid by as many girls as possible. The easier the, girls the better. "Is it for sure?" is one of Huey's most common questions to the other two. Whenever the guys are onto a sure thing they always share it with each other. As the good looking one, Bobby would always be first to bed the girl, while Benji and Huey would wait outside for their turn. Of course they would always watch through the keyhole and, for some inexplicable reason, would strip down to their underwear whilst waiting! Huey would then usually get tricked into going second and get caught with his pants down by the girl's boyfriend! He would then get chased out of the house in his underwear! Alongside this, you get Benji falling in love the first time he claps eyes on a good-looking girl. And you get Benji's Mum (Dvora Kedar) and Dad (Menashe Warshavsky) trying to give the boy some guidance but failing honourably. Some of the best *Lemon Popsicle* moments are spent in Benji's house with his Mum nagging him and his Dad simply shrugging as if to say, "Don't take any notice of her."

The *Lemon Popsicle* films are a wonderful mixture of fun, friendship and sexual adventure, with a fabulous fifties soundtrack. The first thing that hits you about the films is the music. The right song always seems to play at the right time and compliment the film perfectly. Among the many highlights are Curtis Lee's *Pretty Little Angel Eyes* playing in *Baby Love* when the guys are having some fun at the pool. The Popsicle's *I Want My Mama* used in *Private Popsicle* when Bobby, Benji and Huey dress up as girl singers to escape Sergeant Ramirez. Choreographed by Julie Arkin, Huey dancing out of synch to The Champs *Tequila* in *Going Steady* is one of the funniest moments in the entire series.

The films certainly do give you that 'feel-good' factor, there are moments when you just can't help tapping your feet along, but they also deal with serious issues such as abortion, prostitution, deceit and loneliness. Who can forget the perfect use of Paul Anka's *Put Your Head On My Shoulder* in the first *Lemon Popsicle* film, when Benji turns up at a party, hoping to get together with Nikki, but finds out that Bobby has already made his move? Or the closing scene of the film, Benji double-crossed by his friend and the girl he thought was his girlfriend? There, Bobby Vinton's *Mr. Lonely* signals one of the most heart-wrenching moments in the entire series. Then there's the ultimate sad moment in *Going Steady* when Santo and Johnny's *Sleepwalk* is the backdrop to Huey learning that Benji has slept with his girlfriend.

All the things mentioned so far are the formula that goes in to making the *Lemon Popsicle* films so enjoyable. *Lemon Popsicle, Going Steady, Hot Bubblegum, Baby Love* (arguably best film in the *Popsicle* series) followed this formula and, in my opinion, are head and shoulders above the rest. *Private Popsicle* doesn't veer too far from the formula and is very watchable, certainly an enjoyable film, though the jokes are often too corny for my taste. *Up Your Anchor*, the first of the films not written by Boaz Davidson, the writer-director was Dan Wolman, follows the pattern of previous *Lemon Popsicle* films when the guys are on dry land but, once on board the cruise ship Orion, it loses some of the magic and gets a bit silly. *Young Love* seems to have been aimed at the American market, due to the involvement of Warner Brothers. It is a strange film, not at all in the established *Popsicle* style, with the endearing streets and houses of Tel Aviv swapped for a plush hotel. Benji became 'Benny' in the English version and sported an eighties Chris Waddle hair style, and his parents don't appear in the film. Benji's dear old Mum does return in *Summertime Blues*, where the guys are joined by Benji's pre-teen cousin, an annoying brat. But the film gets more serious and the guys finally come of age. Huey doesn't even get caught in his underwear once! It's the end of the road for those Popsicle guys.

The Last American Virgin is an updated and Americanised remake of *Lemon Popsicle* with a little *Hot Bubblegum* thrown in for good measure. The critics of the time incorrectly accused it of being a *Porky's* rip-off but, with recent endorsements by cult filmmakers such as Eli Roth, and an international release on Blu-Ray, its popularity continues to rise.

The Party Goes On is basically a compilation of all the best bits from the previous films, a sort of tribute which sees the guys up to their old tricks again. In a stroke of genius, the legendary Zachi Noy plays the owner of the Montana, the guys' favourite hangout.

Years later, when the popsicles had melted and faded to a distant memory, my interest was re-awakened when Bravo TV aired *Lemon Popsicle* for the first and sadly the last time on British TV. Just like when I watched it for the first time back in the 80's, it gave me a thirst for more! So I went on a quest to track down all of the films on VHS, which wasn't easy back in the year 2000 when the internet was only a pale shadow of its present form. But I tracked them down and I watched them all – again and again! I enjoyed them so much that I wanted to find out more about the films, the music and the actors. Luckily, Lindsay Holmes' wonderful *Lemon Popsicle Forever* website was out there to quench my thirst, but I still wanted to find out more and also pay my own tribute to the films I loved. So, *Popsicle Fanzine* was born. The first issue was released in May 2002. The fanzine has been going for almost 15 years now and has given me the opportunity to contact many of the actors from the films, most of whom have been really helpful and supportive over the years, giving me lots of wonderful memories. So when the historian, publisher, and fellow *Lemon Popsicle* enthusiast, Paul Sutton contacted me about putting together a *Lemon Popsicle* book, I jumped at the chance. Having seen the book he'd written on Ken Russell, I knew by the high standard of his work, that the Popsicle book was going to be special. The material gathered for *Popsicle Fanzine* over the years, together with Paul's writing, expertise, enthusiasm and sheer tenacity have all gone in to making this unique tribute to our favourite films.

Lemon Popsicle

Eskimo Limon

Eis am Stiel

1977

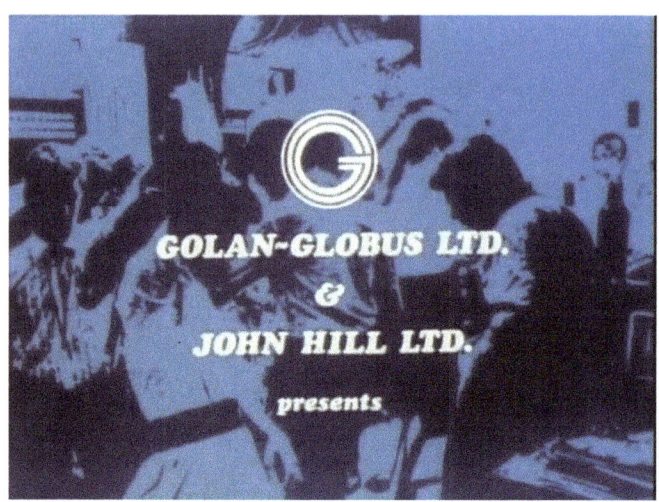

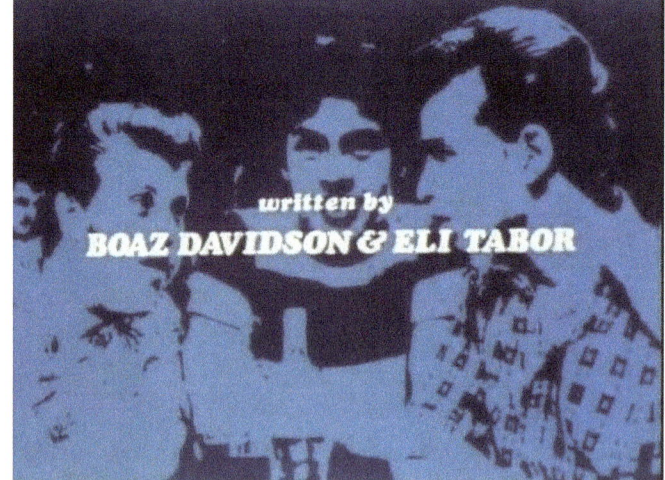

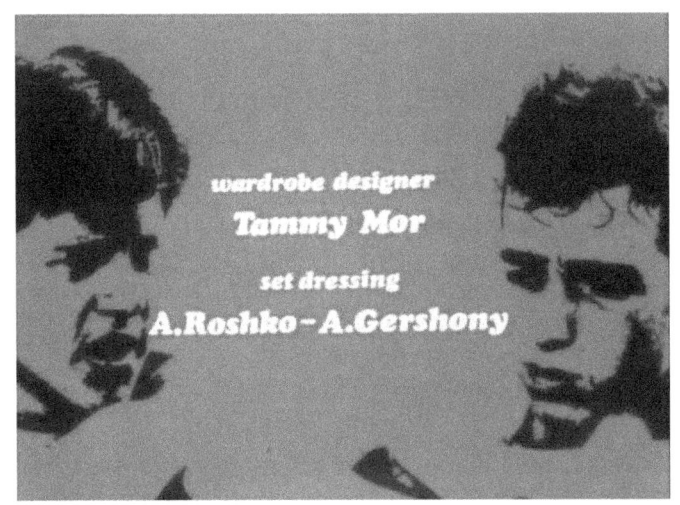

Lemon Popsicle, an appreciation

by Paul Sutton

It starts with a song, not just any old song, or a song-that-will-do, it starts with the perfect song for the film: a song of beauty, of bittersweet memories, lost love and pain - the themes of the film. The song is *Greenfields* by Seattle's The Brothers Four, trimmed to include only the first and last verses:

"Once there were green fields kissed by the sun
Once there were valleys where rivers used to run
Once there were blue skies with white clouds
 high above
Once they were part of an everlasting love
We were the lovers who strolled through
 green fields

But I'll keep on waiting until you return
I'll keep on waiting until the day you learn
You can't be happy while your heart's on the roam
You can't be happy until you bring it home
Home to the green fields and me once again."

Greenfields is scored for two acoustic guitars and a bass guitar and is sung by a close harmony of four male voices. This echoes the film about a young man's wounding fall into rejection in the company of a comedy of two close male friends.

As the guitars fades, the Rock and Roll soundtrack starts with Little Richard singing of *Long Tall Sally* "having some fun" lighting up the mood and the night. It is a black dark night and teenagers are arriving, by polished car and motorbike and on foot, at the red-and-white-neon-light young folks paradise of the Montana ice cream bar. From this 'Paradise' the film will fall to a sort-of teenage Hell. The name Montana is perfectly chosen (perfect is a word I use a lot when talking about this film) not simply because it represents 'America', this is an American-style ice cream parlour playing American pop music, but because the name bridges to the credit song and underlines the film's theme. Montana is a wilderness, traditionally a cowboy place of solo pursuits. The hero walking into an American-style parlour is the teenage equivalent of a gunslinger striding into a saloon bar. Cineaste's remember that The Brothers Four sang the Oscar-nominated song, *The Green Leaves of Summer,* on the soundtrack of John Wayne's film of *The Alamo*, a film about a close community of men standing tall against The World (in the form of the Mexican army) and failing. John Wayne himself will appear in *Lemon Popsicle*, in newsreel presenting an Academy Award. The subtext of the film is that we are going to journey into the wilderness of adolescence, a time when, by virtue of our age, we were necessarily gregarious (we had school to go to) but inwardly, we were often all alone. This set-up is telling us that there will be fun and adventure, with friends to stand by us, but that we will fail in the end because life isn't a Hollywood movie. Life can be cruel. Failure is a part of growing up. *Growing Up* was the Japanese title for the film, a better and more apt title that gave a context for the characters' lewd behaviour and social failings.

With Little Richard continuing to sing, and with the camera picking through the crowd of young dancers, Davidson focuses our attention on the iconography - a juke box, pinball table, slicked hair and active comb, and on a thematically important curiosity, a seaside peepshow viewer. There are peepshow set-pieces in all ten Popislce films. For all their modernity of tone and content and theme, the *Lemon Popsicle* films increasingly became a return to cinema's origins as a carnival sideshow attraction, 'Roll up, roll up and see...'.

And in comes the star of the film, Yftach Katzur as Benji. He is photographed on a long lens from inside the parlour, the camera following him, in an unbroken shot, as he walks in, looks around and sits down at a table where his two best friends, Bobby and Huey, are heartily eating ice-cream. After some chit-chat about an exam in the morning, and a loan of half a dollar ("I'll give it you back, I'm working on the ice truck tomorrow"), in walks beauty like the night, in the form of Anat

Atzmon as Nikki, and Benji is smitten. On cue, the music changes to Del Shannon's *Runaway* (*Hey Baby!* by Bruce Channel plays in the international version). Benji walks over to her and looks at her. She looks back at him. Neither of them speak. There is only music. We are four minutes into the film and three very different pre-recorded songs have played, each perfect for the scene. Davidson finds the right song the whole film through because he understands that the music is not merely the soundtrack to the film, it's the soundtrack to the teenage landscape and the teenage mindset. The music speaks the words and thoughts that the young people can't articulate. These simple songs of love and loss and fun and pain, feed the common and personal feelings of the film's central characters, whilst acting as Pavlovian musical nostalgia for listeners whose own teenage years passed through these same Rock and Roll years.

Back at their table, Benji's friends have spied two girls they claim are ripe for having some rude fun with. Only the sex-desperate can't see that the lank-haired sour-faced girls are the least 'fun' people in the room. The boys' adolescent sex-sap has risen to cloud their judgement. The girls are attractive to them because they have a reputation of being 'easy', i.e. they have a bad reputation. This measure of attractiveness runs counter to sensible adult values and is a reason for the film's popularity with teenagers. Its sense of reality conforms more closely to the real-life morality of teenagers than any film made before it.

Running with the theme of the naturally warped values of teenagers, the 'fun' with the two girls begins with two of the male friends mistreating the third, Huey, who brokered the arrangement. Huey is sent away to put some money in the juke box ("Put it on my bill" says Bobby). Bobby and Benji make off with the girls. Friends misusing friends is rare in films and used mostly as a plot point or crisis point. Here its use is less melodramatic, a simple comedy in the chase for pleasure that is shrugged off by Huey with a look of disappointment and a throwaway line about the boys being "a couple of bastards". This lack of confrontation and the absence of whining, tell-tailing, counselling and tears serves, paradoxically, to emphasize the closeness of the ties that bind the boys. Theirs is not a friendship that is walked on eggshells. Their friendship is stronger than this. As we will see, the boys' friendship is stronger, in fact, than abject betrayal and villainy. This introductory scene is interesting too for the pointers it gives to the appeal of Zachi Noy's character, Huey. Huey is the most materialistic of the trio, with his pocketbook of pencilled loans and accounts and his confident colourful clothes. He suffers his share of disappointments at the hands of his friends, but he's supportive and forgiving, and he has the best way with words. He's also the best actor. Bobby and Benji take the girls to a cinema. Again the relationship between the boys is one of trap and trick. Bobby claims that Benji's father owns the cinema and he sends Benji away to somehow get free tickets. Thinking on his feet, though the implication is that he has done this kind of thing before, Benji climbs in through the cinema's toilet window and he opens the back door. Inside the cinema, the newsreel shows John Wayne presenting Joanne Woodward with the Oscar for *The Three Faces of Eve*, thus setting the film story to March 29th, 1958. It's a clever choice of clip by Davidson. *The Three Faces of Eve* is a fictionalised true story about a woman with three different personalities. This theme is perhaps echoed in Boaz's hopes for the Nikki character. She starts off as the picture of fresh sweet girlhood, but her actions pull the film's finale down to almost Ancient Grecian depths (the end of the world as seen through the eyes of Benji) as she rejects the 'good' and returns to the 'bad', in mirror of what the boys were doing in their introductory scene. We wince in horror at the girl's actions, and watch as our hero walks weeping through lonely streets but we, as adult viewers, understand that the girl's actions have perhaps been misinterpreted by the wounded boy. Theirs was not an equal love.

Lemon Popsicle is not a love story. In the film, a

boy mistakes his infatuation for love and gets hurt when reality bites. Needless to say, though I'll say it all the same, this complexity of character, theme and subtext is rare in films too readily pigeon-holed as teenage sex comedies.

The cinema is showing a Lemmy Caution crime film, which we and the heroes don't get to see (would I be reading too much into a throwaway reference on a bit of set-dressing by saying that this failure to proceed with 'Caution' is a very subtle pointer to the hero's fall?). Inside the cinema, the sour-faced girl's rapid-fire feeding and spitting of peanuts and peanut skins is overdone. It is unrealistic, a low failure of the kind that will increase in proportion to the number of Popsicle sequels. The ticketless quartet are bumped from their seats twice by the usherette and Bobby and Benji are thrown out, turning out their empty pockets in a foyer dressed with a James Dean poster and lobby cards for *Rebel Without a Cause*. The same poster features prominently in the set-dressing of a curling Tel Aviv street, all part of the realistic media landscape that feeds the dreams of adolescents, down which a drunken Benji will stagger propped up on the broad shoulders of a dependable friend, Huey. Benji gets drunk because he is too immature to use alcohol socially. His is the Age of Misinterpretation. "I usually drink three bottles every Friday," is his pitiful and naturally unsuccessful chat-up line at a party, where he sees that his 'true love' has taken up with his best friend. He thinks that the boast makes him sound like a man. To the girl, it confirms to her that he still a boy and it tells her that she has made the right choice in rejecting him as a suitor (with or more likely without the pull of sexual attraction).

And so to sunlight and to school. To the sounds of John Morris singing *Witch Doctor* ("I told the Witch Doctor I was in love with you. And then the Witch Doctor, he told me what to do. He said: "Ooo eee, ooo ah ah, ting tang walla walla bing bang"), fat Huey fails to leap a small pommel horse, shuffling off it without any cat-calling from the class (allowing us to groan at the cleverly comic pre-racist lyric and at the too easy fat joke, the class reaction to which serves to show us that Huey is not a figure of fun, he's respected among his peers). In the changing room, a confident bespectacled boy, 'Froggy', played by Avi Hadash who became a popular featured actor in the series, moves an idealised painting of a school sports day aside to reveal a hole in the wall through which he can watch the girls stripping to their underwear. This leads to the famous comic scene of the boys proudly bulging in their tighty whities in a locker room measure-up contest that's sufficiently original, rude and audacious to get the audience laughing without it being uncomfortably explicit. The audience are given their reaction cue by the way Davidson plays the film off Katzur's expressive face, which is sensible and amused. It's a triumph of staging that the whole scene is free from expressions of prurience, disgust or shame that would have robbed the viewer of its fun.

Helped by Huey's confidence and ready notebook, and by his own low teenage morality that allows him to put others at a disadvantage to further his own interests, Benji intercepts Nikki's bicycle ride to school by deflating the tyre on her own bicycle and giving her a lift on the crossbar of his. This forced meeting is an adolescent jape, but it's one in series of japes that have accumulated to such a degree that they have become a way of life, each a tip-toe to a future tipping point and the inevitable fall. Crushingly, the fall comes at the point when circumstances have prompted Benji's maturity to take an important step forward. In taking that necessary stride towards manhood (arranging and paying for the Nikki's abortion), he puts himself out of kilter with his peers. Bobby and Nikki continue to behave like the kids that they are, and we observe that their attraction came naturally and was equally weighted.

In Germany, the film was rated '16' and given the perfect tag-line, 'Where do you go when the party is over?'. It sold almost three million tickets. In Britain, the film had its biggest impact on video in 1980, helping to usher in The Golden Age of film exhibition there, a brief age that lasted about three years.

For the first time in history, the British public had access to the full riches of world cinema and were allowed to see whatever they wanted to see. Films released on video were not subject to state censorship, nor to the whims and the restricted taste of the six or seven people who imported and exhibited 35mm film in Britain, nor to the American corporations who controlled whole areas of mainstream distribution, particularly advertising and the British press (in 1958, Lindsay Anderson was famously sacked as the film critic of *The New Statesman* for devoting more of his column to Andrej Wajda's *Kanal* than to *The Bridge on the River Kwai*). The video boom allowed anyone to import videos and rent them through pop-up shops and the local corner store. Films that played for one day only at the London Film Festival, now had a shelf run of years at the corner shop of many a Northern, Southern, Eastern and Western town. Video rental stores were legally allowed to show pornography, Italian horror films, Chinese kung fu films, independent French, Greek, Israeli and American films, and German westerns. This liberation removed film exhibition from the snippity hands of the censors and the corporations and gave it instead to people more qualified to decide what they should be allowed to see - the people themselves.

The censors had banned cinema screenings of *Lemon Popsicle* to the under eighteens, but parents and youth workers, now with the full glories of cinema to play with, and who for the first time could readily see the films of the *Deep Throat* genre, knew that *Lemon Popsicle* was perfect viewing for curious children. I saw it for the first time at the Grange Road Youth Club in Haydock, Merseyside, when I was thirteen or fourteen years old. For me, an unsophisticated but intellectually curious pubertal boy, that was absolutely the right age to see it. I had just been knocked upwards by a television screening of Truffaut's *Les Quatre Cents Coup*. Truffaut's film had brought to me the exploding and comforting thought that it was the normal lot of adolescent boys to be unloved and misunderstood, and it brought the important-to-me knowledge that there was more to cinema than Disney films and *Star Wars*. Up until then my thoughts and tastes had been shaped by a corporate media that was both prurient and puritan and by a Protestant upbringing that insisted that sex was obscene and that the repression of sex and sexual images was 'moral'. *Lemon Popsicle* thrilled me and frightened me and moved me. It confirmed to me what I already knew - that sex could be fun - if I could persuade my friends to shake off the puritan shackles that stunted us. The film taught me that sex brought with it responsibilities, the essential building block of adulthood; that rejection hurt badly; that one could grow from the hurt by doing the right thing (perhaps there was something to be said for those do-good puritans after all?) and that life wasn't fair. The good guys don't always win at the end. It also taught me that life is always worth living if you've got one or two friends.

Until the age of broadband, mine was the last adolescence in Britain to enjoy world film freedoms. Stung by their loss of power, the censors and their supporters, a low-class of people who spent their Sundays giggling and tutting into salacious newspapers packed with exposes of errant vicars, pop star groupies and kiss-and-tell whores, a diabolical alliance formed with the American media corporations, who were furious that the British public were ignoring their mass advertised product whilst preferring to watch the films of Golan and Globus. Carried in like plague fleas buried into the backs of rats, and under the guise of a crackdown on so-called Video Nasties, the British establishment stamped in new and all-consuming censorship powers whilst stamping out all but all independent film distribution. In a very few years indeed, film distribution in Britain was almost entirely restricted to mass marketed product from American corporations. Thrillingly, Golan and Globus did the only thing they could do to compete - they rolled up their sleeves and took on the Hollywood majors by becoming an independent Hollywood major! financed in part by a good run of *Lemon Popsicle* films.

Aspects of the *Lemon Popsicle* Film Style

The style of the film is drawn from the subject. The subject is three boys. Thus Boaz Davidson and his cinematographer use a lot of three element compositions:

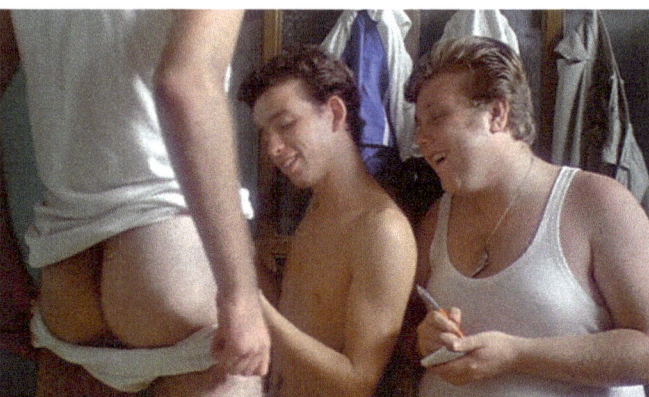

There are ultra close-ups of faces, here to show youthful pleasure and pain. It's possible that this rare style developed as a practical solution to a production problem, i.e. having to film in an enclosed space with coloured lights. The coloured lights provide a party atmosphere but don't give off enough light to provide much depth of focus. Davidson's solution is make the reduced focus an asset by opening the aperture as wide as possible and giving us a photography masterclass that doubles as a study in contrasting emotion.

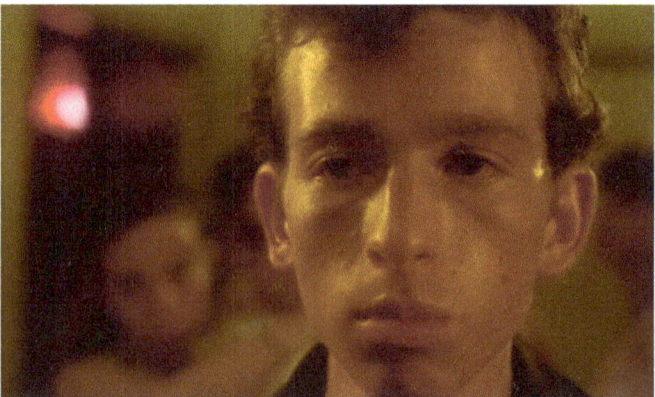

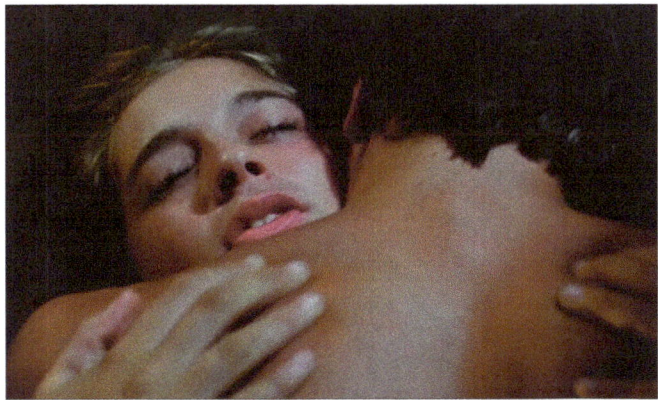 

A close-up that tells of pleasure A close-up that shows loss and shame and emptiness

The two techniques of tri-element composition and ultra close-up combine magnificently in the scene with the prostitute. The scene starts in close-up on Denise Bouzaglo's tough mature face. Hers is not the fresh face of a wounded innocent. The blown smoke almost suggests a dragon. The camera pans to the right and pulls focus to the three boys stepping forward and standing still.

The framing of the boys, distant, low in the frame, and off to the side, emphasizes their fear and uncertainty as does the deliciously full-black backdrop (it's no accident that Segall is wearing a black shirt. The composition wouldn't be as effective if he was wearing a different colour). The panning and focus-pulling are hallmarks of Davidson's film style. They add a fluidity and naturalness that would be reduced if the transition from the woman to the boys had been done using separate set-ups and editing.

There are low-angle shots, high-angle shots, shots taken from waist height and from shoulder height, all to give the film an impressive visual variety and to direct our way of seeing. To reduce the need for dialogue, and with the pop soundtrack giving voice to the characters' thoughts and emotions, Davidson uses the Chaplin/ Chuck Jones approach of using actors faces to tell us what we need to know.

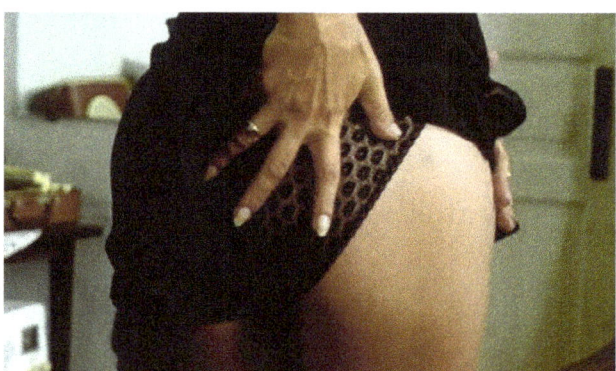

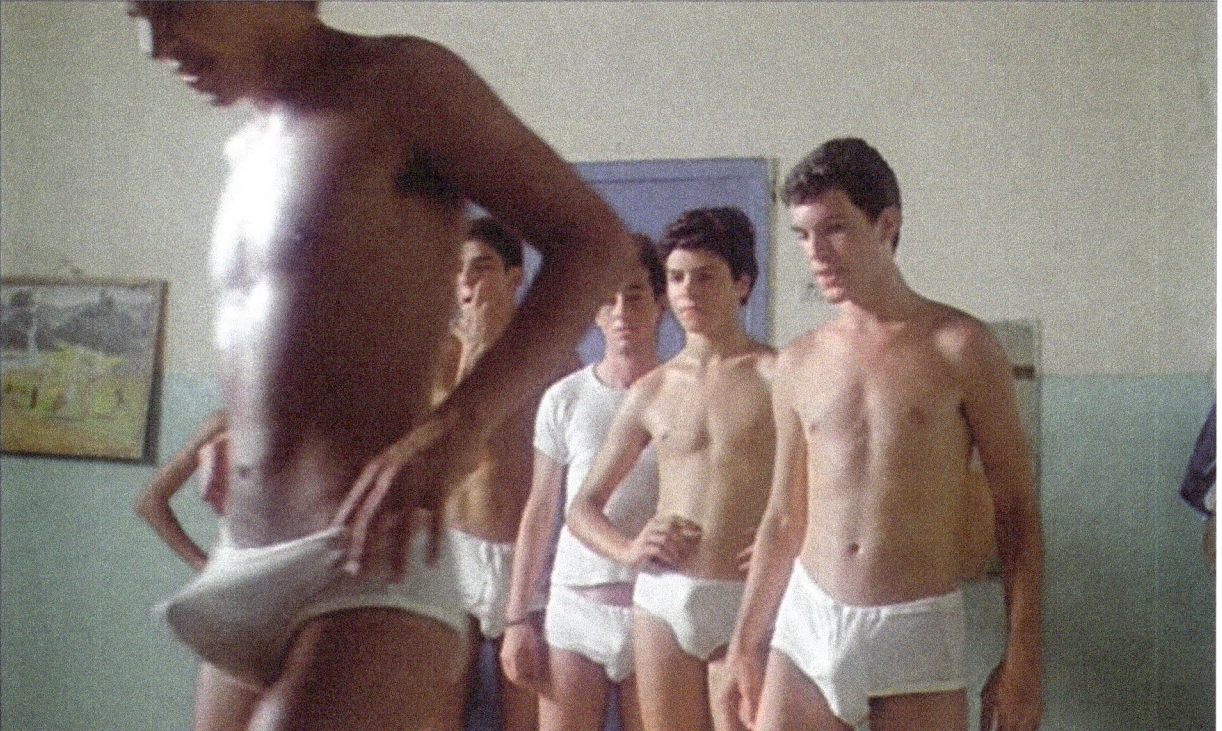

Above - Soft naturalistic lighting and faces full of laughter combine to remove the sleaze and push back the censorship barrier.

Left - Benji in the foreground, Bobby in the middle ground, Huey in the background. A stunning three-dimesional composition that crosses at the focal point, Ophelia Shtruhl as 'Stella', the nymphomaniac with a sideline in algebra and a name to catch Brando.

The set dressing adds layers to the narrative and to the characters. Thus the picture which covers the viewing hole to the girls' changing room is an idealised painting of school sports; the walls of Benji's room are decorated with magazine pages like the rooms of the students in Lindsay Anderson's *if....* (1968). Posters of Elvis, James Dean and Eddie Constantine add period colour and allusion.

It's a film about the long escape from childhood told for the most part through the face of a boy.

Boaz Davidson - writer, director

It wasn't my first film. I had made other films but I needed to make this one for myself. It's all based on my life. I felt this part of my life was still open and decided to go back and touch on those painful moments. I am the main guy, Benji! The real names of Bobby and Huey are Ariel and Arik. The girl in the film, Nikki, her name was Yael and she is now a casting director. I invited her to watch the first cut and she was very moved and so was I. It is unique to see part of your past in the present. About 99% of it really happened. Other people like to believe it was based on them but it wasn't. And the scenes in the film were shot at the same places where they happened to me! The title *Lemon Popsicle* came from the Tel Aviv beach in the Fifties and Sixties where sweaty ice-cream vendors used to carry their ice boxes and scream, "Eskimo Limon! Eskimo Limon!" The music is what I grew up listening to. But to get the music rights was very tough. We had to get originals from many record companies and artists. When we shot the party scene and we put on Paul Anka, or whoever, the whole crew got in to it and had a few tears in their eyes. I wrote the first five *Lemon Popsicle* films. It is unique for a film-maker to shoot scenes from his youth, but after a while I felt I was starting to repeat myself, in a way a bit like a TV series does. After the first few movies I started to invent stuff that didn't happen to me.

The stars with Globus and Davidson at the Berlin Film Festival in February 1978. Patricia Highsmith headed the Jury, which included Sergio Leone, Theodoros Angelopoulos and Larisa Shepitko.

Menahem Golan - producer

"All those movies, especially the first two, were a wild success. The whole country saw the movie. We made seven parts. It had a very erotic romantic atmosphere, and the music softened it. When you entered the movie theatre and saw a scene with bicycles riding to school together etc. you identified with that. You said to yourself, "Yes, that's exactly what I did. That's exactly the way I was." We apparently have a kind of uniqueness in our possibility to bring the way of life/local colour/atmosphere to the movies in a way that's similar to European countries. In Eastern Europe, youths grow up influenced by American culture. In Israel, around 1,300,000 people paid to see the film and then, in the whole world, in Germany ten million and in Japan ten million. At first, the Japanese went in and didn't even smile but we told them, "Look, show it to your children, show it to your youth." The Germans were convinced right away. We took the actors on a tour in Japan and in Germany. They couldn't cross the street. They were the neighbourhood heroes. We arrived in this way to some kind of openness in the international market, and we became international producers."
Speaking on the Israeli DVD of *Lemon Popsicle*. Translated by Susan Hadash

Menahem Golan and Yoram Globus

Peter James, theatre director

Yftach was chosen from an open audition process. As I remember there were about thirty applicants, all in their mid-teens and none with previous professional acting experience. Any risk was considerably reduced by the man playing the psychiatrist, known in the company as 'Hiski, the Older' (there were two actors of that name in the company). He was a very generous partner and looked after the young man throughout the run. I think Yftach quickly realised that this was a huge apprenticeship opportunity. The play was a great success, fuelled by the publicity which surrounded the nudity (which was new to such an official theatre as the Cameri), and by the choice of Yftach. He had big hair with blond highlights and looked like a Raphael angel.

Re. the nudity, I recall the rehearsal during which we confronted the problem. It began with me getting undressed, followed by the two young people, while our female ASM turned her face to the wall! Hard, at this distance, to remember what a big deal it was.

Yftach was naturally gifted, possessed the fearlessness of youth – and the good sense to be guided by Hiski. It was always going to be challenging for him to be without such guidance. What I saw of the films indicated he was staying in his comfort zone much of the time.

Yftach Katzur

My acting career started a year before *Lemon Popsicle* in 1975 at the age of seventeen, when I was discovered in Peter Shaffer's play, *Equus*, where I was playing the lead part of Alan Strang. This famous English stage play, there is also a movie starring Richard Burton, was directed in Israel at Hkameri theater by an English director, Peter James. He is the one who gave me my first acting chance. No-one expected and did not imagine that there was going be a crazy success the size of *Lemon Popsicle*. From *Lemon Popsicle* I have many good memories and I am very happy and grateful for that opportunity I had in my life to make so many people happy for so many years.

It was the first time that an Israeli film touched on global nostalgia. Not our local nostalgia, as shown in the army film, *He Walked in the Fields (Hu Halach B'Sadot, 1967)*, but really global nostalgia. Songs by Paul Anka and songs by Elvis. Suddenly we connected, by means of that film, to the world. You know that it was somehow an autobiographical story, but really it is more in the direction of the story of the unrequited love, of a broken heart. The fact is that that connection between the trio and the love story and all that speaks to every culture. It speaks to the Japanese culture and it speaks to the German culture; it speaks to all of Europe, Western and Eastern Europe, etc. So, beyond the autobiographical story, and who we are and what we are personally, what that film represents, what those characters represent, in some way touches something global, something human.

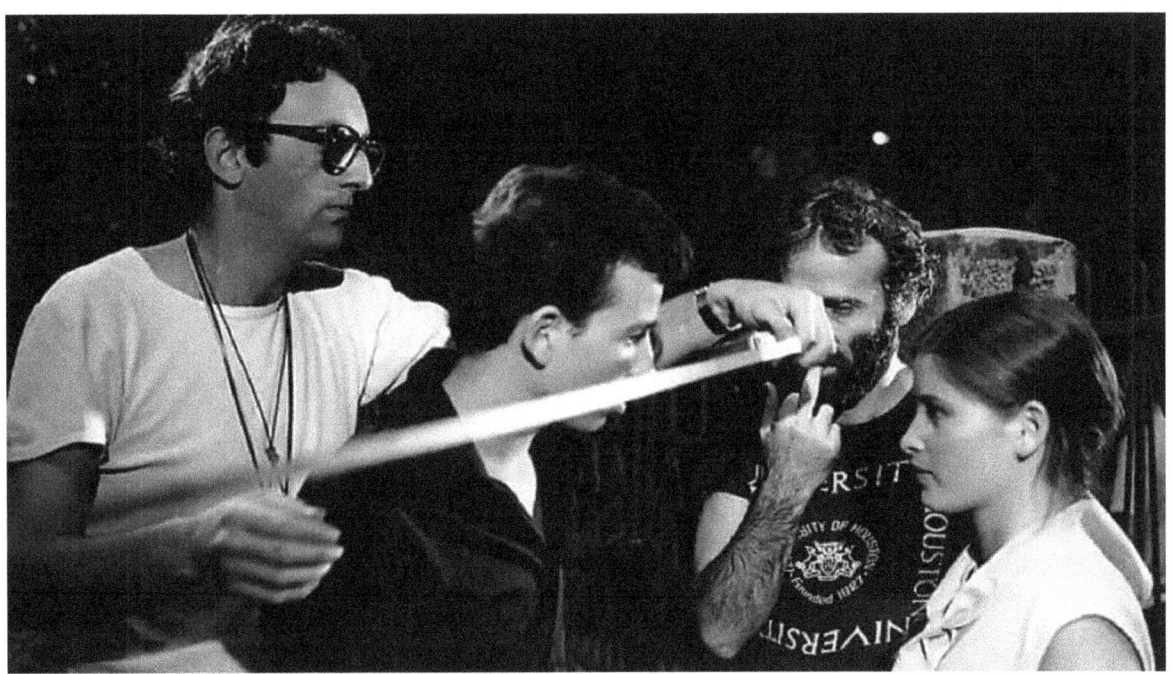

Stills photographer, Yoni Hamenachem sets up a photograph of Yftach Katzur

Zachi Noy

I started as a child actor when I was eleven. My first film role was in a film, *Ha Gan* (*The Garden*, 1975) starring Melanie Griffiths. The director and producers saw me in that and gave me the part in *Lemon Popsicle* without a screen test. Making *Lemon Popsicle* was very hard for me. It was a nightmare for me and I didn't enjoy myself at all. I think that the dosage of my butt in the film was exaggerated and they should have shown my face instead of my butt all the time! I was surprised about the success of the film in Japan.

Alain Jacubowizc, editor

I'm French originally and I moved from France to Israel as an assistant editor. Boaz had a commission to make documentary film about jazz group and we hooked up together just to do that movie, a very small movie. And then he went to do bigger things and I went with him.

We basically both hit the jackpot. I mean, we basically both did all the biggest Israeli hits. He was directing. I was editing. It was probably the best time of my life! I mean, we had so much fun doing the *Lemon Popsicle* movies. I knew then we had something special but I could never imagine that, basically, that's the movie which brought us to Hollywood! I could never project what will happen with that movie and that it would be number one in so many countries around the world.

I can tell you a little story about it. At the beginning, the producers, Yoram Globus and Menahem Golan, really didn't believe in the movie and, during the shoot, they came in to see a few scenes which I'd put together, because they were about to pull the plug on the movie! And I showed them a couple of scenes, then they decided to go on with the movie. So, you never know. You never know! But I had the feeling, I really had the feeling, that it would work because I was laughing while I was cutting! Everything, the characters, I mean *everything* was working so well. And most of all the music, the soundtracks. I had a blast just taking the musuc, which were well-known songs, putting them to the film and cutting sometimes on the beat, not knowing if we would get permission to use the song! And then they went and bought most of the soundtrack! It was really a blast working on the film. I cut the movie to the music. There's a song in it, *My Little One* that I needed to shorten to fit the scene. I worked one day trying to find that cut and I couldn't find it and I went home to sleep. At four o'clock in the morning I woke up. I had dreamed the cut! Four o'clock in the morning I went to the cutting room, made the cut, and it still is the film today. That's the way it's cut!

Interviewed by Mark Boot for the Japanese DVD release in 2004

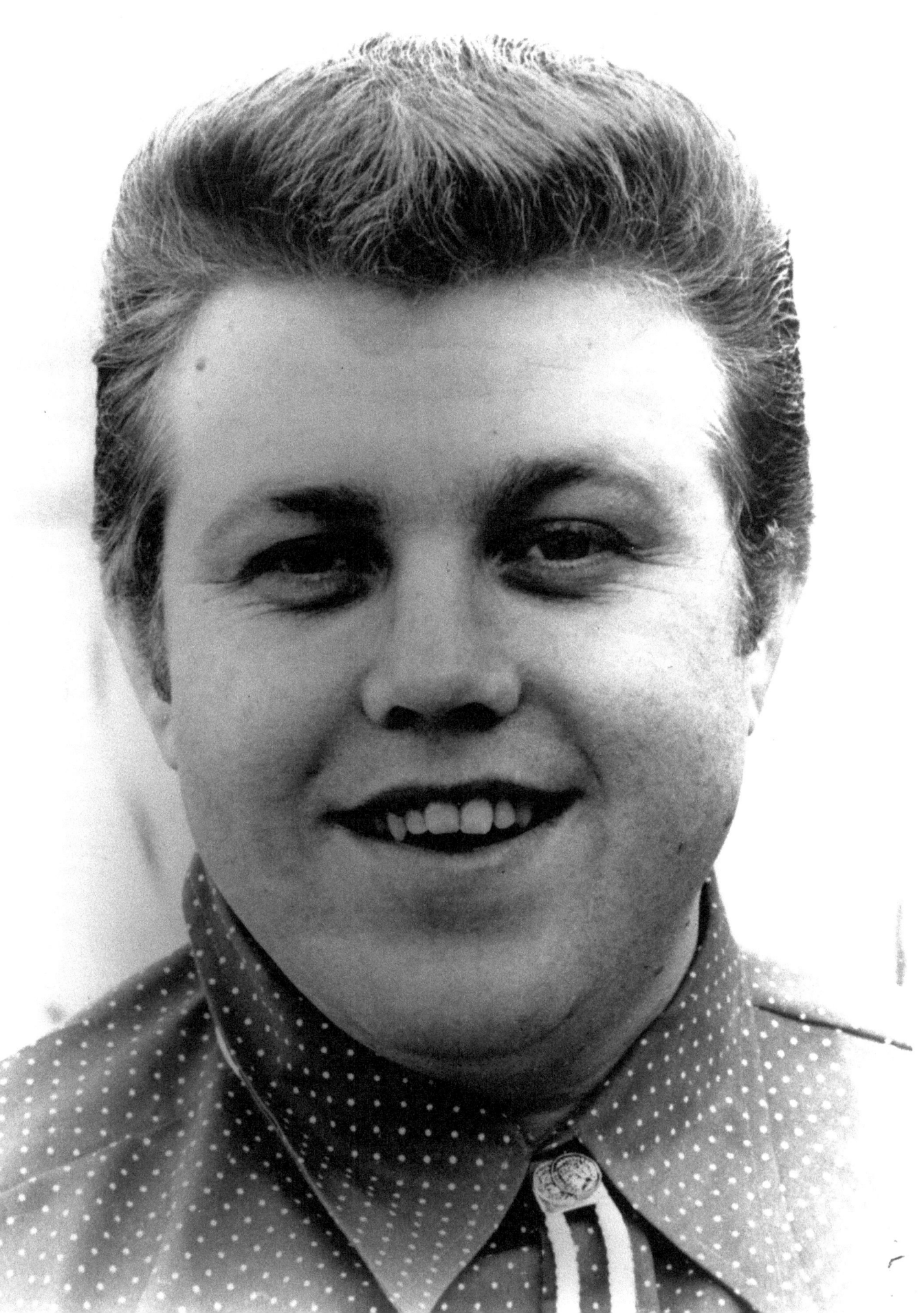

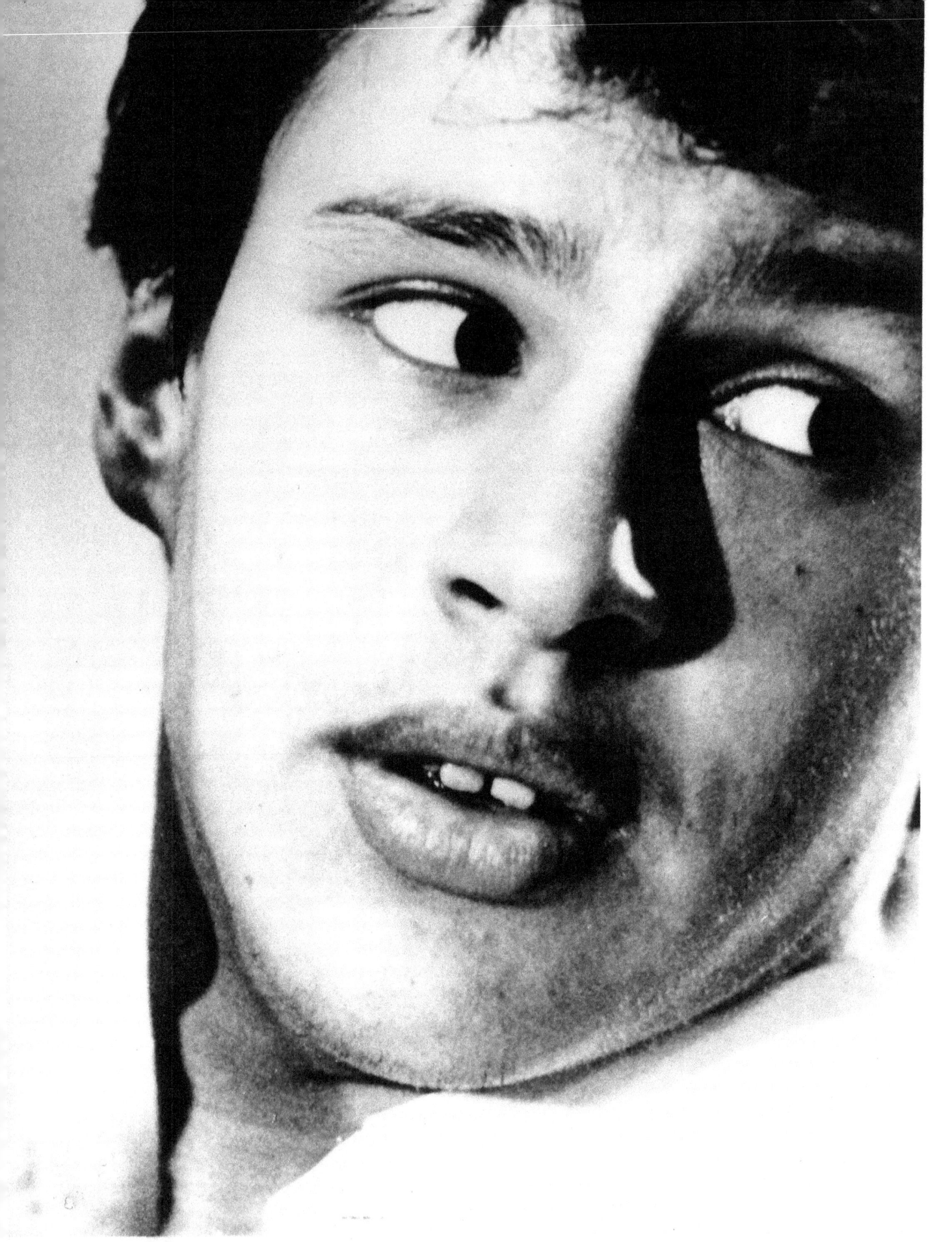

Jonathan Sagall

I was only seventeen. I didn't know anything. Someone just found me and, in three days, I was in *Lemon Popsicle*. I auditioned for it in Tel-Avi just before my army service. I was asked to make a pass at Anat Atzmon, who played Nili (Nikki). I grabbed her and kissed her and got the role. I wanted to be a marine biologist and work in the Red Sea. I was an avid diver then but I have not dived for over a decade. Filming the sex scenes were alright, most of them were with professionals so the air was quite matter of fact. And the reason I got to go first is mere coincidence! It was a relatively comfortable job that beat waitering or bartending any day! The day the film was launched, suddenly my life turned upside-down and I couldn't walk down the street anymore! I look back at the films with a smile. It was good experience. I learnt about filmmaking, about politics, about money, about greed, about intrigue and, well, about people. Part Five was my favorite because the honourable makers of the pops discovered that Bobby could actually talk. Of other filmmakers, Pasolini's films inspired me greatly (I work now as a film director), as do Woody Allen's, Pedro Almodovar, Alan Rudolph.

Anat Atzmon

"I was very innocent. I didn't know you had an abortion with no top on because I had no experience of abortion in my life. Boaz told me that I needed to take off my top, and that nobody was going see my naked body except the actors, and the guys in the room, and I believed him! I think that the secret of the film's magic is its lack of pretentiousness and the innocence that's in it. Boaz and the actors, everyone who had a part in it, tried to bring their best possible work to it, but nobody believed, dreamed, expected, prayed or said, that it would have the success that it did. And maybe that can teach us something about filmmaking, and about the films that some people try to make with pretentiousness and with some kind of hidden intentions, and which, in the end, nothing comes out of them. With *Lemon Popsicle* there was, I think, the right chemistry between the people." (DVD extra)

Dvora Kedar

I studied in the Actors' School of the National Israel Theatre and I had taken part in many plays in Israel, including playing the mother in Arthur Miller's *After the Fall*; the mother in Kafka's *Metamorphosis;* Mother Obu in *Roi Obu,* and many others, when I was invited by the director, Boaz Davidson, to play the part of Sonia in *Lemon Popsicle*. It is customary in Israel for actors to have a Hebrew name. I changed my name from Dvora Halter to Dvora Kedar. The film had a special excitement for everyone participating. I look back very fondly on it.

Avi Hadash

I was always interested in acting from a very young age, and participated in local drama groups. When I enlisted in the Israeli army, I got accepted into the army theatre troupe, which puts on shows around the country for different army units. After the army, I studied theater at Tel Aviv University. Most of my acting has been in the theatre, including the leading role in Neil Simon's *Brighton Beach Memoirs* at Habima, Israel's National Theatre, John in *Peter Pan* (Zachi Noy played Smee), and Motel the Tailor in *Fiddler on the Roof*, with Topol. I have appeared on various TV shows and commercials. The only film work I've done was on the four *Lemon Popsicle* movies.

The first *Lemon Popsicle* movie was filmed in the summer of 1977 when I finished high school and before I went into the army. The director auditioned young people from drama groups all over the country to cast Momo (Bobby). When they saw me they said, "You're not right for Momo but we have something else to offer you", and that was the role of Froike. Froike's character turned out to be larger then originally planned. In the original script, the only scene he was in was the measuring scene in the beginning of the film. Towards the end of the film, when Benzi finds out that Nili went with Momo, the original scene was only between him and Yudale (Huey). The director felt that the scene wasn't working and asked me to join in blurting the information out and receiving a slap for it. Thus a new routine was born which would repeat itself in future films. As for making the part even bigger, the director and the script writers used the character as much as they felt necessary for the storyline, evolving my relationship with Yudale to the point that in the later films I started hitting back.

Shooting a twelve hour day is more work and less play than it looks in the movie. Our main concern in the beach scenes was not getting sunburned; inside the rooms where the party scenes were filmed, it was always very hot and stifling. One of the scenes on the beach was actually filmed as the sun was setting and the most important acting in it was pretending that it was hot and trying not to shiver. The scenes of Yudale amd me slapping each other were done for real. After the the first movie they were actually written into the script, but all it said was, 'Yudale slaps Froike and Froike slaps back.' We took that further, turning it into a slap fight that seemed to go on forever, each one trying to get the last slap in.

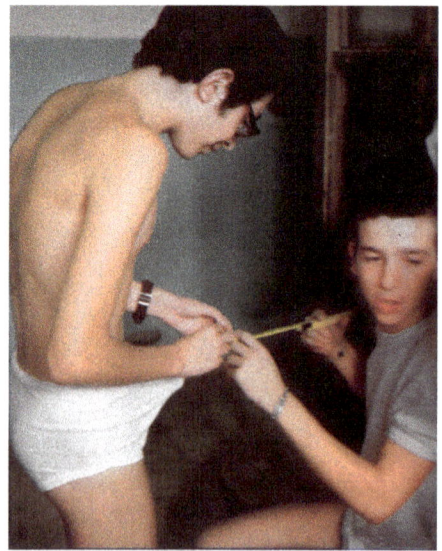

The second film was made when I was in the army and they would not release me. The fourth film was made when I started my acting studies at Tel Aviv University, and I was not allowed to participate in productions outside of the university. I did three, five and six and felt it was enough and time to move on. I do look back on them fondly. I enjoyed making them, but since then I've done so many other things that they're only a small part of my career. It sometimes amuses me when someone on the street recognizes me and says, "I remember you from *Lemon Popsicle*." Then again, after a commercial comes out, everyone remembers me from the commercial, so it changes. I was surprised and delighted to discover that people are still interested in and enjoy the *Lemon Popsicle* movies after all these years.

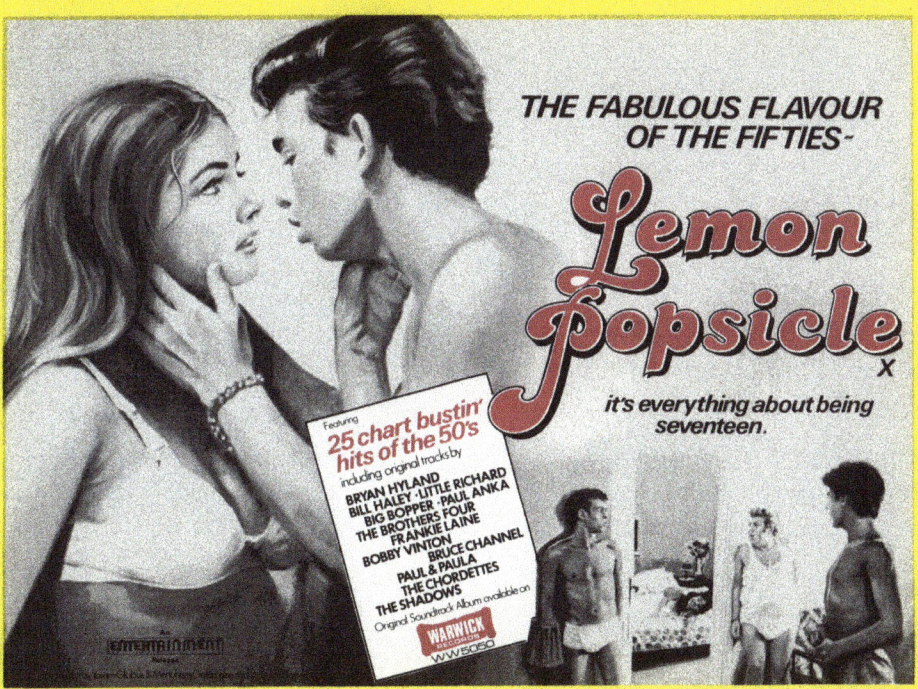

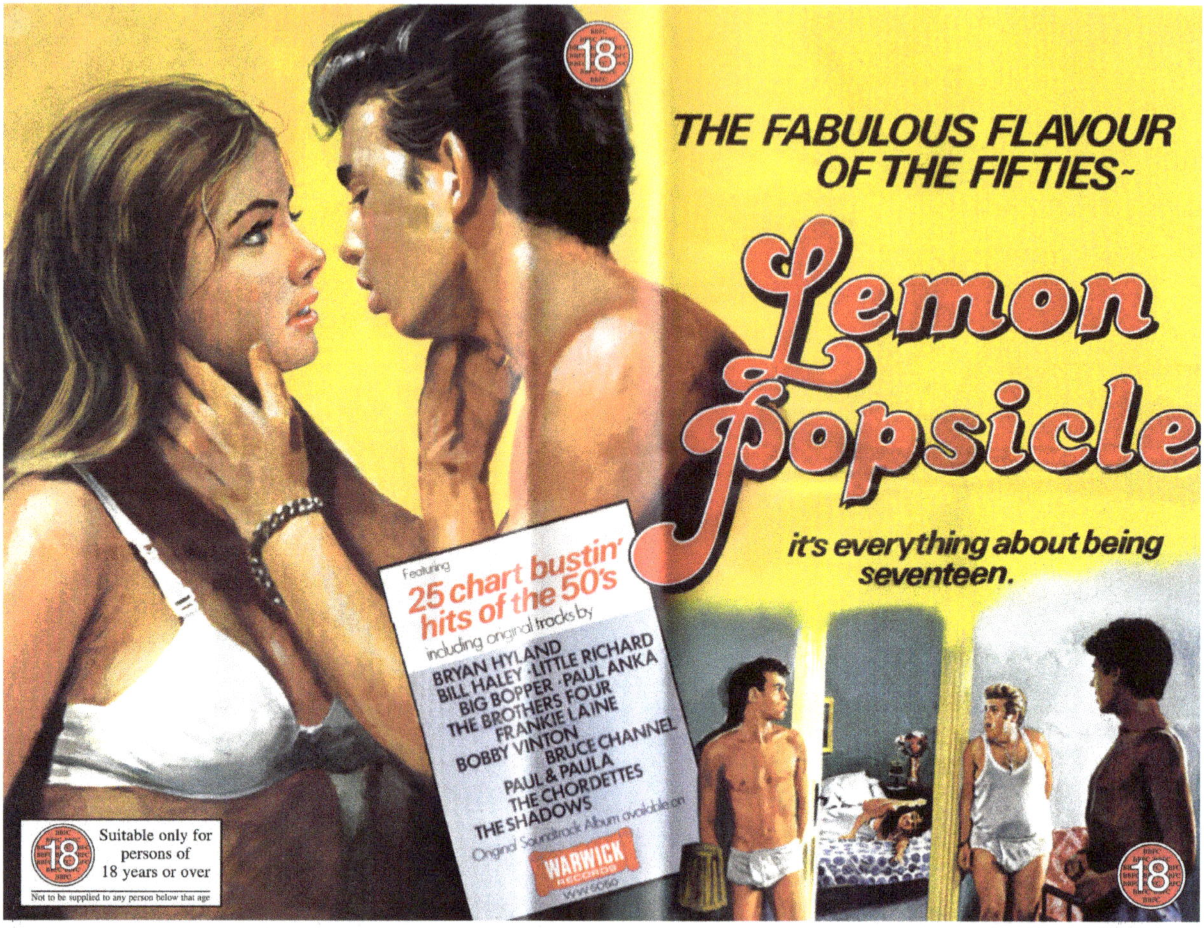
18
THE FABULOUS FLAVOUR OF THE FIFTIES~
Lemon Popsicle
it's everything about being seventeen.
Featuring
25 chart bustin' hits of the 50's
including original tracks by
BRYAN HYLAND
BILL HALEY · LITTLE RICHARD
BIG BOPPER · PAUL ANKA
THE BROTHERS FOUR
FRANKIE LAINE
BOBBY VINTON
BRUCE CHANNEL
PAUL & PAULA
THE CHORDETTES
THE SHADOWS
Original Soundtrack Album available on
WARWICK RECORDS
Suitable only for persons of 18 years or over
Not to be supplied to any person below that age

BBFC
18

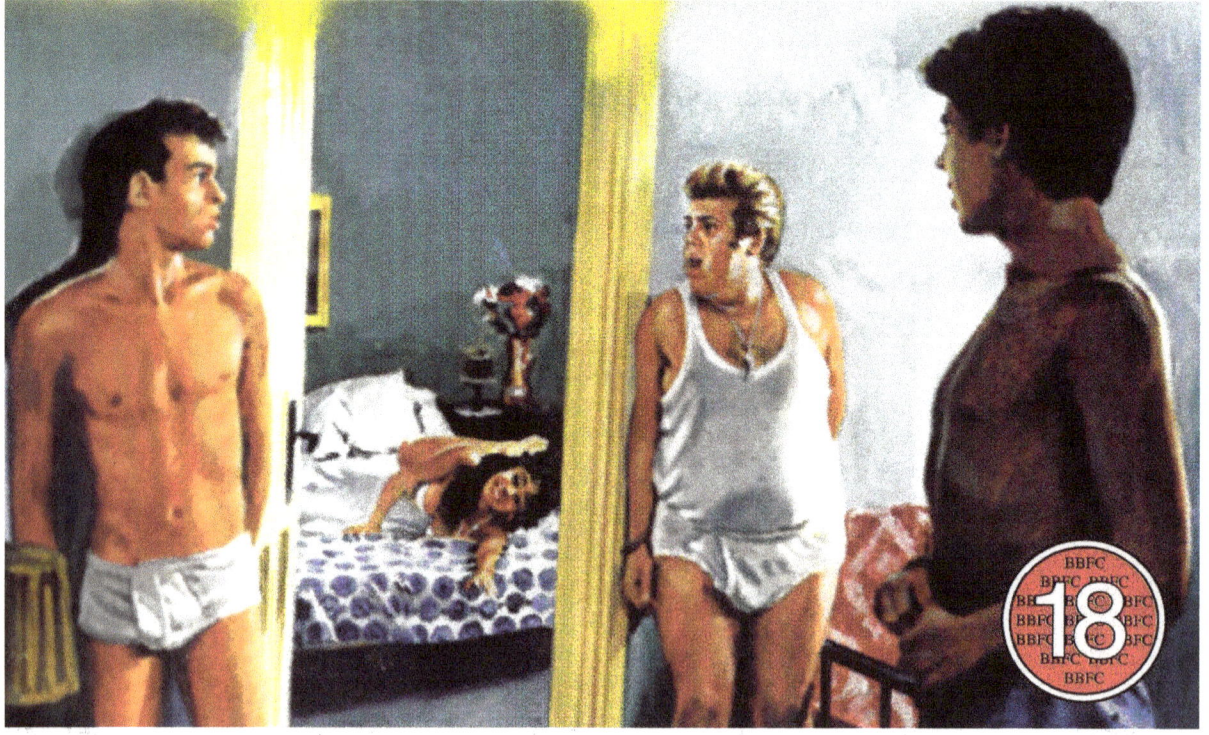

The UK quad poster (left), seen here on VHS box covered with censor labels, was painted by Tom Chantrell, internationally famous for his poster for *Star Wars*. Chantrell painted the posters for the first five Popsicle films released in the UK. This one, with its lemon yellow backdrop and a perfect combination of images that are tender, erotic and funny, has become a favourite with collectors.

Songs used in *Lemon Popsicle*

The most expensive part of filmmaking is clearing the music rights. Songs are often licensed to different companies in different parts of the world, with each company having its own bargaining methods and prices. This led to several different soundtracks being created for the film. The list below identifies the differences between the Israeli and the UK soundtracks.

The Brothers Four, *Green Fields*
Little Richard, *Long Tall Sally*
Paul Anka, *Put Your Head On My Shoulder*
Del Shannon, *Runaway* (Israel version)
Bruce Chanel, *Hey! Baby!* (UK version)
Bill Haley, *Rock Around The Clock*
The Crests, *Sixteen Candles* (Israeli)
Jo Moss, *To Know Him is To Love Him* (UK)
John Morris, *Witch Doctor*
The Chordettes, *Lollipop*
The Everly Brothers, *All I Have to Do Is Dream* (Israel)
Jerry Lee Lewis, *Chantilly Lace* (UK)
Elvis Presley, *It's Now or Never* (Israel)
Paul Anka, *Diana* (UK)
Carl Perkins, *Blue Suede Shoes* (Israel)
Little Richard, *Tutti Frutti* (UK)
The Platters, *The Prayer* (Israel)
Ray Peterson, *Tell Laura I Love Her*
Paul Anka, *Puppy Love* (UK)
The Platters, *Smoke Gets in Your Eyes* (Israel)
Paul Anka, *You Are My Destiny*
Domenico Modugno, *Volare*

Mitch Miller, *Yellow Rose of Texas*
Domenico Modugno, *Ciao Ciao Bambina*
Marino Marini, *Come Prima*
Paul Evans, *Happy Go Lucky Me* (Israel)
Paul Evans, *Seven Little Girls*
Sam Cooke, *Only Sixteen* (Israel)
Bill Haley, *Shake, Rattle & Roll* (GB)
Roy Orbison, *Only The Lonely* (Israel)
Danny & The Juniors, *At The Hop* (GB)
Jo Moss, *To Know Him is To Love Him*
Rosemary Squires, *Que Sera Sera*
Chubby Checker, *Let's Twist Again* (Israel)
Chad Garret, *Can't Help Falling In Love*
Bobby Vinton, *Mr Lonely*
Elvis Presley, *Love Me Tender*
Bryan Hyland, *Sealed With A Kiss*
The Shadows, *Apache* (Israel)
The Shadows, *FBI* (GB)
Paul and Paula, *Hey, Paula!*
Frankie Lane, *My Little One*
Perry Como, *Magic Moments* (Israel)

Eis am Stiel

Israel, 1977
Regie: Boaz Davidson

ESKIMO LIMON

Lemon Popsicle   **Lemon Popsicle**   Esquimau au citron

The film made its international debut at the Berlin Film Festival and was an instant success with the public. Bought for distribution by Sam Waynberg's company, Scotia International Filmverleih GMBH, it sold more than two million tickets in Germany in its first year of release. Sam Waynberg became an increasingly influential producer of the series.

Lemon Popsicle

Tel-Aviv, Ende der fünfziger Jahre: Eine Gruppe von Oberschülern bezieht ihr Lebensgefühl aus der amerikanischen Hit-Parade. Permanent begleiten die Pop-Songs ihre Freizeit, die sich hauptsächlich im Kino, auf Parties und in der Eisdiele abspielt. Selbst die Stichworte zu ihrem Gefühlsleben entlehnen sich unmittelbar all diesen Versen über junge Liebe, Einsamkeit und "Teenage Blues". Die jungen Leute widmen ihrem erwachenden Sexualbewußtsein weit mehr Aufmerksamkeiten als der Schule oder den Ambitionen, die ihre Eltern für sie hegen.

Einer dieser Jungen ist Benz, ein eher schüchterner Sechzehnjähriger, dem sowohl das forsche Selbstbewußtsein seines dicken Freundes Yudaleh fehlt, als auch der Sex-Appeal seines extrovertierten Freundes Momo. Benz fühlt sich permanent von seinen Lehrern und seinen Eltern mißverstanden, insbesondere von seiner recht hysterischen Mutter, die ihn immer noch wie ein Kleinkind behandelt.

Benz verliebt sich auf den ersten Blick in Nili, eine neue Schülerin. Als seine heimlichen Anstrengungen, sie zur Freundin zu gewinnen alle nicht fruchten, verfällt er auf die unkluge Idee, Momo zu Hilfe zu ziehen. Prompt verliebt sich Nili in den "coolen" Momo.

Als Nili schwanger wird, lässt Momo sie fallen. Benz ist glücklich, daß er der deprimierten Nili nun Freundschaft und Hilfe anbieten kann, ja, daß Nili ihn geradezu zu brauchen scheint. Er arrangiert eine Abtreibung, besorgt das nötige Geld. Und während seine Eltern ihn im Ferienlager wähnen, zieht er mit Nili in das leerstehende Haus seiner verstorbenen Großmutter. Nili erholt sich langsam von ihrem Schock. Zunächst verbringen sie die Ferien wie Bruder und Schwester; schließlich gesteht Benz Nili seine Liebe.

Zum Schulanfang kehren die beiden in die Stadt zurück, und von seinem letzten Geld kauft Benz für Nili ein teures Geburtstagsgeschenk. Doch auf der Geburtstagsparty überrascht er Nili schon wieder in Momos Armen. Traurig und allein geht Benz durch die nächtlichen Straßen.

Lemon Popsicle

For a group of highschool students growing up in Tel-Aviv in the late Fifties, radio is "boss". Their extra-curricular activities — consisting mostly of visits to movies and parties, and hanging out in the local ice-cream parlour — are generally accompanied by imported songs from the hit parade; and even when dancing to the music, they still manage to take their emotional cue from the lyrics of all those songs about young love loneliness and teenage blues. Out of touch with the pioneering spirit of their parents' generation, they find their awakening sexual awareness more absorbing than their tudies.

One such teenager is Benz, a shy sixteen-year-old who lacks both the brash confidence of his fat friend Yudaleh and the sex-appeal of his extroverted best friend Momo. Benz feels constantly misunderstood by his teachers and family, in particular by his mother, a hysterical woman who babies him.

Benz falls in love at first sight, with Nili – a new student at his school. When his ingenious efforts to make her his girlfriend come to nothing, he unwisely enlists Momo's help and tries to conceal his misery when Nili promptly falls for Momo.

When, after a while, Momo drops her, Nili becomes unsociable and depressed — not least because she is pregnant. But Benz is less despondent, since she no longer spurns his offers of friendship and even appears to need him. He arranges an abortion for her, obtains the money to pay for it and, while his parents think him away at summer camp, takes her to his grandmother's house to recuperate. They spend the vacation there together like brother and sister, and when Benz eventually declares his love, he is not discouraged by her response.

They return to the city for the start of the new school term, and Benz spends his remaining savings on an expensive gift for Nili's birthday. But when he arrives at her party, he finds her already back in Momo's arms. Sadder and wiser, Benz stumbles out alone into the night.

Esquimau au citron

Pour un groupe de lycéens à Tel-Aviv à la fin des années 50, la radio, c'est le pied. Qu'ils les passent au cinéma, chez eux ou dans le café du coin, leurs soirées sont en général accompagnées des dernières chansons importées des Etats Unis, dont les rythmes les font danser et les paroles – hantées par la joie, tristesse et solitude des premiers amours – leur dictent leurs propres sentiments. Déjà loin de l'esprit pionnier de leurs parents, ils sont surtout absorbés par leur sexualité naissante.

Parmi ces teenagers se trouve Benz, qui à l'âge de seize ans reste toujours timide, n'ayant ni l'effrontement du gras Yudaleh ni le sex-appeal décontracté de Momo, son meilleur ami. Il a le sentiment que personne ne le comprend – ni ses professeurs, ni sa famille, et surtout pas sa mère hystérique.

Quand Benz voit Nili, une nouvelle élève, c'est pour lui le coup de foudre. Et quand, malgré des efforts aussi ingénieux que circonspects, il ne réussit pas à la faire sortir avec lui, il a l'idée imprudente de solliciter l'aide de Momo, dont Nili tombe tout de suite amoureuse. Benz trouve difficile de dissimuler sa peine.

Quand Momo la laisse tomber, Nili se montre insociable et déprimée- d'autant plus qu'elle est aussi enceinte. Mais Benz se sent moins découragé, car elle ne rejette plus l'amitié qu'il lui offre et semble même avoir besoin de lui. Il lui procure un avortement, obtient le fric pour le payer et, pendant que ses parents le croient dans une colonie de vacances, amène Nili se remettre chez sa grand-mère. Ils passent les vacances ensemble comme frère et sœur. Benz finit par se déclarer, et Nili ne semble pas le rejeter.

De retour en ville, Benz dépense le peu d'argent qui lui reste pour offrir à Nili un magnifique cadeau de fête. Le jour de son anniversaire, il arrive chez elle et la retrouve de nouveau dans les bras de Momo. Benz quitte tristement la maison et se promène seul dans la nuit.

Herausgeber: Internationale Filmfestspiele Berlin 1978
Redaktion: Jan Dawson, Bodo Fründt
Layout: Atelier Noth & Hauer/Reinke

"If there is still a public vote at the Berlin Film Festival, like in the early years, then this contest entry was certainly one of the favourites. There was great applause for the director and the actors. Using music from 1958, Boaz Davidson told an autobiographical tale of shy love and first sex with rude humour and pubescent sensitivity." Spandauer Volksblatt

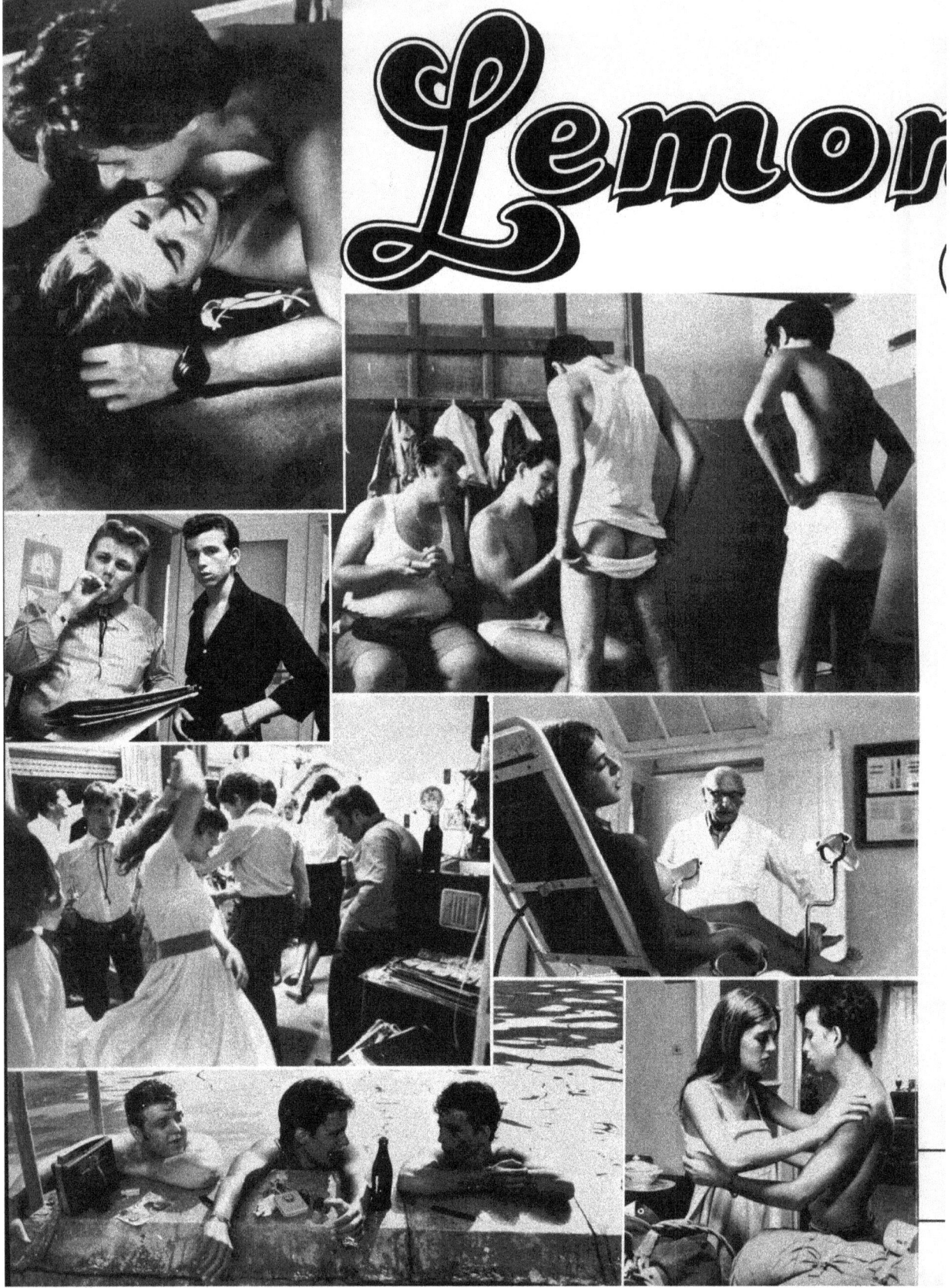

THE STORY

Bengie, Bobby and Hughie are typical of their age and generation. Seventeen year olds in their final year at High School, children in the eyes of their parents, but physically and mentally men, they are anxious to break away from parental influence in the transition from adolescence to manhood. And increasingly aware, of course, of the opposite sex.

Bengie is shy, sensitive, much misunderstood and ill at ease with girls. Hughie is an overweight hanger-on, philosophical about his lack of sex appeal. Bobby, on the other hand, is handsome, outgoing and irresistible. He doesn't even have to try...

It is 1958 and the boys spend most of their free time at the local ice cream parlour, going to parties, to dances, to the cinema, and listening to loud contemporary pop music. When Bengie falls head over heels in love with Niki, a very attractive new girl at school, he simply can't express his feelings and she treats him with cool disinterest. Instead she takes up with the popular Bobby and an affair soon develops.

The boys' fumbling steps into manhood land them in adventures which are both sad and hilarious. Earning pocket money by delivering ice, Bengie encounters Stella, nymphomaniac girl-friend of an absent sailor, who invites him and his friends into her flat and insists on initiating them one by one. Enjoying the experience, and itching for more, the trio hire the services of a sleazy streetwalker named Martha but end up with an unwelcome bonus. They are still itching the next day...

When Bobby boasts to Bengie about his conquest of Niki and claims that he's made love to her, Bengie is consumed with jealousy and disbelief, but it's true. Niki is pregnant and Bobby casually breaks off the relationship.

Gallantly, Bengie steps in. He declares his love to Niki and arranges for her to stay at his grandmother's vacant flat during the school holiday. He steals money from his parents to help pay for the inevitable abortion.

Niki appears grateful and warms to Bengie, but his passionate love for her remains unrequited. They return to school and resume the usual round of social gatherings. At a party Niki returns to Bobby: seeing them passionately embracing Bengie can stand it no longer. He leaves, heart-broken, in tears...

CAST

Bengie	YIFTACH KATZUR
Niki	ANAT ATZMON
Bobby	JONATHAN SEGAL
Hughie	ZACHI NOY
Sonya	DEVORAH KIDAR
Stella	OPHELIA SHTRALL
Zizi	DENIS BOUZAGLO
Martha	RACHEL STEINER
Romak	MENACHE WARSHAVSKY

CREDITS

Produced by YORAM GLOBUS and MENAHEM GOLAN : Directed by BOAZ DAVIDSON : Director of Photography ADAM GREENBURG : Editor ALAIN JACKUBOWICZ : Written by BOAZ DAVIDSON and ELI TABOR : Dialogue Director LOUIS ELMAN : Music Supervision by JACK FISHMAN : Set Dressing A. ROSHKO and A. GERSHONY : Wardrobe Designer TAMMY MOR : Sound Editor ROY TAYLOR : Sound Mixer PETER MAXWELL : English Translation MAGGIE DICKIE and MEIR Z. RIBALOW.

Running Time 95 minutes   Certificate 'X'   Reg. No. F. 39728

AN ENTERTAINMENT RELEASE

THE FABULOUS FLAVOUR OF THE FIFTIES - Lemon Popsicle

LEMON POPSICLE (X) Featuring on the soundtrack 25 great songs by the original hit artists.

Released by Entertainment Film Distributors Ltd.

German Lobby Cards

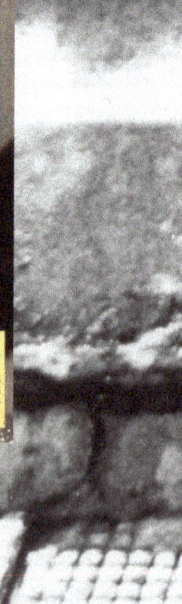

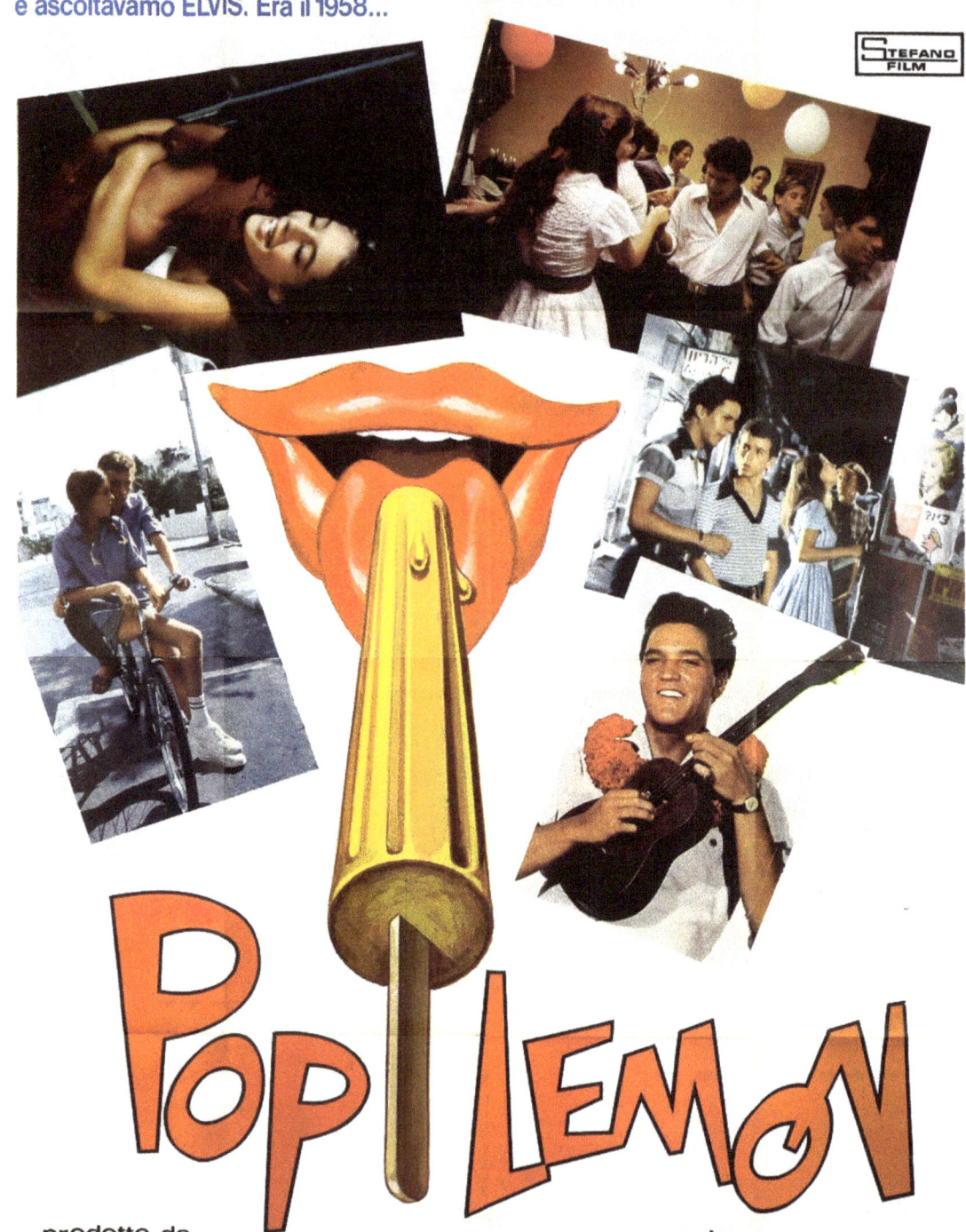

Italian poster

French poster

UK film magazine

Japanese programme cover

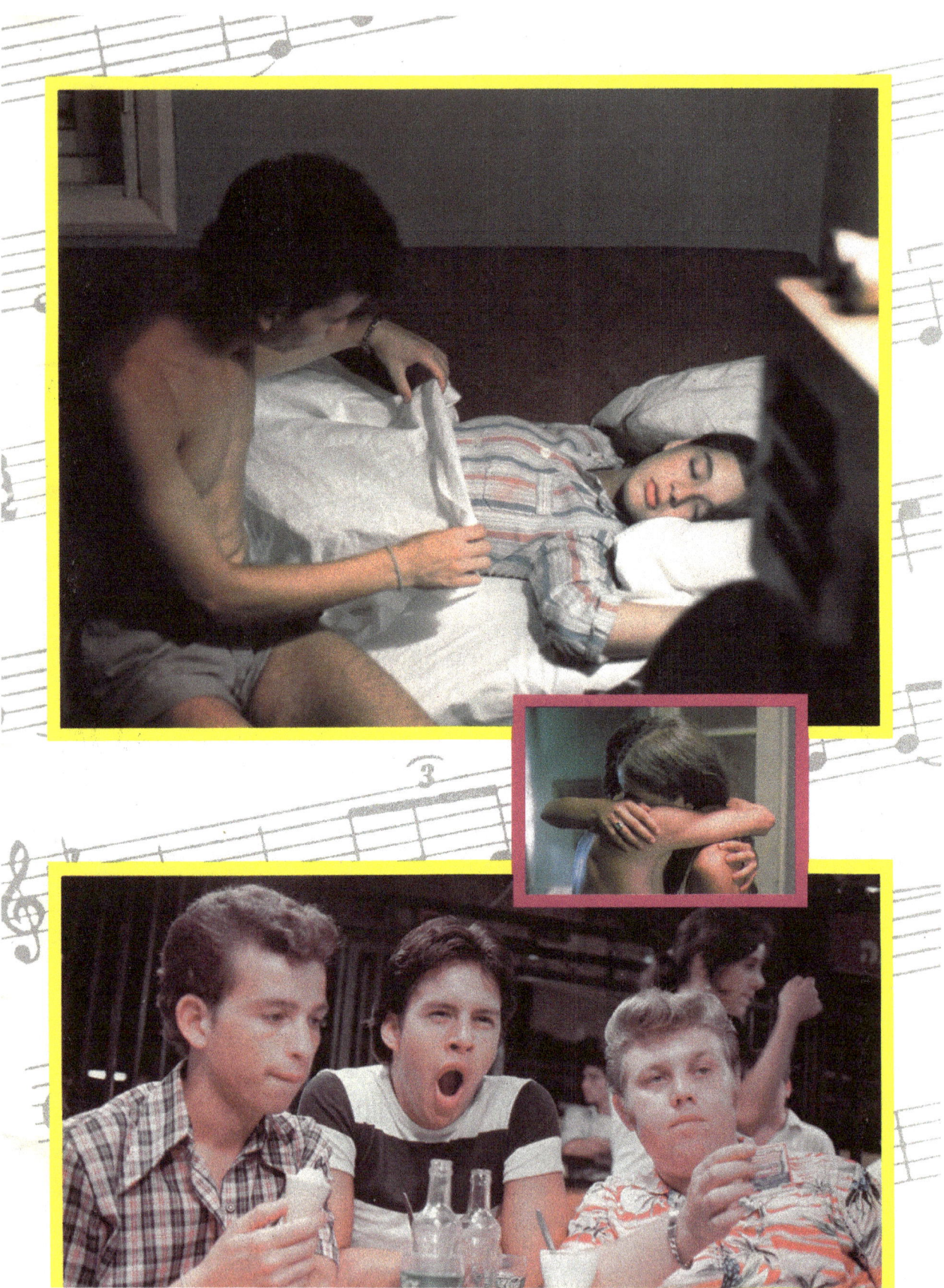

やるせなさ

ない。ベンジーが明日の自分の姿でないと、だれがいえよう。

「グローイング・アップ」が、私をゆり動かす理由の第二は、音楽である。

メロディとリズムの奔流に身をひたしながら、目くるめく思いだった。「ロック・アラウンド・ザ・クロック」が、「アット・ザ・ホップ」が、文句なく陶酔を運んでくる。

といって、それらはノスタルジックな媚薬の働きをしただけではなかった。登場人物と、当時の私が同じ条件で音楽に接している実感が、記憶をより鮮明によみがえらすのである。

私は、1950年代の日本でロックンロールに出会い、打ちのめされた、「グローイング・アップ」のイスラエルの若者と同じように。

私も彼らも、異国のメロディとリズムに、烈しい衝撃を受けた。と同時に、異質な文化への抵抗感がいつのまにか共感に変わっていくプロセスを経験した。「アメリカン・グラフィティ」のロックンロールより「グローイング・アップ」のそれが身近かに感じられるのは、50年代のカルチャー・ショックが、あまりに強烈だったからだ。

私にとって、「ロック・アラウンド・ザ・クロック」や「アット・ザ・ホップ」は、単なる"懐かしのメロディ"ではない。今日までの20年間、絶えず耳元で鳴りつづけてきた"覚醒の音楽"だった。

それにしても……あの頃は、まだ若かった、彼らほどではないけれど。

"The other thing that moved me about this film is the music. The melody and the rhythm seem to just flow through my body and evoke a lot of images in my mind. Songs like *Rock Around the Clock* and *At the Hop* seem to lull me into this sense of nostalgia. The music links me to the main character, who was not too different from me at that time. Both he and I felt the melody and rhythm of a different country. The music seems to freshen up my memory. In the 1950s, I was in Japan and I'd just got started in rock n' roll. The situation was not too different from the Israeli teenagers in *Lemon Popsicle*. I felt the pressures of the cultural difference and, before I knew it, I processed the difference and it became a part of me."

A behind the scenes shot of Anat Atzmon and Yftach Katzur that is, in essence, the film in miniature. A one-sided romance played without words.

Going Steady

Yotzim Kavua

Eis am Stiel 2: Feste Freundin

1979

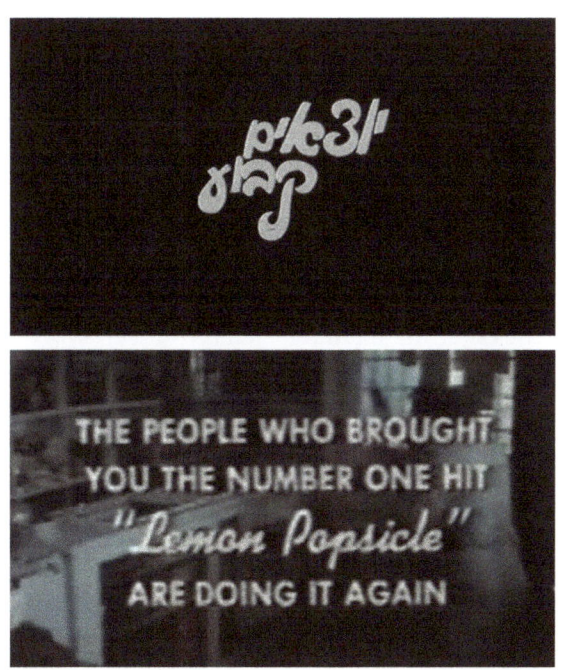

Israeli title card (top). UK trailer on VHS (bottom)

Going Steady

The three main approaches to sequels are *The Empire Strikes Back* approach, the *Karaoke*, and *The Sitcom*. The first extends and illuminates the narrative line and characters, and can include the breaking of the narrative chronology (such as the use of flashbacks). The Karaoke method is more or less straightforward imitation, albeit often with a wink. The third approach, The Sitcom or The Cannon Variation, serves up variations of the things (situations, action, characters, dialogue, songs) that made the first film so popular. This approach harks back to the carnival dawn of cinema and the trick films of George Méliès in the 1890s, through to the slapstick comedies of the silent age, and Disney's *Silly Symphonies* and the popular cartoons of the twenties and thirties, i.e. it produces films that are as far from real life as it is possible to be. This third approach reached a pinnacle with *The Honeymooners*, the Fifties foundation of the sitcom (that inspired *The Flintstones* cartoon series). A downside to this method is that depth is lost in direct proportion to the flight from reality (although real life is routine and repetition). The other main failing is that the main strength of The Cannon Variation, its entertainment value, quickly becomes its Achilles heal. The chase for romps and laughs takes it ever further away from reality.

The *Lemon Popsicle* films evolved into a long-running series because of the intelligence used in shaping a sequel template out of the structure and the situations of the first film. In *Going Steady*, Davidson and the producers hit the ground running. In fact, they hit the ground driving. After a perfect bittersweet song gently sung over the credits, *Tammy* by Debbie Reynolds, whom we remember best for *How The West Was Won* (1962), *Going Steady* opens at night with Little Richard now singing about Lucille ("please, come back where you belong") and a tracking shot of teens making their way, by cars and motorbikes and on foot, through the night streets of Tel Aviv to the Montana ice cream parlour. So far so imitative, but this opening scene is on a bigger scale than the one which opened the first film. In American parlance, it gives the viewer more bang for their buck. We don't expect that from a sequel! The three heroes are riding along in a big beautiful car. They are relaxed and happy and enjoying themselves. Their happiness is infectious. This grand-scale opening scene is much more like a movie than *Popsicle's* first scene and it is much less like real life. It puts us in an artfully contrived *Honeymooning* world.

On the whole, the clientele at the Montana are older than in *Popsicle*. Many of the familiar extras are missing, though, in a wry bit of set dressing, the happy blond kid we saw dancing by the juke box in the original film has his mirror image smiling down from a huge painted billboard for Coca Cola (an improvement on the in-store advert for cigarettes in the first film).

From their table in the Montana, again to the sounds of Del Shannon singing *Runaway*, Huey, Bobby and Benji observe the arrival of The Diary Queen with the Horny Twins (I'd pay to see a film with that title!), who stroll in like characters from a Western (we notice a poster of a cowboy-hatted James Dean on the wall). This variation improves on the original film but, alas, the DQ and HT characters, and their place in the *Popsicle* universe, are not sufficiently developed in the film that unfolds.

Bobby speaks: "What's love's got to do with it? If you see a mattress, you lie on it". The dialogue is more consciously crafted (more tuneful but less real) than the dialogue in the first film. The boys drive the girls to the beach, go night swim skinny dipping, and the girls run off with their clothes. Similar repetitions and variations work well in the scenes at home with Benji's parents but less so in the wooing of the new lead actress, the object of Benji's attentions, Yvonne Miklosh as 'Tammy'.

Miklosh is a curious piece of casting. I'm not sure that the Hungarian actress was right for the part or that she was not absolutely right for the part. She's almost as stunningly beautiful as Brooke Shields, and she looks as articulately intelligent as Jodie Foster. This is quite the wrong combination to work satisfactorily on screen with the expressive almost mime-like approach of a leading man like Yftach Katzur playing a sex-and-love-obsessed adolescent called Benji. Nothing sparks. Miklosh is too cool, too distant, too uninvolved except... except that the final scene works beautifully.

It has been documented in print and on-line at the excellent *Popsicle Forever* website that Miklosh was unhappy with the nude scenes, and that she sued to have them cut before the film was released. To me that doesn't speak of a happy set, or of a particularly intelligent actress. Did she not see the first film? or understand the theme? It helps to explain the on-screen lulls in the courtship scenes, scenes stretched to cover gaps - their kiss reunion is too long, particularly when a few minutes later there is a long long scene in an empty apartment when they look long long long into each other's eyes and stroke each other's hair. But then again, the final scene works beautifully.

The set dressing is generally less effective than in the first film. Taken as a whole, the visual/aural tapestry isn't as rich as it could be, with the exception of the drive-along opening scene and a nice big choreographed party scene: a gym hall, dressed with balloons and streamers, full and alive with a colour coordinated cast, the boys and girls all in white or all in black, except for Huey of course. But I do I like the explicit allusions to James Dean with Benji's *Rebel Without a Cause* red windcheater jacket and, following on from *The Three Faces of Eve* wink in the first film, I like the reference to another Oscar-winning Sixties film that failed to enter the canon, the eating scene from *Tom Jones* is referenced here with raw food in a school library.

Rachel Steiner

I learned acting at the Beit Zvi Acting School and at the Kibbutz Seminar Acting school. I made my film acting debut as Martha in *Eskimo Limon*. I had an audition, plus the director liked the character I created and so increased the role. Martha is a character who behaves very differently to the way I do. The film does not reflect the era of my own years in high school but something like fifteen years before. It was a fun and an exciting experience for me but the success of the film did not change my life. The producers contacted me to be in the fourth and the fifth films but we did not come to an agreement.

BIG RECORD TIE-UP WITH

WW 5078

Warwick Records are releasing an LP and cassette tapes from the original soundtrack of "GOING STEADY". The distribution is very large, particularly through W.H. Smiths, Boots and Woolworths stores. Not only will Woolworths stores display point of sale material tied in with the film, but in some cases will show extracts from the film in the store on video display units. Make the most of this great record tie-up in your area with Woolworths or any leading record store. Ensure that stills and posters for these displays are on hand to arrange with your local store managers. Warwick Records are buying a huge TV and radio advertising campaign to support their sales effort using material from the film. Watch out for the ads. Below is a list of Warwick Records personnel. Contact your local representative to arrange joint promotional campaigns.

FIELD SALES MANAGER
Paul Halliwell
152 Cannock Road
STAFFORD
Staffs.

AREA SALES MANAGER
Tony McGinty
153 Langstone Drive
EXMOUTH
Devon

AREA SALES MANAGER
Rex Walton
410 Bexhill Road
ST. LEONARDS-ON-SEA
Sussex.

Iain A. Campbell, 187 Main Street, Uddingston, GLASGOW, Scotland.
Lyn Davies, 55 Ketton Close, LUTON, Beds.
Richard Hughes, 29 Griffiths Drive, Hesketh Park, SOUTHPORT, Merseyside.
Max Mortimer, 84 Ventnor Road, St. George, BRISTOL.
David Pearson, 34 Milford Way, Hallgarth Estate, BOWBURN, Co.Durham.

David Pyk, 34 Southgate Road, CANNOCK, Staffs.
David Rose, 5 Ively Road, FARNBOROUGH, Hants.
Stephen Wilmott, 1 Kings Chase, BRENTWOOD, Essex.
Max Bloor, 80 Witney Road, Baswich, STAFFORD, Staffs.
Peter Lincoln, 17a Veronica Road, Balham, LONDON SW17.

GREAT SONGS BY THE ORIGINAL HIT ARTISTS

* "SPLISH SPLASH" — Bobby Darin
* "TAMMY" — Debbie Reynolds
* "KISSES SWEETER THAN WINE" — Jimmie Rodgers
* "ITSY BITSY TEENY WEENY YELLOW POLKA DOT BIKINI" — Bryan Hyland
* "TELL LAURA I LOVE HER" — Ray Peterson
* "BE BOP A LULA" — Jerry Lee Lewis
* "YAKETY YAK" — The Coasters
* "SMOKE GETS IN YOUR EYES" — The Platters
* "I'M SORRY" — Brenda Lee
* "RUNAWAY" — Del Shannon
* "A SUMMER PLACE" — Percy Faith Orchestra
* "HIGH SCHOOL CONFIDENTIAL" — Jerry Lee Lewis
* "LUCILLE" — Little Richard
* "ONLY YOU" — The Platters
* "TEQUILA" — The Champs
* "LITTLE DARLIN'" — The Diamonds
* "END OF THE WORLD" — Skeeter Davis
* "LET'S TWIST AGAIN" — Chubby Checker
* "ALL ALONE AM I" — Brenda Lee
* "WHY?" — Frankie Avalon
* "SLEEPWALK" — Santo & Johnny
* "SAVE THE LAST DANCE FOR ME" — The Drifters

Extracts on video display units in Woolworths in 1980! And to think I only remember the singles counter and the Pick 'n' Mix. The soundtracks to the Popsicle films were big sellers internationally and continue to sell in healthy numbers today. *Going Steady* was released in the UK by Rank on 6th April 1980, supported by *Gambling City* by Sergio Martino. Rank re-issued it on 10th May 1981 on a double-bill with *Lemon Popsicle,* and again on the 6th June 1982 supporting *Rosemary's Killer. Lemon Popsicle* was re-released nationally an astonishing four times, including twice on a double-bill with *Flesh Gordon*.

58

ベンジー
イフタク・カツール

ボビー
ジョナサン・シーガル

ヒューイ
ツァッチ・ノイ

Eagle-eyes viewers will spot the same Lemmy Caution poster on the wall that we saw outside the cinema in *Lemon Popiscle*. The red phone box is a symbol of the British occupation of Israel and of Boaz Davidson's film training in London.

Yftach Katzur in his James Dean jacket

The pyjama party descends to a rock and roll tribute to the boys' school anarchy of Jean Vigo's *Zero de Conduite* (1933).

The boys have graduated from bicycles to cars, and not just any old cars. The Popsicle films now became a treasure trove of vintage American motors.

Rachel Steiner with Zachi Noy. She played Huey's girlfriend, Martha, in the first three films: "You know why I'm with him? (Benji). So I can be near you. I never even slept with him. I waited for you."

Katzur exhibiting a James Dean-like passion. Yvonne Miklosh in her only film as an actress. She became a cinematographer.

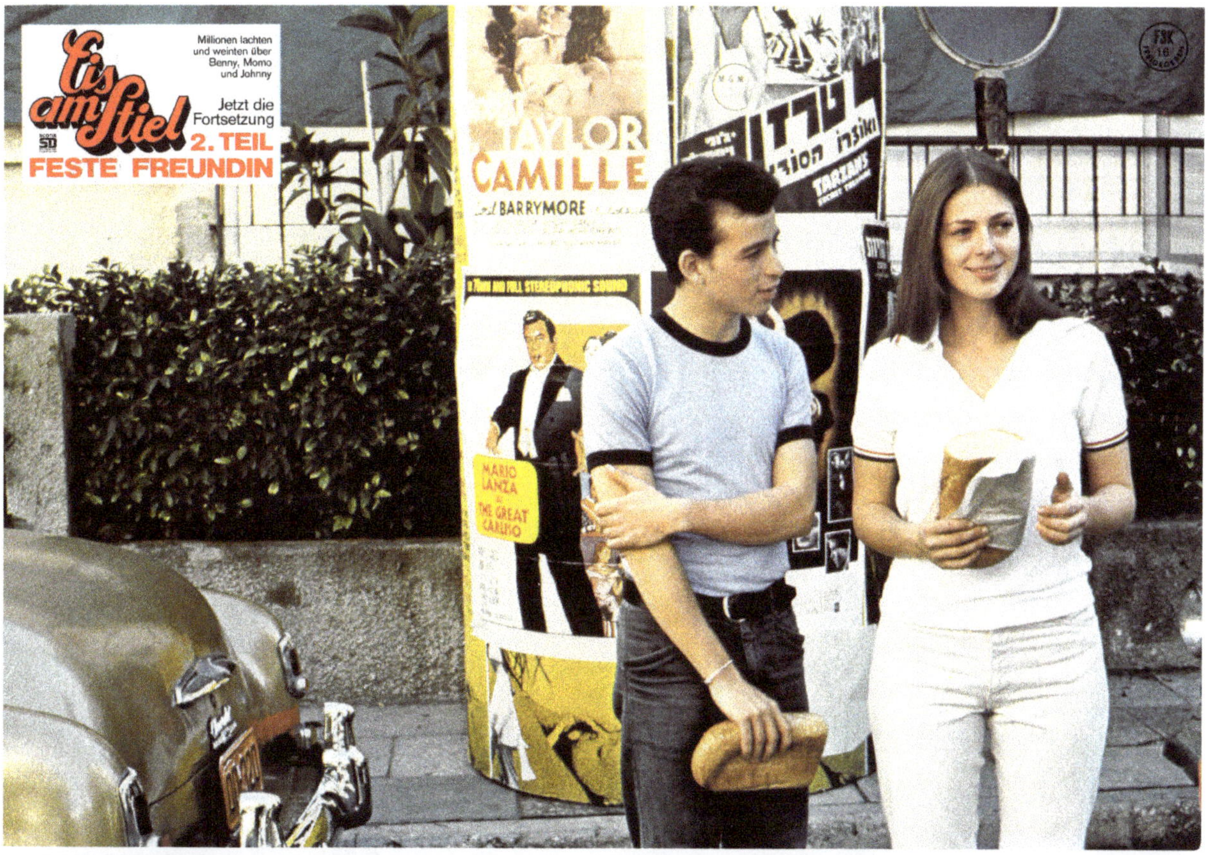
Eis am Stiel
Millionen lachten und weinten über Benny, Momo und Johnny
Jetzt die Fortsetzung
2. TEIL
FESTE FREUNDIN
TAYLOR
CAMILLE
BARRYMORE
MARIO LANZA
THE GREAT CARUSO
FSK

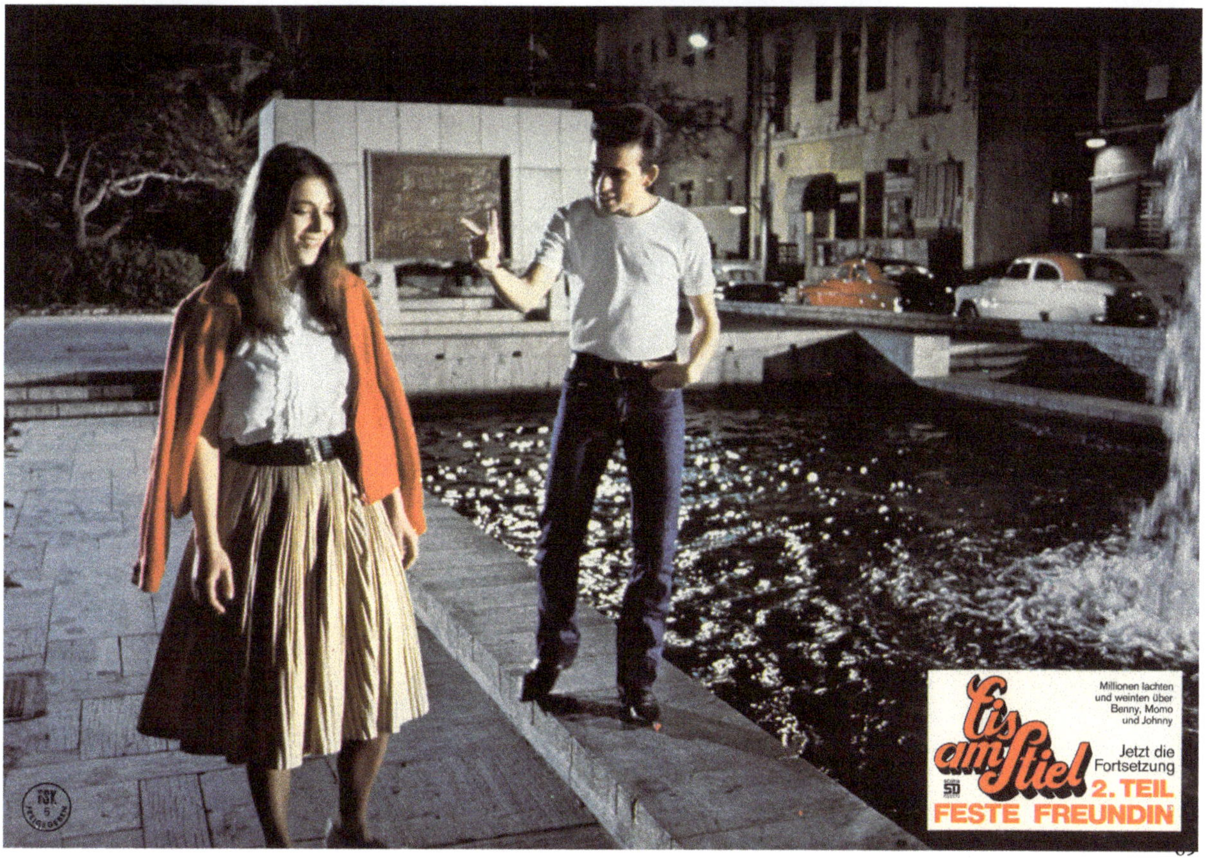
Eis am Stiel
Millionen lachten und weinten über Benny, Momo und Johnny
Jetzt die Fortsetzung
2. TEIL
FESTE FREUNDIN
FSK

Alternative takes were shot in Hebrew and English of several scenes.

The picture sleeve for the Japanese re-release of Debbie Reynolds's *Tammy*.

Songs used in *Going Steady*

Debbie Reynolds, *Tammy*
Little Richard, *Lucille*
Del Shannon, *Runaway*
Bobby Darin, *Splish Splash*
Brian Hyland, *Yellow Polka Dot Bikini*
Frankie Avalon, *Why*
Jimmy Rodgers, *Kisses Sweeter than Wine*
The Drifters, *Save the Last Dance for Me*
The Platters, *Only You*
The Platters, *Smoke Get's in Your Eyes*
The Teddy Bears, *To Know Him Is to Love Him*
The Percy Faith Orchestra, *A Summer Place*

The Diamonds, *Little Darlin'*
Brenda Lee, *I'm Sorry*
Little Richard, *Lucille*
The Coasters, *Yakety Yak*
Chubby Checker, *Let's Twist Again*
Skeeter Davis, *End Of The World*
Frankie Lane, *My Little One*
Jerry Lee Lewis, *Bep Bop A Lula*
Jerry Lee Lewis, *High School Confidential*
Santo & Johnny, *Sleep Walk*
The Champs, *Tequila*
Ray Peterson, *Tell Laura I Love Her*

"Going Steady"

Running Time 90 minutes   Certificate 'X'   Reg.No. F.40278

Benjie	JEREMY KATZUR	Shelley	DAPHNA ARMONI
Bobby	JONATHAN SEGAL	Martha	RACHEL STEINER
Huey	ZACHI NOY	Bazoom	NURIT MANNE
Tammy	YVONNE MICHAELS	Twins	ORIT and DORIT KROIZER

Directed by BOAZ DAVIDSON : Produced by MENAHEM GOLAN and YORAM GLOBUS : Screenplay by BOAZ DAVIDSON and ELI TAVOR : Director of Photography ADAM GREENBERG : Editor ARIAL ROSHKO : Sound Mixer CYRIL COLLICK : Music Supervision by JACK FISHMAN.

Hot Bubblegum

Shifshuf Naim

Eis am Stiel 3 - Liebeleien

1981

Hot Bubblegum

The two most difficult things about making independent films, particularly films with an eye on the international market, are raising the necessary money to pay for the production costs (and the many dozens of professional salaries) and distribution, so when a German producer, Scotia owner, Sam Waynberg, stepped up to share some of the costs, and offered ready markets in Germany and Austria, and some very marketable support-cast 'talent', Golan and Globus sensibly shook Waynberg's hand and took the film further down the *Honeymooners* fantasy line than Davidson could possibly have imagined. It made for some good scenes. At the midpoint of the film, Benji and his parents go to pick up their German relative, Frieda. She turns out to be a long-legged blonde played by Sibylle Rauch, June 1979's 'Playmate of the Month'. And she looks fantastic, completely out of place in Davidson's humdrum but not unattractive Tel Aviv. She notches up the glamour levels so high that they stir life and a hitherto unseen situational comedy spark in Benji's downtrodden Dad. In fact, the idea of importing a foreign glamour model into a homely Israeli setting is a good one, once one accepts that we are no longer in the original Popsicle Land, and not enough mileage is made from it in *Hot Bubblegum*. Rauch is mostly kept indoors. Her stay is brief but she'll be back.

There being no need to start with a bittersweet song, for this is not a bittersweet film, it's a Sibylle stride into fantasy, the opening music is Ritchie Valens singing *La Bamba*. It's good to hear it and it gets the film off in the right party mood. We hear it again later in the film. And then we hear it again. It's a good song but it's not *that* good. In the international version, the credits play over a painted backdrop of people at the beach done in a style and colours suggestive of the artwork for Fellini's seaside/home town masterpiece, *Amarcord*. Fellini has replaced James Dean as the bringer of the iconography. We've moved away from the dark misunderstood fifties of *Rebel Without a Cause* to the sunny early sixties of *La Dolce Vita*. There will be light music, outdoor dining, and statuesque women. The glamour extends to a lip-gloss version of Nikki, the girl from the first film who fell from grace and who has now metamorphosised into a similarly named but new and dangerously attractive and cruel character played by Orna Dagan, a German actress. And Benji is smitten all over again.

But *Hot Bubblegum* starts at the beach. The beach had featured only in two brief night scenes, one each in *Popsicle* and *Steady* and, being a natural hangout for teenagers, and an easy source for eroticism and fun, it's good to see the film open in sunlight and with Huey, Bobby and Benji enjoying the girls. The girls are changing and showering in a not very solidly built shack. Benji and Bobby are peering through eyeholes cut by Huey, who now climbs onto the changing room roof. The wooden planks shake under the weight, and in anticipation of what is to come. Huey crashes through the ceiling to be chased around the beach by a hard slapping old woman. He escapes by being buried up to the chin in the sand, and is accosted by the polar opposite of a moral old woman, the sweetest looking but naughtiest infant in all Israel. We're five minutes in and it's clear from the tone, the sunlight, the rudeness and the humour, that we are looking at a better box-office prospect than the two hugely popular films that went before it. And that proved to be the case.

Publicity Information

CANNON DISTRIBUTORS (U.K.) LIMITED
111 WARDOUR STREET, LONDON W1V 3TD.
Tel: 01-439 0111

. In the UK, the film opened on 5th July 1981.
The support film was *Seed of Innocence*, also directed by Boaz Davidson.

THE STORY

It is the beginning of the revolutionary sixties, pre Beatles and just at the point where Bobby Soxers are on the way out. Benji, Huey and Bobby are on the beach where they spend hot summer days girl watching. Having left their steady girlfriends sunbathing, the three discover a peephole into the women's changing rooms. Fat Huey unable to get a look in, scrambles onto the roof which collapses and the boys are chased off. Further down the beach Benji runs into an ex-schoolfriend Lilly, who although sexy is something of a tease; he dates her but later cannot shake off his regular girlfriend Doris and is unable to enjoy the delights of Lilly.

One evening Benji's parents are out and the three boys bring their girls over and head for the bedrooms. Huey manages to talk his reluctant girlfriend into bed after promising to stay out on the fire escape and count to one thousand whilst she undresses. Meanwhile Benji's parents return unexpectedly causing pandemonium as three half naked girls flee, the oblivious Huey having finished his countdown jumps into bed.... with Benji's mother!

When Benji's gorgeous blonde cousin Frieda arrives from Germany everyone makes a play for her, including her uncle. Benji quickly discovers that juggling two girlfriends gets very complicated but Doris solves the problem by leaving him thus freeing him for Lilly. She, however, finds no difficulty in juggling with two or more boyfriends. A disenchanted Benji eventually meets up with a lonely Doris and under the moonlight once again re-discover true happiness.

STARRING

YFTACH KATZUR as Benji   ZACHI NOY as Huey   JONATHAN SEGAL as Bobby

Screenplay by BOAZ DAVIDSON and ELLI TABOR

Produced by MENAHAM GOLAN and YORAM GLOBUS

Directed by BOAZ DAVIDSON

Certificate X   Colour   Running Time 94 minutes.

An Interview with Ariella Rubinowich

Rubinowich first appeared as an extra in Lemon Popsicle in the playground after Benji had given Nikki a lift to school on his bike. She also made an appearance at the end of the film, dancing with Huey. In Hot Bubblegum she played the part of Benji's girlfriend, Doris (Nurit in Israel; Sally in the German version). This interview took part in London in 2011.

Ariella, great to meet you, what brings you to London?

I came with my niece. Three days ago she finished the army. She's never been to London.

What have you got planned, some sightseeing?

Yes, for me it's the third time. But it's been so long, it's been fifteen years so I don't remember anything. And you won't imagine, but I have only been in the hotel room for two minutes! We just entered. Oh God, what a day! We came too early for the check-in so we went out and we just came in. I can't feel my feet! We've been walking around for seven hours, even more (laughs)!

Can you tell us a little about your family?

I live in Tel Aviv, in the West, on the seashore. I am married. I'm not Rubinowich anymore. I have two kids, one is a boy. He's 13 years old. His name is Or. And the other one is a girl called Bar. She will soon be ten. And she is the biggest rising star in Israel! Already she's done twelve commercials, three series for the television and, just three months ago, she finished the leading role in a new Israeli film.

Is that something you encouraged her with, acting, or was it something she wanted to do herself?

It came naturally from her. And I'm glad. And she's brilliant! She's gonna make it.

Maybe she will be in a remake of Lemon Popsicle in a few years time!

(laughs) Nobody's going to do another *Lemon Popsicle*!

We live in hope!

You do?

There was talk about it a few years ago but it died a death unfortunately. Did you always want to be an actress and work in the movie business?

My career started at twelve in a play of Tom Sawyer, That was young for those times. I went to the only high school in Israel at that time that was like *Fame*. It was for acting, painting and music. I did acting. And when I finished that I went into the army, for the army theatre. *Lemon Popsicle* was between high school and the army.

Is National Service still compulsory in Israel?

Yes, it is still. You give something to your country.

Which actors inspired you when you were young?

Israeli actors?

Any actors really.

Well, you have to understand the situation. I was ten years old when we got a television. The first series I can remember was *The Saint* with Roger Moore. He was young then and I used to watch it just to see him! I didn't understand English. I learned English from watching television. My parents both came from Poland. They were Holocaust survivors. Nobody spoke English. So I studied English from television and was actually a very good student! I spoke very well. I wrote with terrible spelling mistakes but I spoke very well.

Did you have to audition or did your agent get you the part?

Nobody gives you a part, you have to audition (laughs). Nobody gives you anything!

You are in a couple of scenes in Lemon Popsicle. You were in a scene at the beginning of the film and also at the very end dancing with the main character, Huey.

I was an extra there. I don't remember how I got there, if it was before I had an agent or through an agent, I don't remember that anymore. But I do remember being there. Looking with those big, big eyes! I was fifteen and I said, "Wow, I want to do that!"

In your next film you play a babysitter in Moments de la vie d'une femme.

Where did you get that information? I'm dying to know that?

The internet. There's the internet movie database with that on but other than that there's very little about you. Do you remember much about that film?

Moments was a short film. I think I'd just finished film school when I did that part. It wasn't that important.

But you starred alongside two of your Lemon Popsicle co-stars, Menashe Warshavsky, who played Benji's father, and Yehoshua Luff, who played the ice-man. Did they remember you from Lemon Popsicle?

No, no, no. Nobody did. When you're an extra nobody remembers you! Nobody knows you.

Well somebody must have been impressed by you because you came along to play the leading lady in the third film, Hot Bubblegum.

It was even better than you think! For the second part I was still in high school so nobody talked about it. For the third one actually there was a woman, not a woman a girl, who was supposed to do the part. She was from a kibbutz. And two weeks or one week before the shooting she suddenly decided she doesn't want to do it anymore. So they were stuck without an actress. And I remember getting a phone call, not through the agency but directly from the director's assistant, Renen Shorr, who later became a director himself. He'd seen me in something else and he recommended me. So I came to the office and did a reading for Boaz Davidson, the director. And that was it! They told me it's your part!

Straight away?

On the spot. I thought I'm fainting! Imagine it, there was one channel of television in Israel at that time. Everybody went to see the movies because you didn't have anything to watch on television. So you went to the movies. And Lemon Popsicle was the biggest hit! It was huge then.

The most popular film in Israeli history.

And to get the lead on the third one, when I'm just finishing high school, was incredible. I couldn't believe it! And actually, the following day or two days later I was on the set already! There was not enough adjusting time even to digest! Thirty years later people recognise me and I'm like, it's thirty years ago! But they say you have the same voice so I say, 'Okay'.

Unfortunately that's one thing we don't get to hear over here, your voices. Because it's dubbed in to English.

Oh that's terrible.

But when a film is good it stays in the memory. It was a very nice capture of the Sixties.

Yes, it was great fun. It was a big success, they did it right. I had some difficult scenes because I was crying most of the film (laughs)! And I got great reviews for that because I'm not using artificial tears. It was real, so everybody liked it.

Benji was very cruel to you wasn't he? (laughs)

He's actually the nicest person you can meet. But working with those guys was intimidating because they were big stars. But they made me feel very, very comfortable. And actually, I'm jumping now thirty years later. We did a small reunion a few months ago because Zachi Noy's daughter got married. So he invited me to the wedding. And I was there with Yftach and Anat. It was a nice gathering.

A few years ago, on the Israeli Lemon Popsicle DVD release, there was a bonus feature which showed you being interviewed. Was that the same boating lake from the film?

Nah, but it was the same river. I have to tell you a secret. We don't have that many rivers! (laughs) Maybe it's the same boat, maybe not. Who knows?

Did any funny incidents happen while you were on set?

Well, I was terrified about one thing. I should have had a scene on the boat, on that river, when we were making out! And Yftach was supposed to take off my shirt. And you know I never did anything like that. I was hysterical. I was frightened! And then, the real moment came, but everything stayed in place. And the only thing he did was touch my knee (laughs)! That was my sex scene, he touched my knee! But they didn't know that was going to happen because I thought I was going to take off my shirt. A week earlier I had gotten some press, in the biggest Israeli newspaper, a woman's paper with a spread. The title, 'The new Israeli actress who will take off her clothes'. (laughs) Something like that. But all they saw was him touching my knee! So you can imagine what it was like in my house! (laughs)

Your parents weren't too happy then?

Uh uh! But all ends well and nothing happened. So I definitely do remember that day vividly! I remember the dancing. I remember the music. I remember the clothes, because it was different. It smelt different. And the hair, it really took you back in time.

Most Lemon Popsicle fans agree that, apart from the characters in the films, the one thing that stands out in their memory is the great music. A great fifties and early sixties soundtrack. Do any of the songs now, if you hear them on the radio, bring back any memories?

Yes, immediately. Immediately. Even my kids, they tell me, Mum that's from your film!

Songs used in *Hot Bubblegum*

Ritchie Valens, *La Bamba*
The Latin Rhythm Section, *Patricia*
Chad Garrett, *Teddy Bear* and *All Shook Up*
Chad Garrett, *Don't Be Cruel and Love Me Tender*
Chad Garrett, *Can't Help Falling In Love With You*
Ritchie Valens, *Donna*
Bill Haley, *Rip It Up* and *Shake, Rattle And Roll*
Ray Peterson, *Tell Laura I Love Her*
The Fleetwoods, *Come Softly To Me*
The Drifters, *Dance With Me*
Johnny Tillotson, *Poetry In Motion*
Little Richard, *Tutti Frutti*

Little Richard, *Long Tall Sally*
The Fleetwoods, *Come Softly To Me*
The Shirelles, *Dedicated To The One I Love*
The Diamonds, *Little Darlin'*
Frankie Avalon, *Why*
The Four Aces, *Three Coins In The Fountain*
The Four Aces, *Love Is A Many Splendoured Thing*
The Chordettes, *Lollipop*
Chuck Berry, *Johnny B. Goode*
Bobby Vee, *Devil or Angel*
The Teddy Bears, *To Know Him Is To Love Him*
Duanne Eddy, *Rebel Rouser*

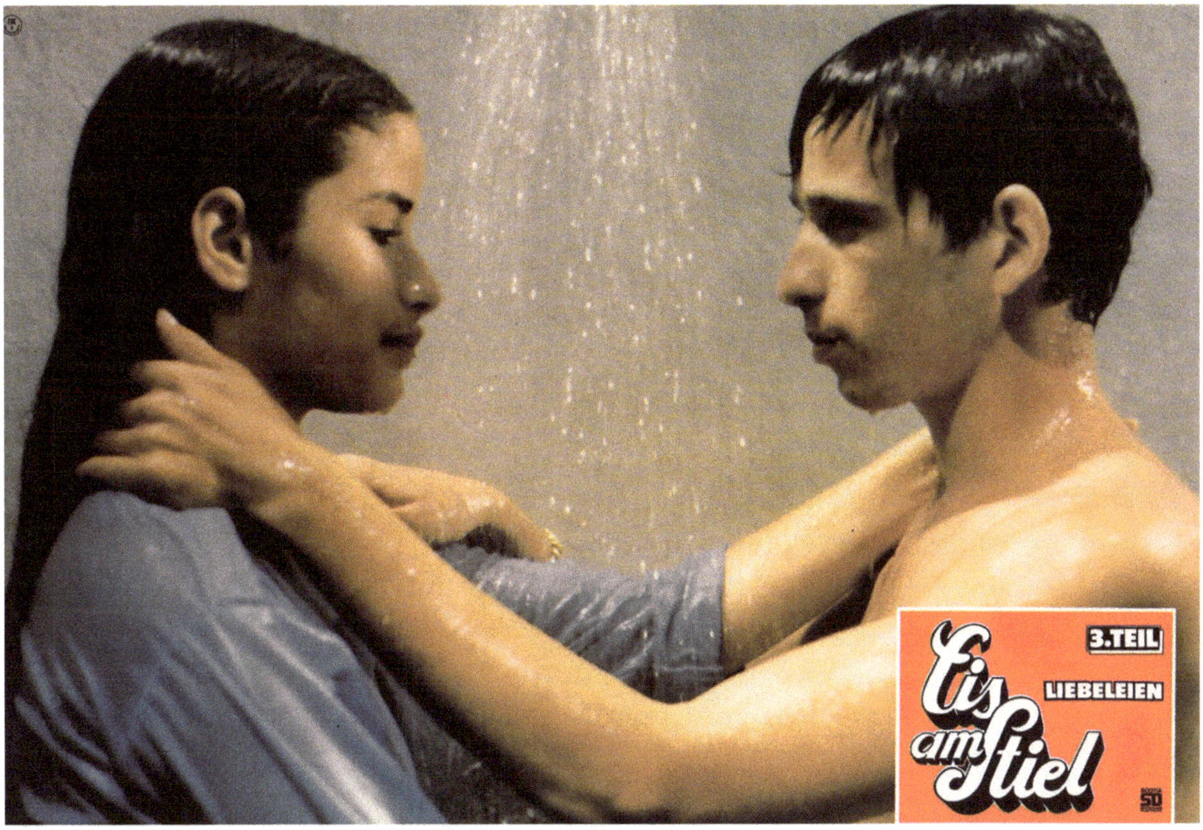
3.TEIL
Eis am Stiel
LIEBELEIEN

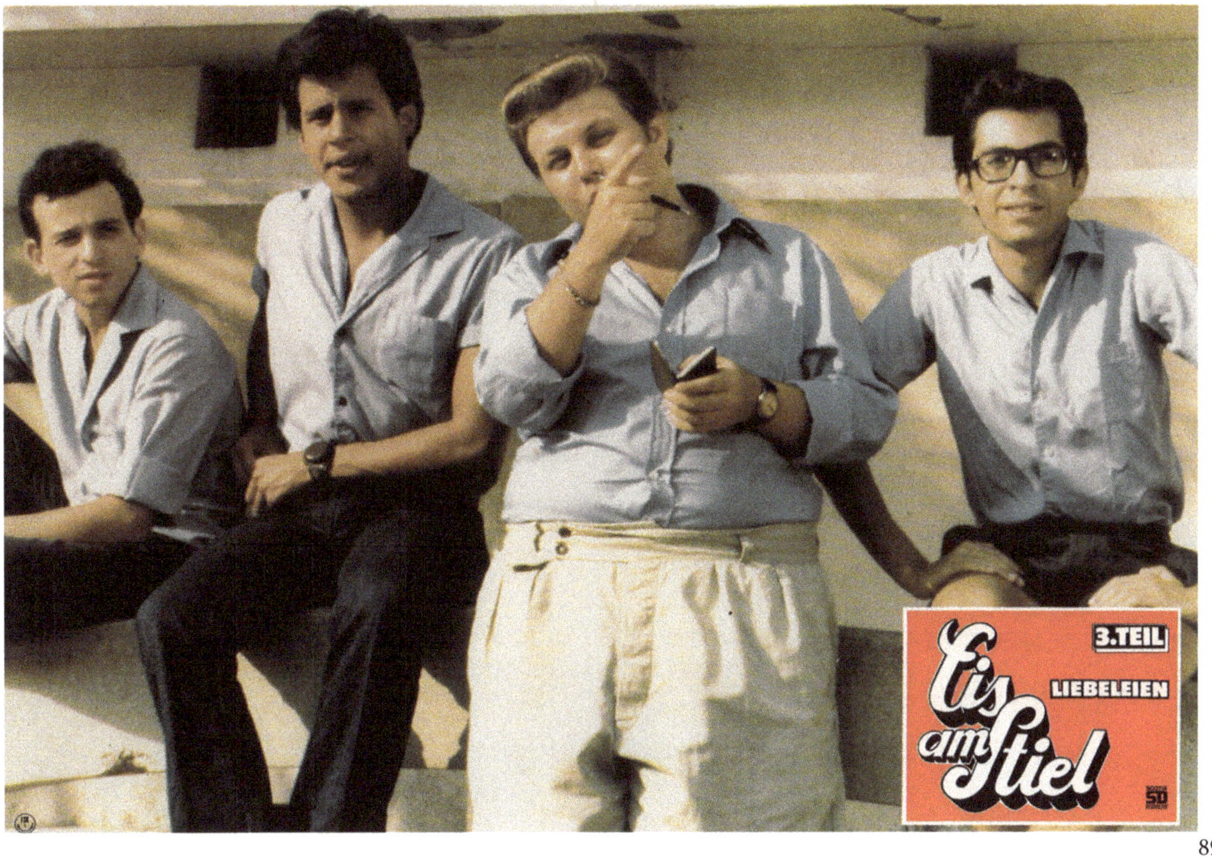
3.TEIL
Eis am Stiel
LIEBELEIEN

Christiane Schmidter

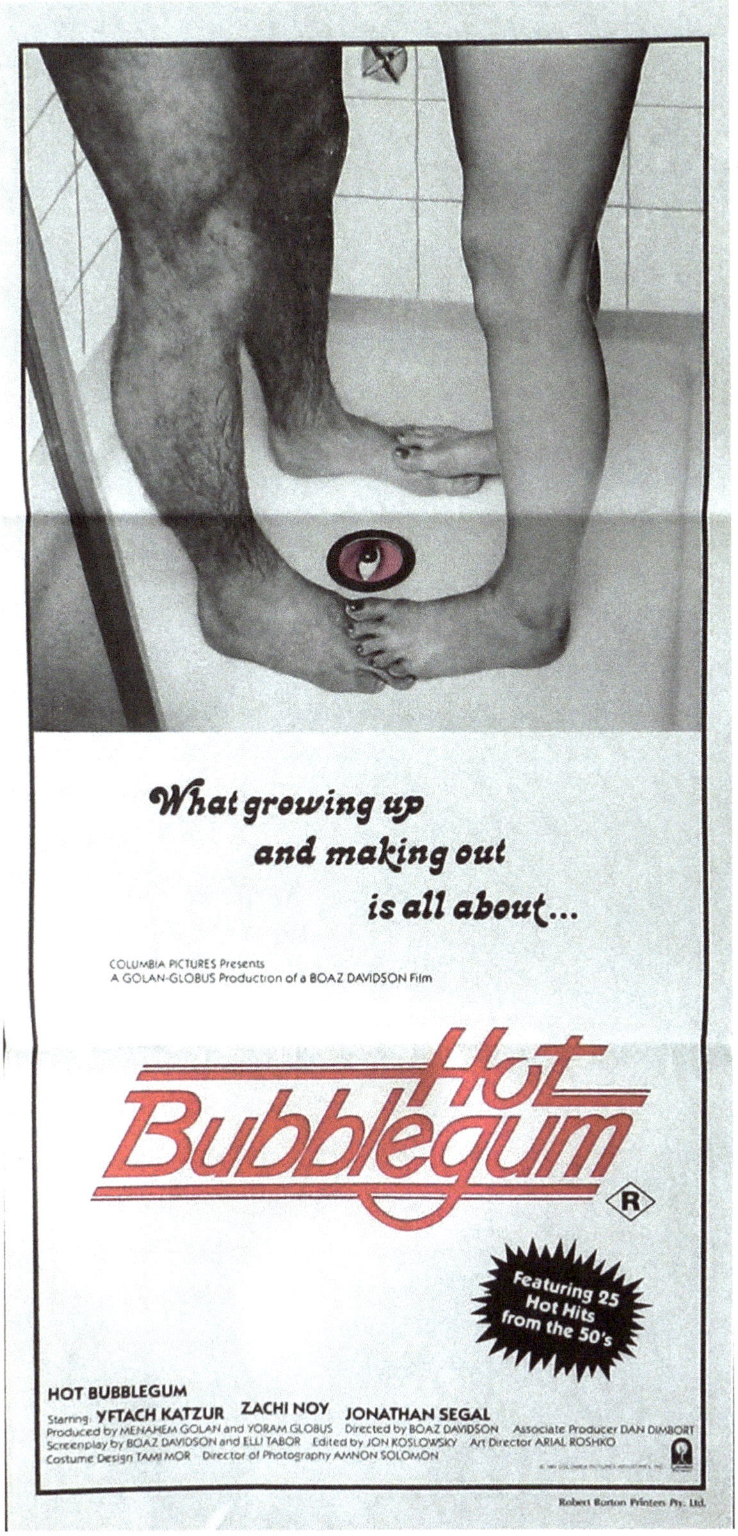

The Australian daybill poster uses the best image from the film, the feet on feet, and adds an eye to the plug-hole to bring in the shower spy theme.

Hot Bubblegum
Lemon Popsicle III

イフタク・カツール　ツァッチ・ノイ　ジョナサン・シーガル
オリジナル・サントラ盤〈ポリドール・レコード〉

Columbia Picture ©1980 Columbia Picture Industries Inc.

97

Private Popsicle

Sapiches

Eis am Stiel 4 - Hasenjagd

1982

Private Popsicle

All Israeli citizens reaching the first bloom of adulthood are rewarded with three years in the army, an understandable requirement for an embattled country in the very heartland of Creation and civilisation, so it was natural for the *Popsicle* series to follow the boys on the rites of passage that is their patriotic duty. Patriotism and duty are fine as far as they go but, this being a *Popsicle* film, the main thought on the minds of our heroes are 'women'. Actually that's true only for Bobby and Benji, who again falls for the best-looking woman around, Viennese model, Sonja Martin in her film debut. Huey's main thought is for making money.

He arrives with so much stuff to sell that the Sergeant gives him the nickname 'kitbag'. Actually, Huey spends the funniest parts of the film trying to escape from romance and lust, on account of him being the object that men are lusting after! Twice the trio dress up in drag, and it has to be said, for it is absolutely true, that Zachi Noy makes the best looking woman of the three. His drag act is played for laughs, of course, but his is a very skillful performance. If John Waters was ever wanting to replace Divine?

Two new characters make a good impression, Joseph Shiloach (spelt 'Shiloah' in the British version) as Sergeant Ramirez, and the mighty Devora Bakon, in the Hattie Jacques role of the big woman lusting after the little man played by Ramirez. Her Carry On is forthrightly vulgar, muscular and funny. Bizarrely, Ramirez is dubbed with a Bombay Indian accent in the English-language version. The dubbing is poor throughout. The voices aren't well cast, Sagall is given a Joe Pesci gangster voice, and everyone overacts. Curiously, the English dubbing was done by Mel Welles and his company. Welles cameos as the pharmacist in *Last American Virgin* and is rather good there.

The main location is an ex-British army base, and the opening song is a favourite by an old British war horse, Cliff Richard singing *Lucky Lips* (a good title for a *Popsicle* film). The 'army' adventure is preceded by a ten-minute stunt as the boys endeavour to return to the spirit of 1977 and have sex with a welcoming nymphomaniac played by Bea Fiedler. The variation, and it is a good one, is that the Fiedler's husband (Shumel Eiser) is unconscious, drunk, huge and needs to be put to bed.

On the downside is an accumulation of scenes that don't work as comedy or drama because they have no connection to real life - such as Sergeant Ramirez holding up a banana skin and thinking he is going insane because the three *Popsicle* boys pretend they can't see it. This dislocation with reality, which began with the spectacular opening scene of *Going Steady*, was the main reason why Davidson withdrew from the series.

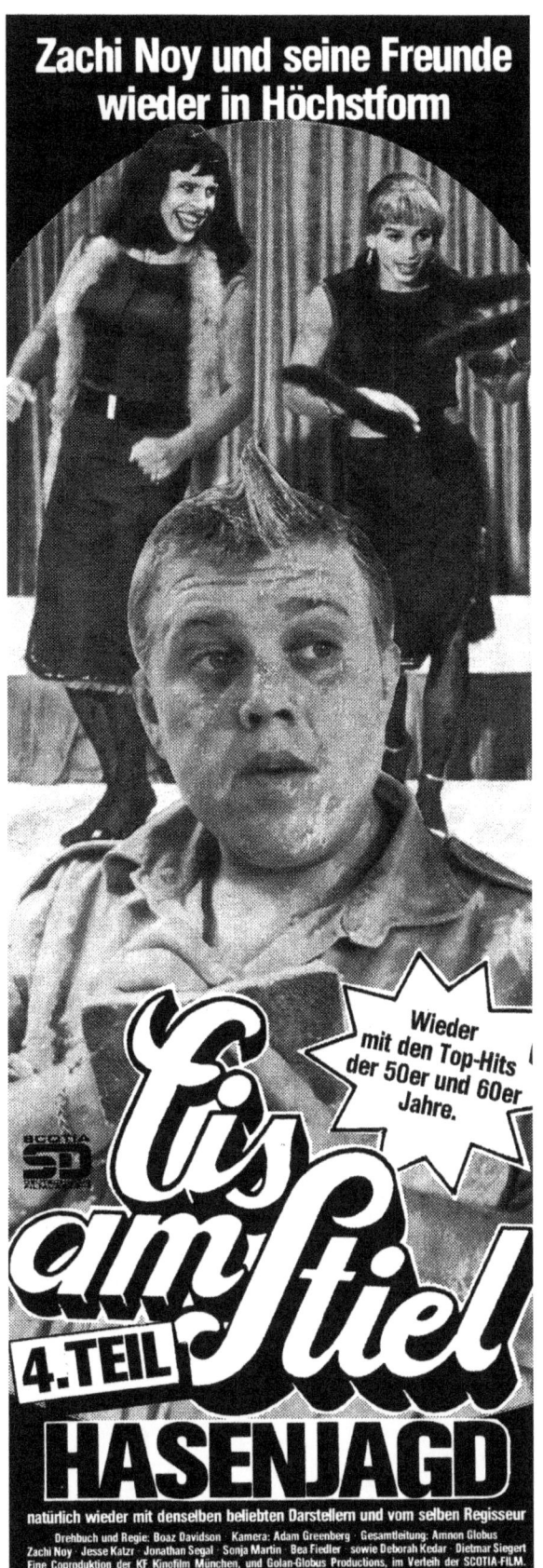

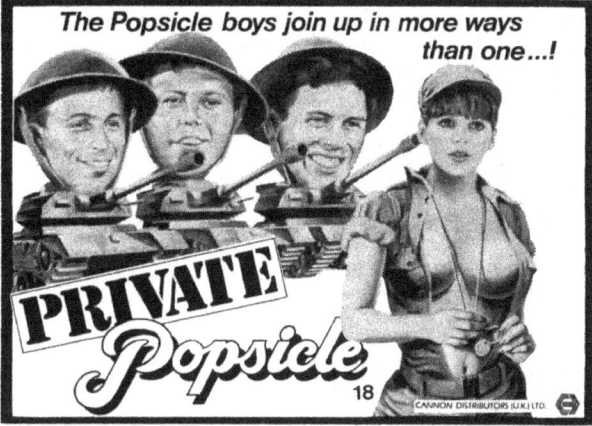

Production Notes

By overwhelming demand, the mischievous trio of Benji, Bobby, and Huey, from "Lemon Popsicle," "Going Steady," and "Hot Bubblegum" reprise their antics in a fourth sequel, PRIVATE POPSICLE, another outrageous escapade from writer-director Boaz Davidson.

PRIVATE POPSICLE starts with Benji (Yftach Katzur), Bobby (Jonathan Segall), and Huey (Zachi Noy) signing up for a three year stint in the Army. Not too thrilled with Army life, the three scamps contrive every means to outsmart, confuse, and bamboozle their superior officers - and with hilarious results.

Most of the film takes place in an Israeli Army camp. It was the duty of the location manager to find one that was not in use - not an easy task! An old British Army camp was discovered just outside Tel-Aviv. The base was in such a state of disrepair that everything had to be rebuilt - and rebuilt again when one of the new bunkhouses burned to the ground three days before shooting began.

The camp is the site of a large archaelogical excavation where 2,000 year old Roman ruins have been uncovered. One day while shooting, Yftach Katzur had to dig a hole under the scrutiny of his drill sergeant (Joseph Shiloah) as punishment for one of his pranks. Several takes later, Yftach couldn't dig anymore. He had dug all the way down to an old Roman road. Not only did he uncover antiquity, but also four snakes, very much alive.

Shooting went along smoothly under Boaz Davidson's direction. Everyday the hilarity in front of the camera was matched by the hijinks in back. Asked if any of the characters were autobiographical, Davidson replied that Benji is very much a young Boaz, going through many of the same growth pains and zany adventures that Davidson had in his life.

Cinematographer Adam Greenberg has shot all of the "Popsicle" pictures with the exception of the third, "Hot Bubblegum." Among his credits are the TV movie "Golda," Samuel Fuller's "The Big Red One," "Paradise," "The Last American Virgin," and "10 to Midnight."

PRIVATE POPSICLE was produced by Menahem Golan and Yoram Globus in conjunction with KF Kinofilm of Munich.

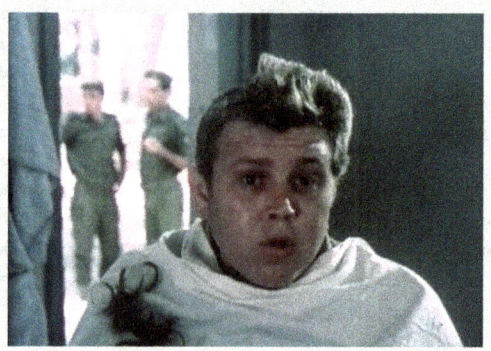

YFTACH KATZUR

Yftach Katzur is the total opposite of the gawky, lovelorn Benji he portrays in PRIVATE POPSICLE. In reality, Yftach is confident, intelligent, and in control of his life, but he had created such a sincere character on screen that the public is convinced Yftach and Benji are one and the same.

A native of Tel-Aviv, Yftach's acting career began when he was looking for something to keep him busy after school. Taking an acting improvisation class at the urging of a friend, Yftach excelled to the point where he won the lead role in a production of "Equus" by the age of eighteen.

Yftach stayed in the theatre for a year after graduating from high school, and then Boaz Davidson snatched him up to play Benji in "Lemon Popsicle." The film and Yftach were overnight sensations, but Yftach didn't have long to dwell on it. Soon after the film opened, he was off to the Army to serve his three years. He continued to hone his craft in the Army theatre group and also worked as an Army radio broadcaster.

While Yftach was still in the Army, Davidson managed to get him out just long enough to shoot the sequel. "Going Steady" was so successful that the third sequel, "Hot Bubblegum," was soon under way.

Yftach enrolled at a film school in Tel-Aviv after leaving the army. While he loves acting, he would like to direct even more.

ZACHI NOY

Zachi Noy's first appearance in drag was as the Ugly Stepsister in a production of "Cinderella." Although only twelve at the time, his hilarious performance stopped the show. As Huey in PRIVATE POPSICLE, Zachi plays a private in the Israeli Army who puts on a wig, makeup, and cocktail dress to masquerade as a zaftig blonde on a date with his drill sergeant.

Drag and army fatigues are both familiar to Zachi. The former he wears purely for comedic convention, the latter he wore in a more sober situation: his mandatory three years in the Israeli Army. An actor since his early adolescence, Zachi broke the blues of being a private by joining the Army Ensemble. He continued his work as an entertainer in nightclubs, radio, and television after his tour of duty was over.

Zachi has played the role of rotund Huey in all four of the "Popsicle" films. His other screen credits include "The Garden," "My Mother the General," "The Magician of Lublin," and "Enter the Ninja."

Although a gifted comedian, Zachi's acting ambitions are quite serious. He eventually wnats to be well known by audiences in the United States. Ideally, he wishes to emulate the styles of Charles Laughton and Peter Lorre, two men whose work he admires tremendously.

JONATHAN SEGALL

Jonathan Segall continues his successful role as Bobby, the confident, handsome member of the trio in PRIVATE POPSICLE. Jonathan's teen idol looks have propelled him into being the John Travolta of Israel. He retains a private secretary just to handle the bundles of fan mail that come in regularly.

Born in Toronto, Canada, Jonathan and his parents moved to Israel in 1964. His mother Ruth Segall, a very famous stage and film actress in Israel, introduced Jonathan to director Boaz Davidson while he was casting "Lemon Popsicle." Although Jonathan never felt the calling to be an actor, he accepted Davidson's request for a screen test and won the role of Bobby over hundreds of young, aspiring actors.

So far, Jonathan's film career has only consisted of the four "Popsicle" features, but he has taken his new profession seriously, studying voice and drama at London's Guildhall Academy of Music and Drama.

BOAZ DAVIDSON

Director Boaz Davidson's PRIVATE POPSICLE continues the zany, madcap exploits of Benji, Huey, and Bobby that "Lemon Popsicle" first spawned. That film, written in collaboration with Elli Taylor, was set in the fifties and concerned the mischievous antics of three sexually precocious teenage boys. Based on Davidson's life experiences, "Lemon Popsicle" was a tremendous hit in Israel, and it went on to enjoy unprecendented popularity abroad. It spawned three sequels, "Going Steady," "Hot Bubblegum," and the fourth, PRIVATE POPSICLE, in which the three reck havoc in the Army.

Davidson, always having the desire to make motion pictures, made his first step when he won the coveted Israeli Government scholarship to the London Film School where he studied for two years.

Upon his return to Israel, he began his close association with Menahem Golan and Yoram Globus and their company, Noah Films, Ltd. Davidson wrote and directed a string of comedies which include "It's a Funny, Funny World," "The Tzani Family," and "Lupo Goes to New York." When Golan and Globus purchased controlling shares in The Cannon Group, Inc., Davidson moved to Los Angeles becoming Vice-President of Creative Affairs with Cannon. He continued to expand his repertoire into drama with "Seed of Innocence," a tender story about teenage parents, and "Hospital Massacre," a horror-shocker starring Barbi Benton.

Recently, Davidson translated his "Popsicle" series to the screen for the American public. The result was "The Last American Virgin," set in the punked-out Los Angeles of the '80's.

Songs used in *Private Popsicle*

Cliff Richard, *Lucky Lips*
Cliff Richard, *Livin' Doll*
Paul Fishman, *The Private Popsicle March*
Gerry and The Pacemakers, *I Like It*
Jerry Lee Lewis, *Whole Lotta Shakin' Going On*
The Platters, *Only You*
Robin Merrill, *Mr. Sandman*
The Coasters, *Charlie Brown*
Bill Haley, *See You Later Alligator*
The Crystals, *Da Doo Ron Ron*
Barry Mann, *Who Put The Bomp*
Sandy Nelson, *Let There Be Drums*
Pat Boone, *Speedy Gonzales*
The Tymes, *With All My Heart*

Mimon Ruth, *Temptation*
The Shirelles, *Dedicated To The One I Love*
The Popsicles, *I Want My Mama*
The Popsicles, *El Cumbachero*
Amen Corner, *Bend Me, Shape Me*
Bobby Helms, *My Special Angel*
The Shirelles, *Soldier Boy*
The Chordettes, *Lollipop*
Chuck Berry, *Johnny B. Goode*
Bobby Vee, *Devil or Angel*
The Teddy Bears, *To Know Him Is To Love Him*
The Tremeloes, *Silence is Golden*
The Fleetwoods, *Mr. Blue*
The Rookies, *Rise & Shine* and *Strictly Private*

Private Popsicle was rated X by the British censors on 6th July 1982 (all the *Lemon Popsicle* films were banned in Britain to the under eighteens). It was released in cinemas in July 1983.

THE CANNON GROUP, INC.
THE MAJOR AMONG THE INDEPENDENTS

presents

A GOLAN-GLOBUS production
of a BOAZ DAVIDSON film

PRIVATE Popsicle
(Lemon Popsicle IV)

Starring
YFTACH KATZUR   ZACHI NOY   JONATHAN SEGAL

Produced by Menahem Golan and Yoram Globus
Written and directed by Boaz Davidson

© 1982 Noah Films, Ltd.

CANNON INTERNATIONAL, INC
6464 Sunset Blvd., Suite 1150
Hollywood, Ca. 90028
Tel (213) 469-8124
Telex 18-1270 Answerback GG LSA

At the AFM
Westwood Plaza Hotel (Holiday Inn)
Office No. 1115 and 1117
Tel (213) 475-5284

In CANNES
Hotel Carlton, Suite 241
Tel 68-91-68
Telex CARLT A 470720 F

PRIVATE Popsicle

Benji, Huey and Bobby, the three perpetual adolescents, are out of high school and have joined the army for a three year stint.

Trouble starts immediately after induction when the boys discover that their army camp is divided between the sexes, and the women are strictly out of bounds. Libido overrides Sergeant Ramirez's orders when the three disguise themselves as officers and enter No Man's Land.

In the middle of the night, the girls are roused out of bed with a bogus lice alert. They are ordered to march, double time, to the showers. Benji, Huey, and Bobby ogle at the girls through peepholes. Their fun abruptly comes to an end when they are caught by an amazon lady sergeant, known and feared as Marshmellow. She catches Huey and gives him a beating while the other two run away.

Benji finds sanctuary in the guardhouse where he stumbles across Renee, asleep at her post. Benji falls head over heels in love with the sleeping beauty. She awakens to see an officer standing over her, and instead of a reprimand she gets a date.

Renee and two girlfriends join the boys (dressed as officers) at a nightclub. While ordering drinks, Sgt. Ramirez and his date, Marshmellow, enter the club. They order the girls back to the army base. When the boys return from the bar, they see the two sergeants. They run into a dressing room, pull off their officer uniforms, and disguise themselves as women. The night club manager, thinking that they are his new act, ushers them onto the stage where they quickly improvise a musical revue directly in front of the two sergeants.

Sgt. Ramirez falls in lust for Huey, a ravishing buxom blond. Marshmellow notices his quickened pulse and warns him that if ever he steps out of line, he is as good as dead. She leaves him, however, and Rodriguez makes his play. Benji and Bobby fend him off and leave Huey alone in Rodriguez's clutches.

Benji and Renee continue to see each other. He wants to tell her he isn't an officer, but just can't get the words out. Renee soon discovers that Benji is a common private. Heartbroken and enraged, she seeks to get even for his deception.

They meet for a date in a warehouse. Renee seduces Benji, undressing him totally. After he is naked, she takes his uniform and tells him where to get off.

Sneaking back into camp, Benji is caught by Ramirez. The sergeant takes the boys' plight to heart and they exchange the woes of their love lives. Ramirez is very much in love with Julie (Huey). Benji has a brainwave. He will arrange a date with Julie for the sergeant if he can get three passes.

Benji leaves the base and goes home to call Renee who is also on leave. His parents observe his erratic behaviour over this girl and become quite concerned. Benji tells Renee where he will be, but she hangs up on him. Meanwhile, Ramirez breaks his date with Marshmellow on the pretence that Benji is having family trouble and he must help the boy out.

Suspicious and jealous, Marshmellow pays a visit to Benji's house. The parents think she is Renee. Benji's mother is sick to think that her son could fall in love with such a beast. When the truth comes out, Marshmellow rushes over to the nightclub where she discovers Huey in Ramirez's arms. During the ensuing scuffle, the boys lose their wigs and flee for their lives.

Just outside the nightclub, Renee is waiting for Benji. She calls to him, and the two are reunited in love...

CAST

Benji . . . . YFTACH KATZUR	Sergeant Major . . . . DVORA BAKON
Huey . . . . ZACHI NOY	The Captain . . . . MOSHE ISH KASSIT
Bobby . . . . JONATHAN SEGALL	Eva . . . . BEA FIDLER
Renee . . . . SONJA MARTIN	Sonya . . . . DVORA KEIDAR
Sergeant Ramirez . . . . . JOSEPH SHILOAH	Romek . . . . . MENACHE WARSHAWSKY

Produced by MENAHEM GOLAN and YORAM GLOBUS ·
Written and Directed by BOAZ DAVIDSON · Associate Producer AMNON GLOBUS ·
Director of Photography ADAM GREENBERG · Editor BRURIA DAVIDSON ·
Art Director ARIEL ROSHKO · Music Soundtrack Supervision JACK FISHMAN ·

Running Time: 100 mins.   Certificate '18'   Reg. No: F41478

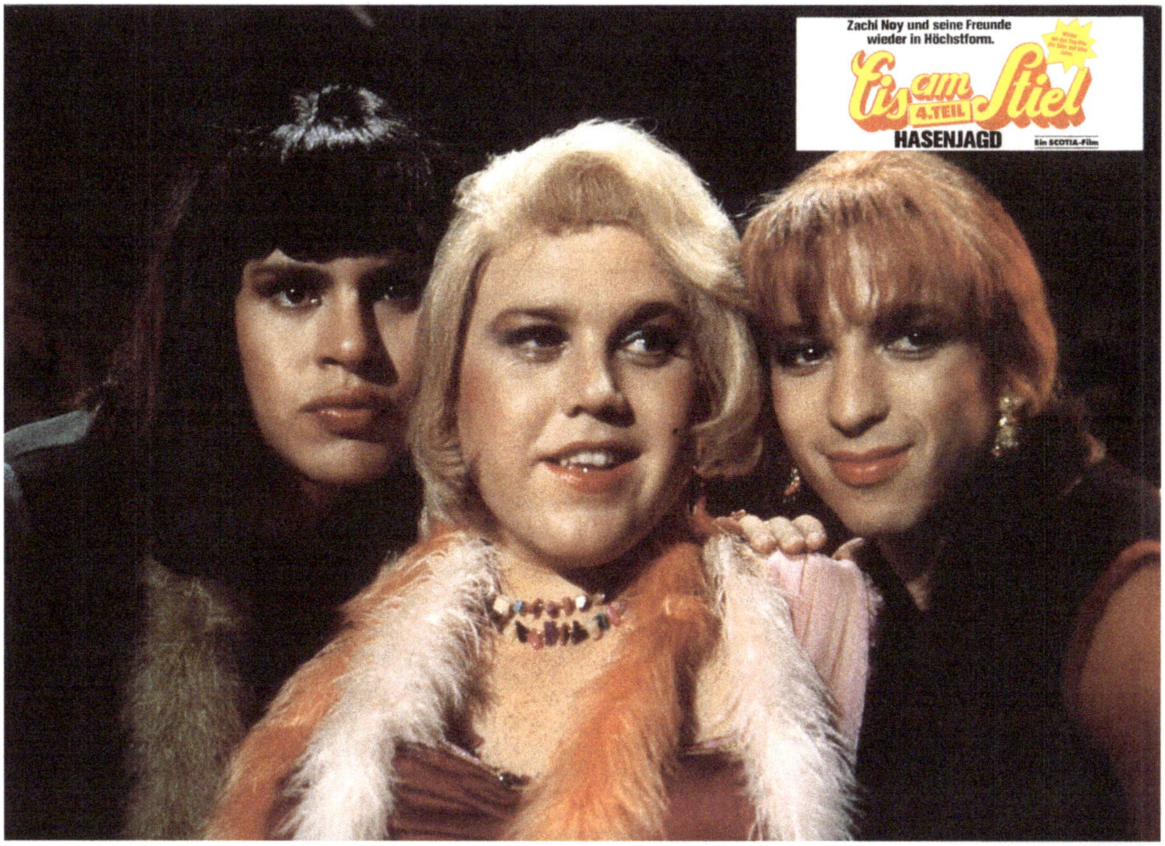
Zachi Noy und seine Freunde
wieder in Höchstform.
Eis am Stiel
4. TEIL
HASENJAGD
Ein SCOTIA-Film

Zachi Noy und seine Freunde
wieder in Höchstform.
Eis am Stiel
4. TEIL
HASENJAGD
Ein SCOTIA-Film

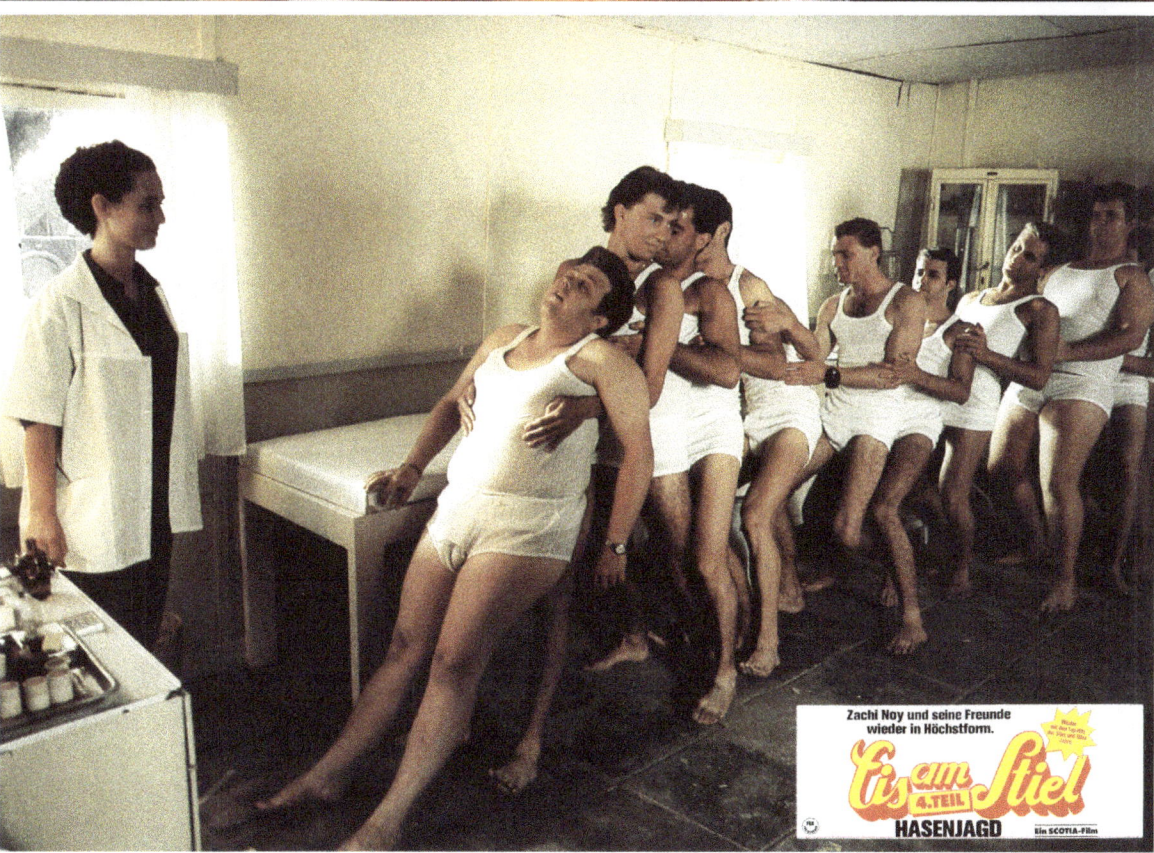

When Bobby is making the moves, you know that Benji and Huey aren't too far away and they're stripping to their underwear. The spectacular Bea Fiedler makes her Popsicle debut. She returned in *Baby Love* and *Up Your Anchor*, and appeared in two 'nourishing' Popsicle cash-ins, *Popcorn and Ice Cream* and *Hot Chilli*.

Sonja Martin as Rina. She returned as 'Sandy' in *Young Love*.

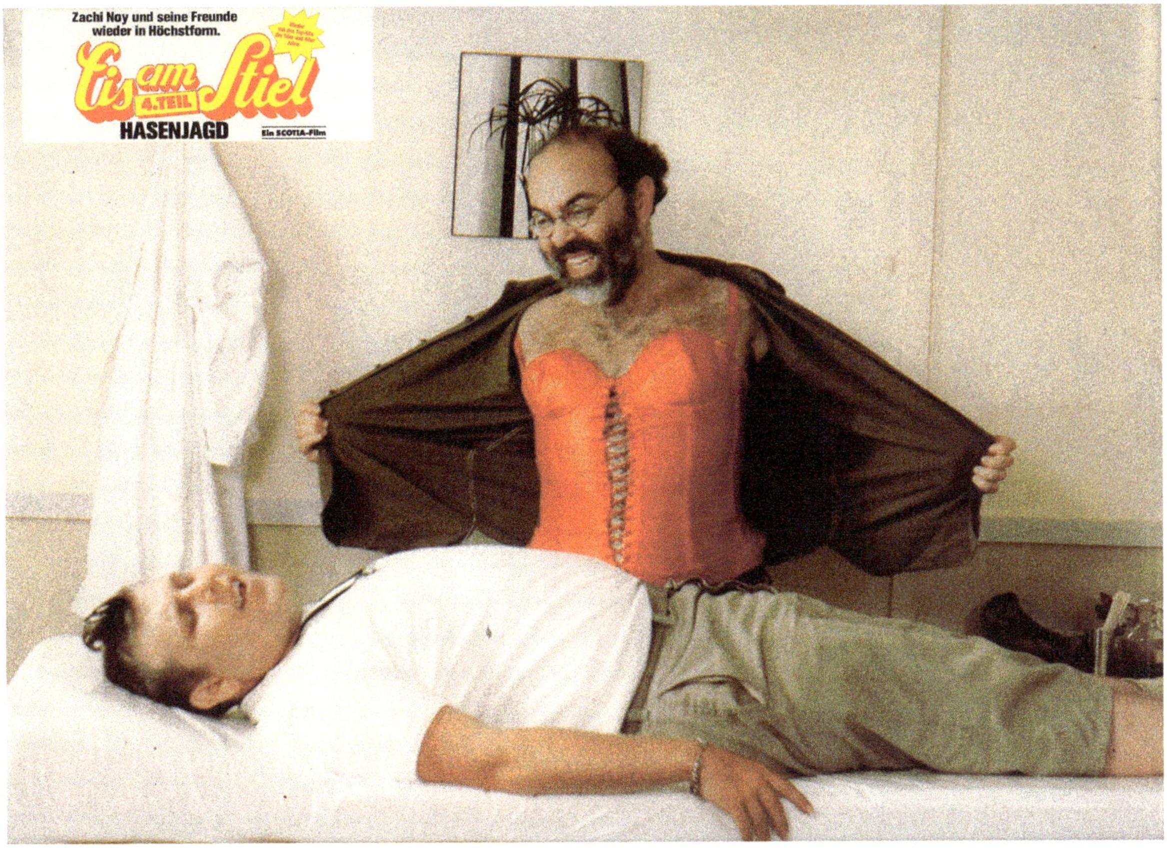

Zachi's scheme to get a leave of absence by pretending to be an insatiable homosexual backfires as the skeletons come rattling out of the psychiatrist's closet. Louis Rosenberg is great as the crazy doctor. He played the pharmacist in the original film.

'Yftach Katzur and Sonja Martin arrived in Japan on June 23rd to do the publicity campaign for their movie. The reporters met up with them to interview them. Having just cranked out *Growing Up 5, Baby Love*, the two show no sign of stopping.'

Katzur: "I don't think I was as good as Dustin Hoffman at cross-dressing. The makeup took two hours and the entire cross-dressing scene was shot in three days. My friends were all laughing about it but I personally don't have any interest in cross-dressing!"

Four Films with Zachi Noy

Private Manoeuvres (*Sababa; Eis am Steil 4, Teil - Hasenjagd 2, Teil,* 1983)

This sequel to *Private Popsicle* doesn't star Katzur or Sagall, but Zachi Noy returns as Huey to run Ramirez (Joseph Shiloach) ragged again, and Dvora Bakon returns as Marshmallow to complete Ramirez's misery. The story builds to the annual war games battle between Captain Fletcher (Moshe Ish-Kassit) and Captain Shag (Shmuel Omani), with Fletcher determined to upset the form book. On or about the thirty-seven-minutes-and-twenty-seconds mark, Sibylle Rauch strides in as the English-speaking wife of a visiting ambassador. She, Shiloach and Zachi Noy speak English during their scenes together. There is a bit of confusion over the credits - Noy is top-billed on the press-releases and posters but, on the screen, Rauch gets top billing. A similar arrangement was done for Clint Eastwood and Burt Reynolds for *City Heat*. The direction is credited on the film to Tzvi Shissel, but the promotional material co-credits Boaz Davidson. Davidson wrote the screenplay, which is more expansive than that of *Private Popsicle*.

p Golan & Globus *ph* Adam Greenberg *ed* Bruria Davidson, Karen Hoenig *pd* Yoram Barzilai

Wenn Sie wissen wollen, wie
EIS AM STIEL 4. Teil – HASENJAGD
weitergeht, dann gehen Sie in
HASENJAGD 2. Teil
Regie: BOAZ DAVIDSON/Z. SCHISSEL
Ein SCOTIA-Film

Wenn Sie wissen wollen, wie
EIS AM STIEL 4. Teil – HASENJAGD
weitergeht, dann gehen Sie in
HASENJAGD 2. Teil
Regie: BOAZ DAVIDSON/Z. SCHISSEL
Ein SCOTIA-Film

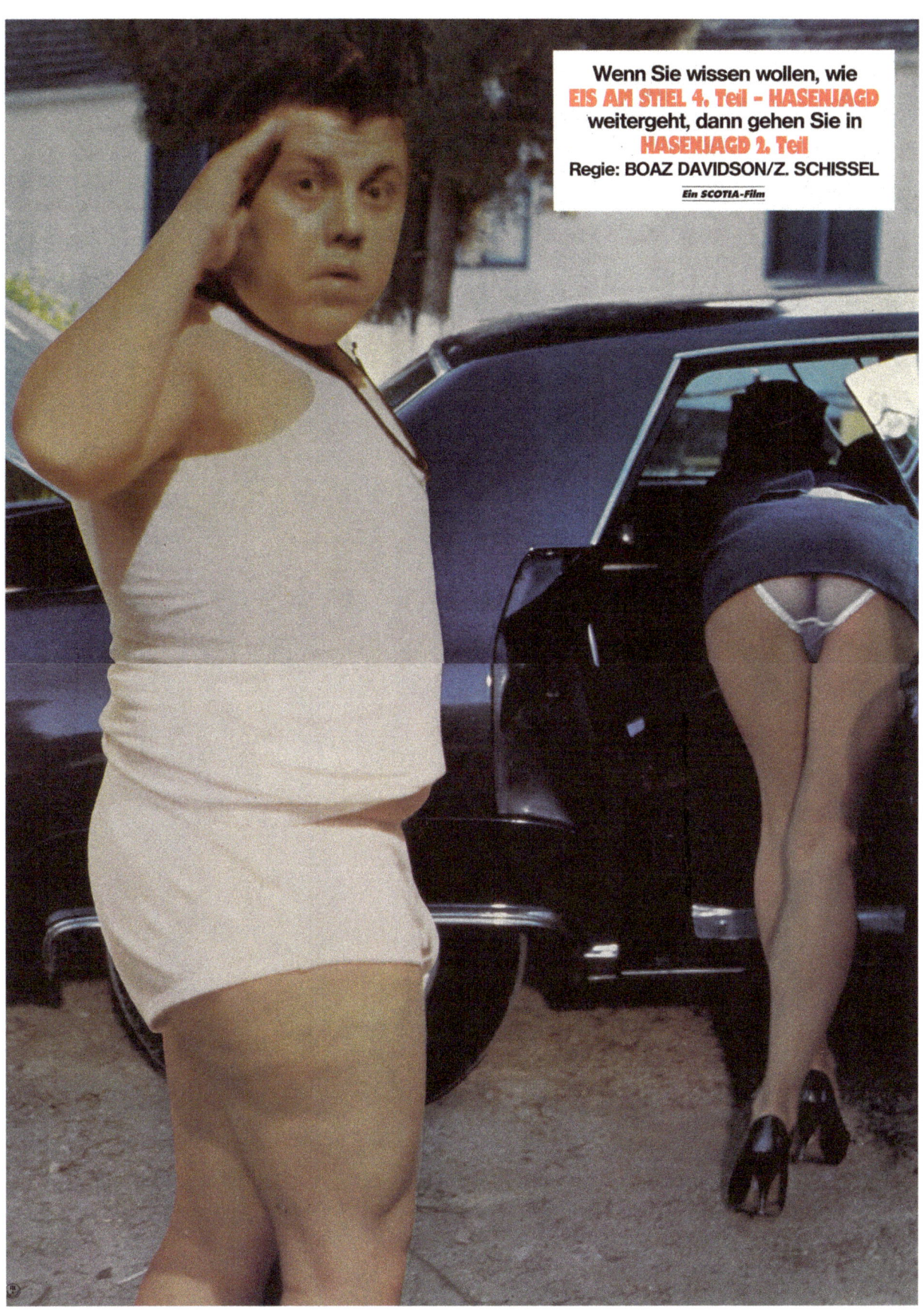

The *Private Manoeuvres* Soundtrack

The film has a more orchestral and eclectic soundtrack than a full Popsicle style song score as such. It starts with what sounds like a chorus of Bengali women singing over the opening credits (of the Israeli version), and it closes with a yodeling song that is also used during the first Rauche-Noy sex scene. In between come four favourites, *Whole Lotta Shakin' Goin' On*, *Mr. Sandman*, *La Bamba*, *Yakety Yak*, and *The Liberty Bell* (The Monty Python Theme).

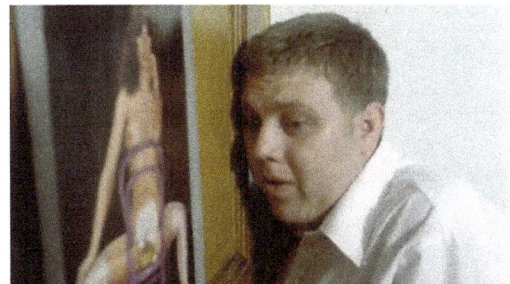

Zachi Noy and Christine Zierl would famously reunite for the party scene in *Baby Love*.

Popcorn and Ice cream (1978)

The film with which the Popsicle series took a tentative (bold) step into Germany, with Zachi Noy imported into Munich as a holiday season waiter and billed before the title. It sold 575.000 tickets at the German box-office, therefore it was only a matter of time before a German producer bought into the full Popsicle cast. It's a sexy summer film with poor slapstick comedy sequences, long disco scenes, and Zachi briefly in drag as a nun. A lemon-yellow VW Beatle leads to lost money and hotel sex adventures for two liberated young women. There is so much VW product placement that it is almost unsurprising to see the Formula One World Champion, Nikki Lauda, make a cameo appearance. That said, it would be rather like Gary Lineker turning up in a Robin Askwith sex romp.

d Franz Josef Gottlieb sc Erich Tomek m Gerhard Heinz. It starts with an electronic version of *The Benny Hill Theme*, thereby establishing the aim and the tone.

Soundtrack Tommi Ohrner, *Nochmal Schwein Gehabt*
Suzy Quatro, Chris Norman, *Stumblin' In*
Bogart, *Black Magic Woman*
Cliff Richard, *We Don't Talk Anymore*
Marshall Hain, *Dancing in the City*
Exile, *I Wanna Kiss You All Over*
Peter Kent, *It's a Real Good Feeling*
La Bionda, *One For You, One For Me*
Hank The Knife & The Jets, *Guitar King*
The Cats, *One Way Wind*
Charly, *Santa Barbara*
Peter Griffin, *Step by Step*

Die Unglaublichen Abenteuer des Guru Jakob (1983)

Zachi Noy took time out from getting chased in his underwear to, er, get chased in his underwear in *The Unbelievable Adventures of Guru Jakob*. The film centres around the Bavarian exploits of Jakob (Zachi Noy) and his mate Tommi (ex-child star, Thomas Ohrner) and their attempts to make a fast buck. Noy is mistaken for a religious Guru! The strong *Popsicle* connection is boosted by the welcome appearances of Sonja Martin and Sibylle Rauch. Noy's character has romantic aspirations towards Suzi (Martin) but, in keeping with *Popsicle* tradition, she only has eyes for his good-looking friend.

d Franz Marischka *sc* Franz Marischka, Leon Pulver *ph* Ernst W. Kalinke

The Ambassador (1984)

The *Popsicle* connection was kept going in Golan and Globus' *The Ambassador* (1984), a film about the Israeli-Palestinian conflict. It was shot on location in Israel with a cast of superstars, Robert Mitchum, Donald Pleasance, and Rock Hudson in his last film, supported by Popsicle regulars. Most of the action focuses on the U.S. Ambassador's attempts to formulate a peace plan.

The *Lemon Popsicle* interest starts early in the film with Yftach Katzur's stalking the Ambassador's wife (played by Ellen Burstyn) in order to find out information about her affair with Hashimi (Fabio Testi). Zachi Noy and Joseph Shiloah also make early appearances. Zachi plays Ze'ev, a dubious character involved in all sorts of shenanigans. Joseph plays the equally dodgy Shimon. Both characters are out to make a fast buck, and don't mind at whose expense, and both are involved in negotiations with a hit-man who is hired to kill the American Ambassador (Mitchum). Rachel Steiner appears briefly as a laboratory technician. The cinematography is by *Popsicle* regular, Adam Greenberg.

p Menahem Golan, Yoram Globus *d* J. Lee Thompson *sc* Max Jack, suggested by the novel *52 Pick-Up* by Elmore Leonard *ph* Adam Greenberg *ed* Mark Goldblatt *ad* Yoram Barzilai

"... the only real surprise comes from the fact that the film under review has a totally different ending from the one in the distributor's synopsis. There, something to do with the blackmail plot - here entirely forgotten - provides the climax... the rest of the film involves an inordinate amount of cross-cutting between the many and largely unrelated plots, and an even greater amount of driving round the streets of Jerusalem and Tel Aviv, presumably in search of some degree of authenticity. In fact, the only authenticity comes in two brief but powerful scenes between Robert Mitchum and Ellen Burstyn, in which they discuss their marriage in terms which could almost refer to their presence in the film. Otherwise, *The Ambassadors* is the epitome of the Cannon style of market-orientated motion picture: a dash of controversy, a hint of topicality, pretty (but low-cost) locations, a touch of nudity, a lot of guns, and as big a bunch of ill-assorted international stars as the budget will bear." Nick Roddick (*Monthly Film Bulletin* UK, January 1985)

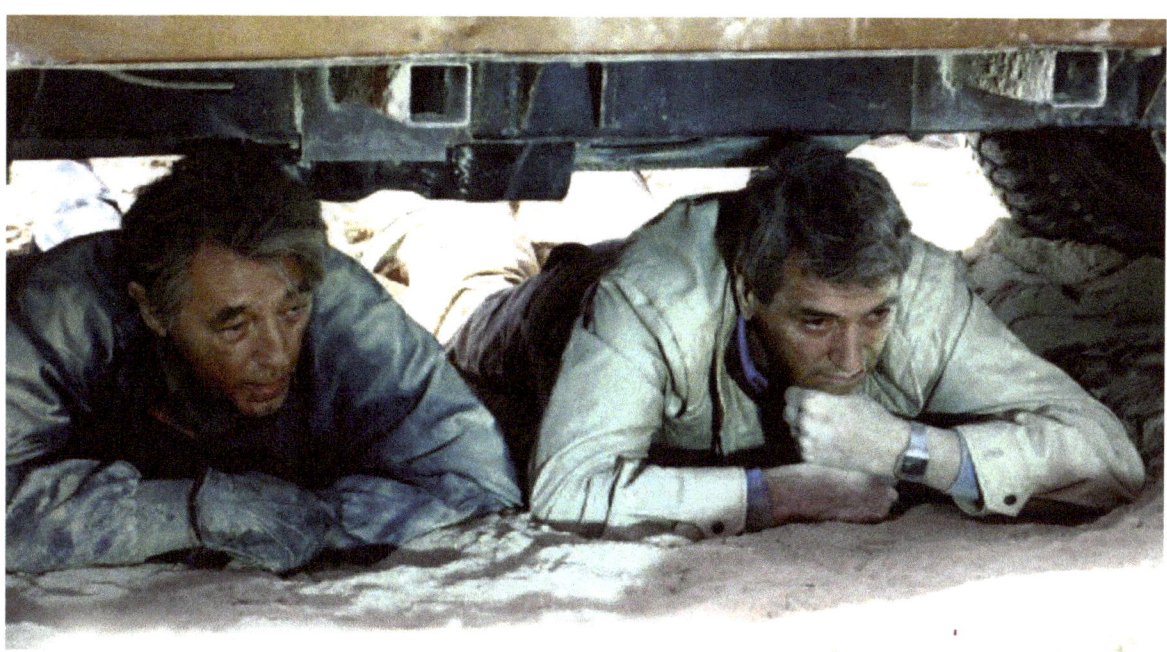

Baby Love

Roman Za'ir

Eis am Stiel 5 - Die große Liebe

1984

Baby Love

We like *Star Wars* films to start with a shot of star-dotted space and the camera panning down to a spaceship. We like *Lemon Popsicle* films to begin with the three heroes travelling through the streets of Tel Aviv en route to the Montana. Here they are on big loud motorbikes. An illogical but thrillingly cinematic edit takes them from the dusk-dark city to the sun-bright beach and to comic variations on scenes of spying at a woman in the shower, and sex stunts which end with Huey being chased and slapped on his big bare backside. On then to the Montana to watch the girls come in. This time, the arriving girl is Bobby's kid sister, Ginny, played German newcomer, Stefanie Petsch. The film that emerges is a puppy love romance between Ginny and Benji. Petsch has the right bloom of youth to contrast poignantly and uneasily with the increasing adulthood of Benji and his friends. She's fine in the role, although the dramatic high is somewhat neutered by a lack of detail and screen time, i.e. Ginny takes an overdose but is up and about again that very same night. The film pulls too many punches to be really effective as drama.

Around this main narrative line are pranks at the pool, a visit to the local nymphomaniac (Bea Fiedler now playing a dental nurse) and laughs with Benji's parents. The tone, the colours and the playing, are more confident than any previous Popsicle film, doubtless because the actors have grown in life as they have in their art, and because new blood has been brought to the production, particularly in the form of a new director, Dan Wolman, and a new cinematographer. Boaz Davidson supervised the production and wrote the script with Eli Tabor.

It's possible to see *Baby Love* as an inspired combination of James Dean and Elvis films, a would-be sensitive and hard-hitting film about young love set within an easy-go-lucky frame and a rock and rock soundtrack, with Benji's character drawn from the James Dean prototype of the sensitive, misunderstood, handsome rebel without a cause. *Rebel Without the Cause* is the inspiration for the film's beach cliff motorcycle stunt, but when it comes to directing action scenes, Wolman is no John McTiernan (and no Nicholas Ray). He fails to create a sense of speed and danger. James Dean images dominate the set dressing. There are photographs of James Dean on at least four different sets/locations including a cinema billboard for *Rebel Without a Cause* still playing at their local cinema! (It will be back again for *The Party Goes On*). And in this film, Huey gets to wear the red *Rebel* windcheater.

Jonathan Segall's, Bobby, is a sort of Elvis-Brando variant (his nickname in *Private Popsicle* was 'Elvis Presley'). Elvis himself appears on screen in the form of his in-the-army newsreel (a wink to *Private Popsicle*) and his image appears in the set dressing, notably on reproductions of the superb poster for Elvis's 1962 film, *Girls! Girls! Girls!*. The poster features prominently on the wall of the Montana ice-cream bar and, in cut down form, as the centrepiece of the wall collage in Benji's bedroom. Bobby, is given a more central role than he has been given thus far (he was the cause of the drama of the first film but absented himself from the resolution), but the emphasis, i.e. the main narrative line, stays with Benji, and it is right that that is so. Benji is a more potent audience identification figure than the big strong handsome Bobby who always gets the girl. The world has more Benjis than Bobbys.

But Christine Zierl (who found fame under the pseudonym, Dolly Dollar) almost steals the whole show. She made her film debut alongside Zachi Noy and Bea Fiedler in *Popcorn and Ice Cream* (see page 135). Here she is hindered by overly crude make-up (a faceful of over-large black spots that change in almost every shot) and bottle-glasses. But, when she stops knocking things over and spilling things (yawn) she gets the biggest laughs. She generates real energy and excitement when, spiked with alcohol, she strips and swings her big beautiful breasts.

The soundtrack, framed by performances of Chuck Berry singing *Sweet Little Sixteen*, features the expected favourites and also a surprising tune for cineastes - the acoustic guitar theme from René Clement's heartbreaking masterpiece, *Forbidden Games* (about an orphan girl lost in the French countryside in wartime). It is played by an extra on the beach when Ginny's romance has broken up, and it continues across to the scene where she is weeping in her bedroom.

Audacious transition edit from the dark dusk of Tel Aviv's streets to the bright sunlight of the beach.

Above, Tom Chantrell's rough sketch for the UK poster. Below, his approved and finished painting.

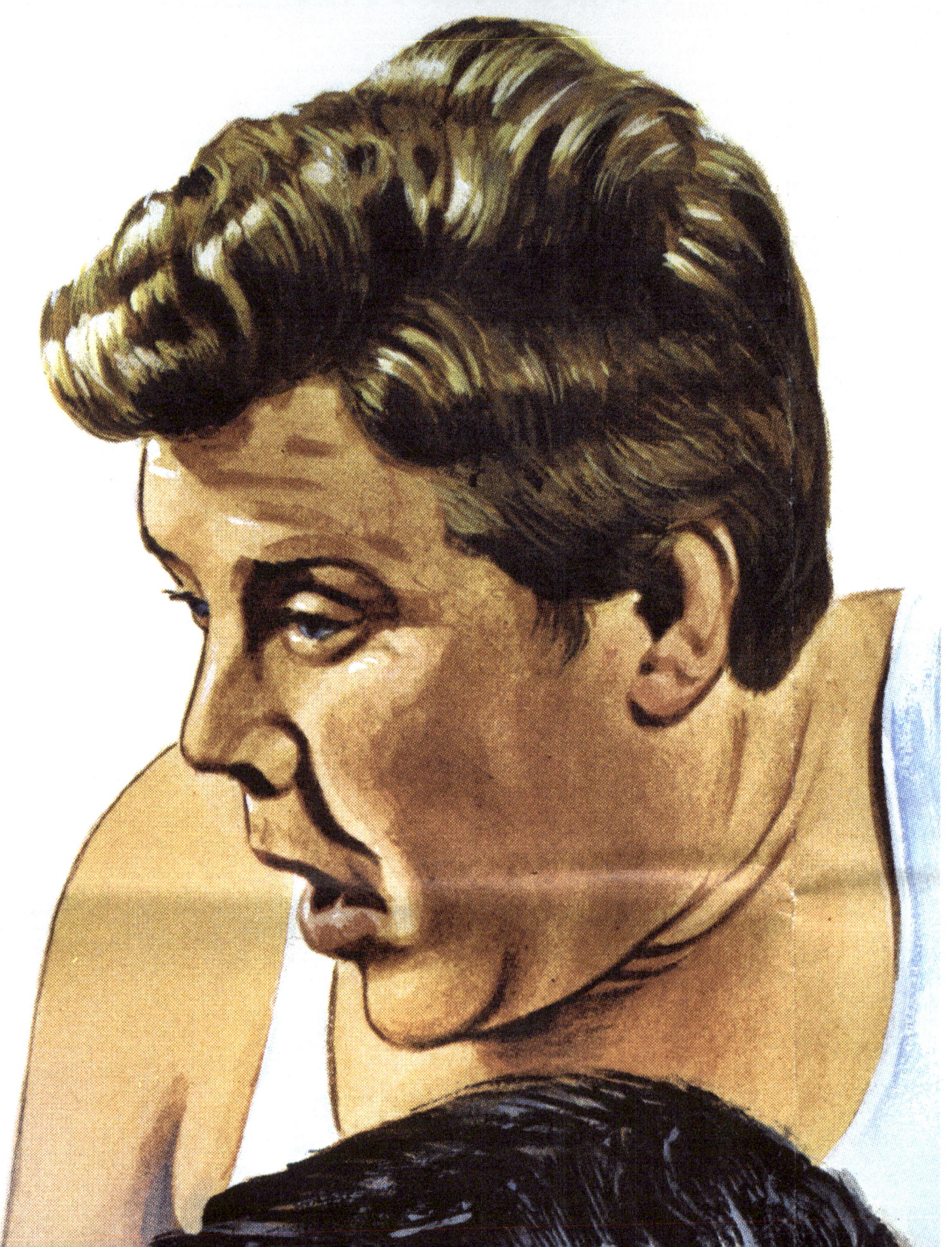

'BABY LOVE' begins with Benji, Bobby, and Huey out of school and closer than ever as friends. It is summer, and their days are occupied by excursions to the beach and humorous escapades.

In addition to their obsession with the fairer sex, the boys have a new preoccupation — motorcycles. During the day, they enjoy showing off their bikes by racing around a barrel perched precariously by the edge of a cliff. For evening fun and frolic, they hang out at the Cafe Montana.

One night, the boys run into Bobby's sister, Gili, at the cafe. Benji is quite taken with her as she is with him. Over the course of the next few weeks they see each other often and grow quite affectionate. Bobby becomes anxious about their relationship and tries to cut it off. When he does, Gili becomes emotionally distraught. This leads to further conflict between Benji and Bobby. Having lost his girlfriend and his best friend within a short period, Benji attempts a a very foolish and dangerous stunt with his motorbike. Bobby comes to the rescue, but soon it is he who needs aid. When Benji saves him, the two work out their differences to everyone's satisfaction.

CAST

Benji	YFTACH KATZUR
Huey	ZACHI NOY
Bobby	JONATHAN SEGALL
Gili	STEFANIE PETSCH
Ruthi	SABRINA CHEVAL
Cousin Frieda	DOLLY DOLLAR
Lifeguard's Girlfriend	RENATE LANGER
Romek	MENACHE WARSHAVSKY
Dental Assistant	BEA FIEDLER

Executive Producers: Amnon Globus and Rafi Adar
Director of Photography: Ilan Rosenberg
Editor: Mark Halfrich
Written by Boaz Davidson and Eli Tabor
Produced by Menahem Golan and Yoram Globus
Directed by Dan Wolman

Running Time: 1hr 25 mins   Certificate '18'

Baby Love was given an 18 certificate by the BBFC on 13th January 1984. It was released in UK cinema release in March 1984.

Ah, this really should have been Louis Rosenberg, our favourite crabs chemist and crazy doctor.

Renate Langer as the lifeguard

Avi Hadash balances the glasses on this rare Greek lobby card. Christine Zierl prepares to dance.

Stefanie Petsch plays peek-a-boo. Sabrina Cheval kisses Jonathan Sagall

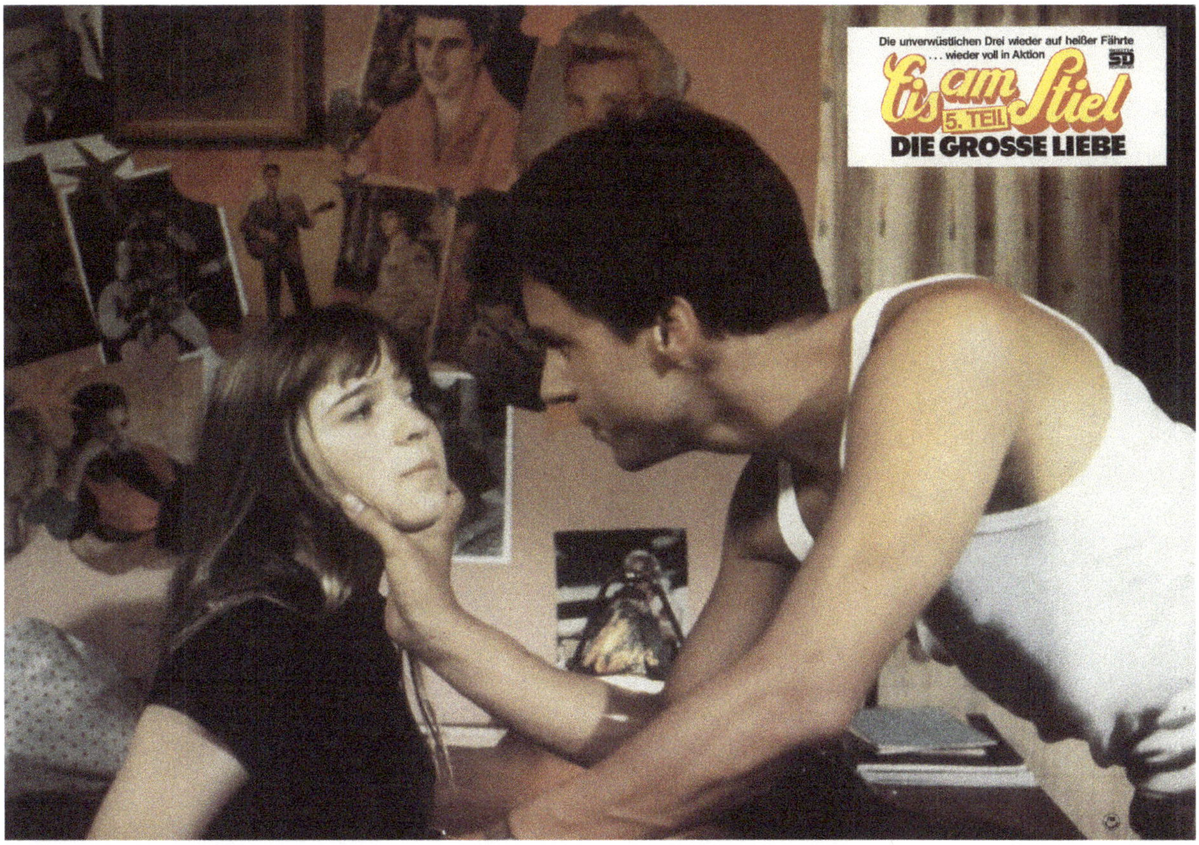
Die unverwüstlichen Drei wieder auf heißer Fährte
... wieder voll in Aktion
Eis am Stiel
5. TEIL
DIE GROSSE LIEBE

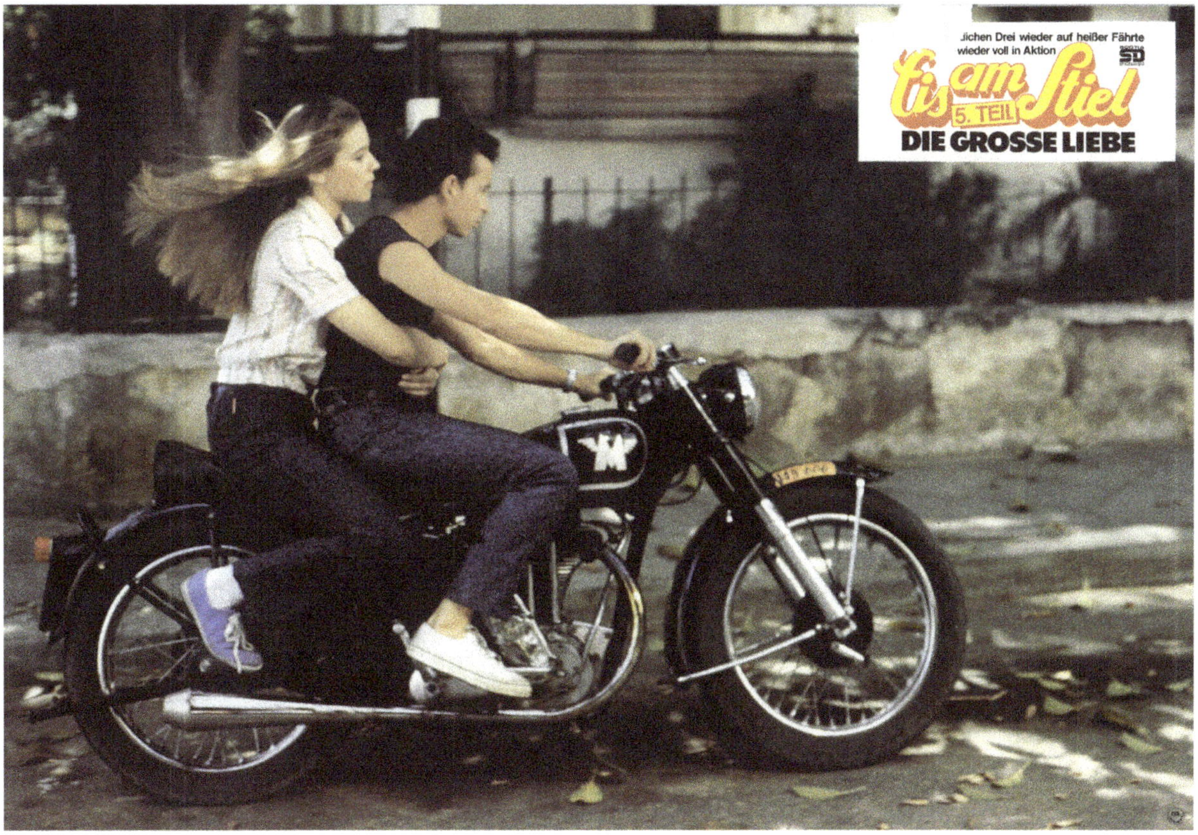
wieder voll in Aktion
Eis am Stiel
5. TEIL
DIE GROSSE LIEBE

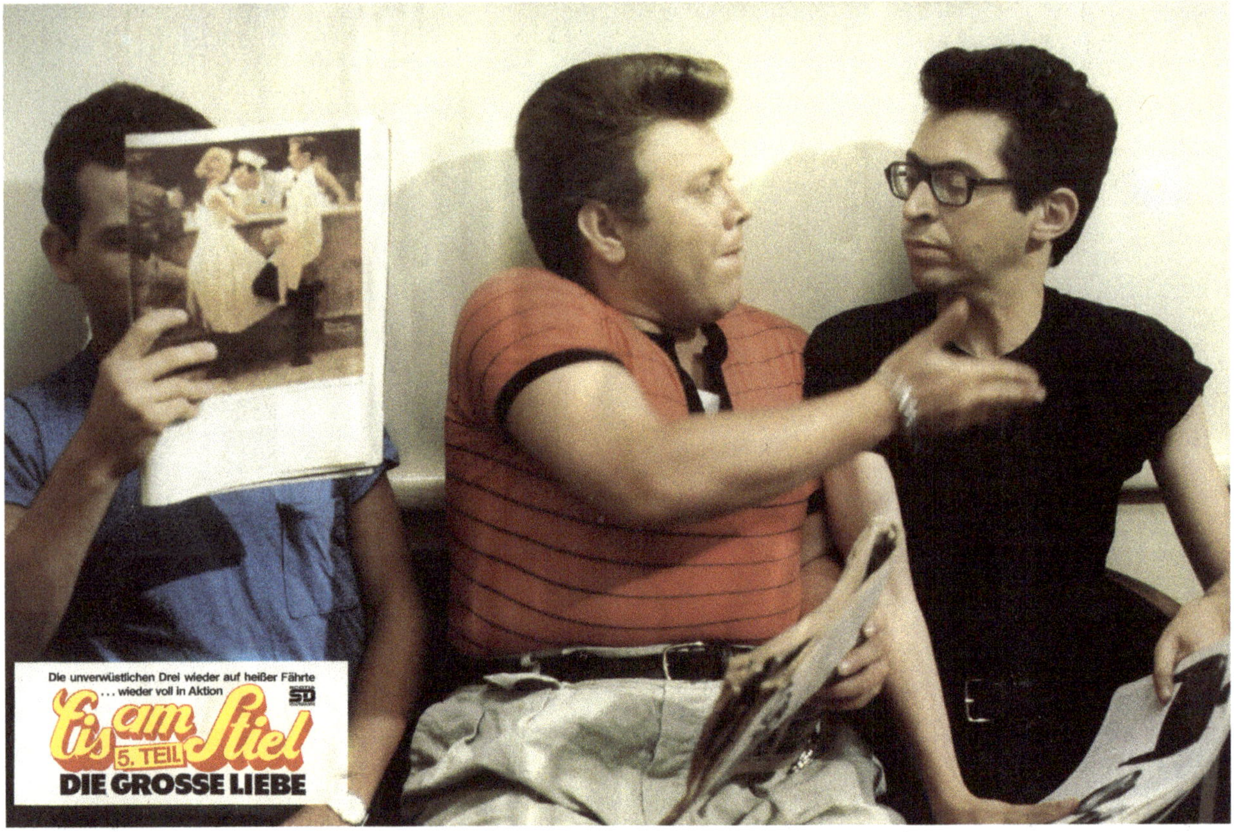

A very civilised Norman Rockwell painting in Benji's magazine is used to add to the fifties flavour and to contrast with the very uncivilised behaviour of the slap-happy Huey.

Set dressing images of James Dean in *Rebel Without in a Cause* are there to suggest that this tale of infatuation will not end happily.

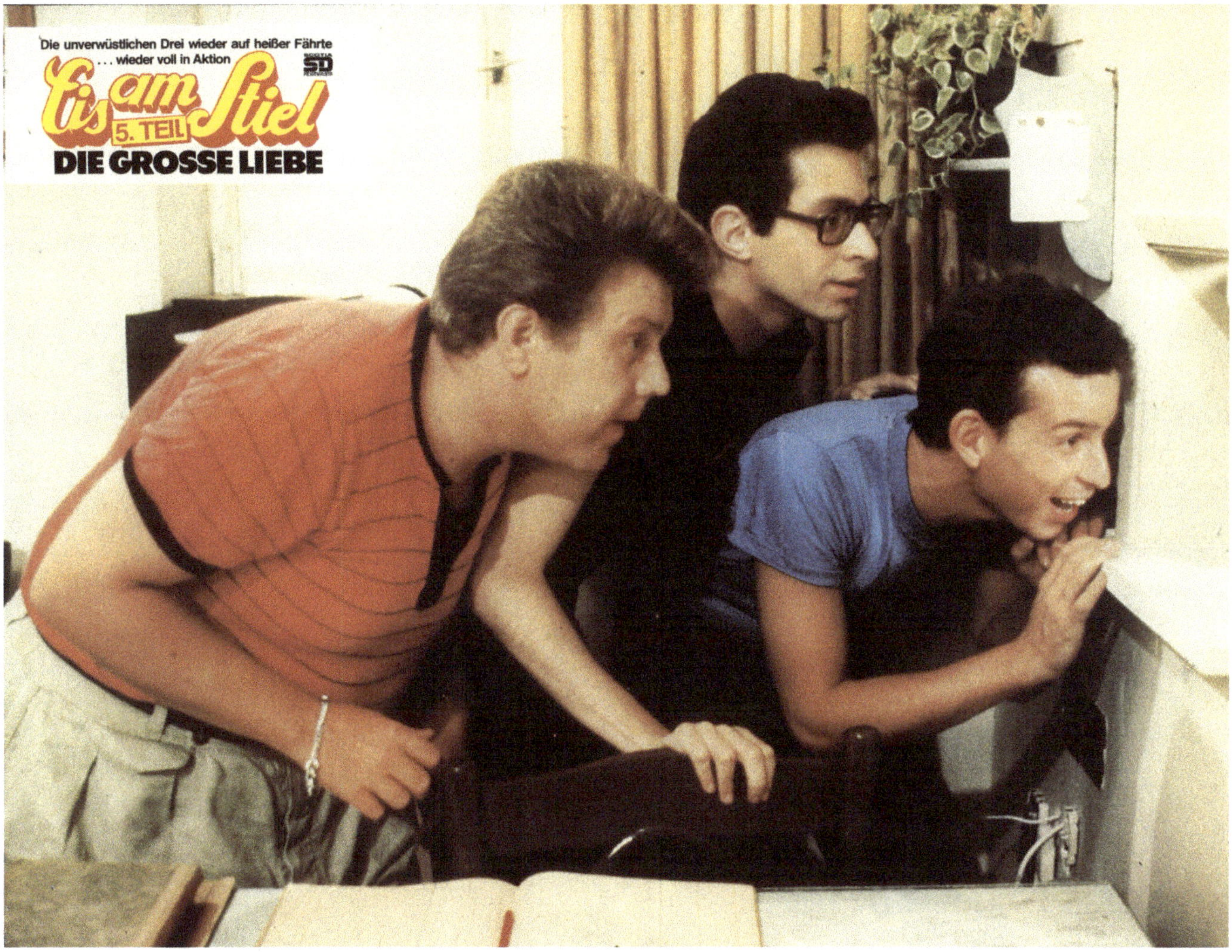
Die unverwüstlichen Drei wieder auf heißer Fährte
... wieder voll in Aktion
Eis am Stiel
5. TEIL
DIE GROSSE LIEBE

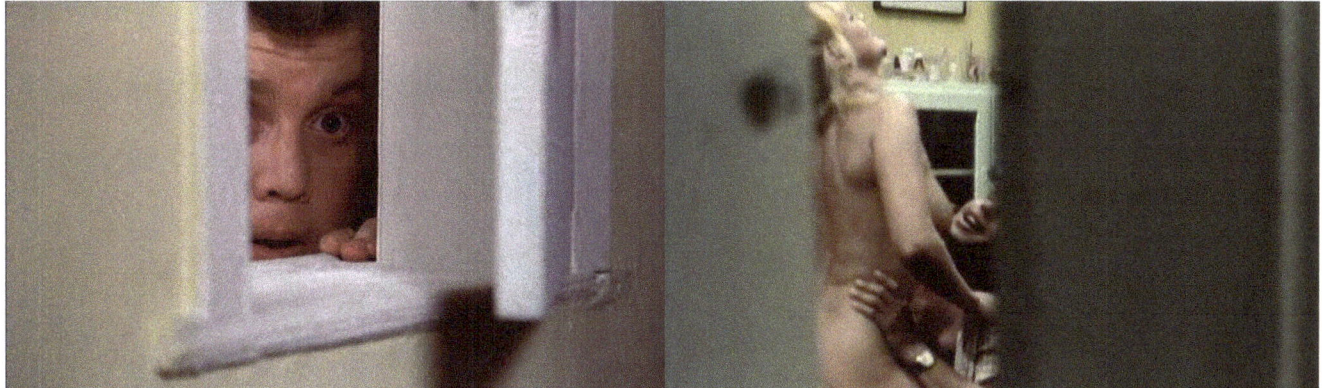

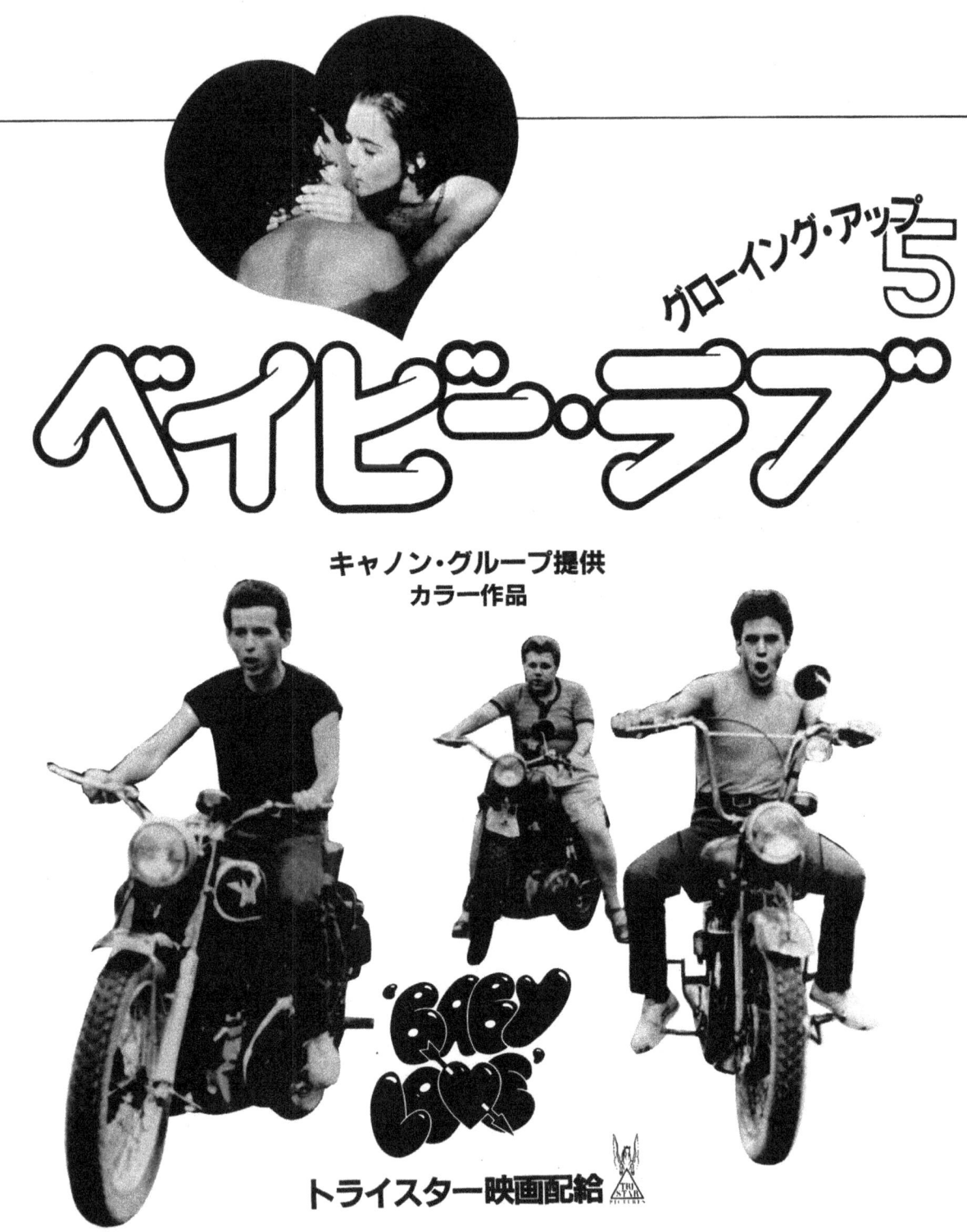

Japanese programme note: "In my poor knowledge, I equate Israel with Christ. But these movies have completely changed that. Ever since these movie have been made, Israel has become a hit country for me. And bit by bit, I have come to like Israel. During this time period, movies used a lot of violence, occult, panic and special effects to rope in a bigger audience. The audience received such shocks that they didn't have a chance to think. It's times like this that realistic everyday life movies have the most appeal. I'm sure there are movies all over the world that go against the grain like *Baby Love*."

Songs used in *Baby Love*

Chuck Berry, *Sweet Little Sixteen* and *Maybelline*
Bobby Darin, *Splish Splash*
Fontella Bass, *Rescue Me*
Eddie Cochran, *Summertime Blues*
The Crests, *Sixteen Candles*
Dion, *The Wanderert*
Bobby Vee, *Take Good Care Of My Baby*
The Surfaris, *Wipeout*
The Cherokees, *Apache*
Little Eva, *Locomotion*
Curtis Lee, *Pretty Little Angel Eyes*
Little Richard, *The Girl Can't Help It*
Sam Cooke *You Send Me*
Bobby Darin, *Multiplication*
Little Richard, *Keep A Knockin'*
The Chiffons, *He's So Fine*
The Platters, *Twilight Time*
Bill Justis, *Raunchy*
Bryan Hyland, *Ginny Come Lately*
Bobby Darin, *Dream Lover*
Sam Cooke, *What A Wonderful World*
Sam Cooke, *Only Sixteen*
Fabian, *Tiger*
Dion, *The Wanderer*
The Cherokees, *Apache*
Skeeter Davis, *End Of The World*
Sandy Nelson, *Teen Beat*
The Cascades, *Rhythm of the Rain*
Bryan Hyland, *Ginny Come Lately*
Paul Anka, *Crazy Love*

Elvis doesn't sing on the soundtrack but he does an in-film cameo on newsreel, and his image plays a prominent role in imagery in the set dressing.

Luridly coloured credit cards used on the UK prints.

Text from the German pressbook: "The *Lemon Popsicle* films have developed into a brand name and, when evaluated as a phenomenon, each film in the series became better in its design. Countless imitators have made that clear. Therefore, for the fifth time, happily and originally, we have the joys and sufferings of young love. It's ONE FOR ALL - AND EVERYONE FOR HIMSELF!
As a trio they are more like The Andrews Sisters than Alexandre Dumas' Three Musketeers. The Marx Brothers, Groucho, Harpo, Zappo and Chico, who strained our laughter muscles, are like the adopted fathers of our trio - Benny, Bobby and Johnny - although *Lemon Popsicle* never had the praise which these much loved and much praised anarchists of the cinema screen had."

Eine deutsch-israelische Coproduktion der KF KINOFILM, München, und GOLAN-GLOBUS PRODUCTIONS, Tel Aviv, im Verleih der SCOTIA

Kinostart: 9. März 1984

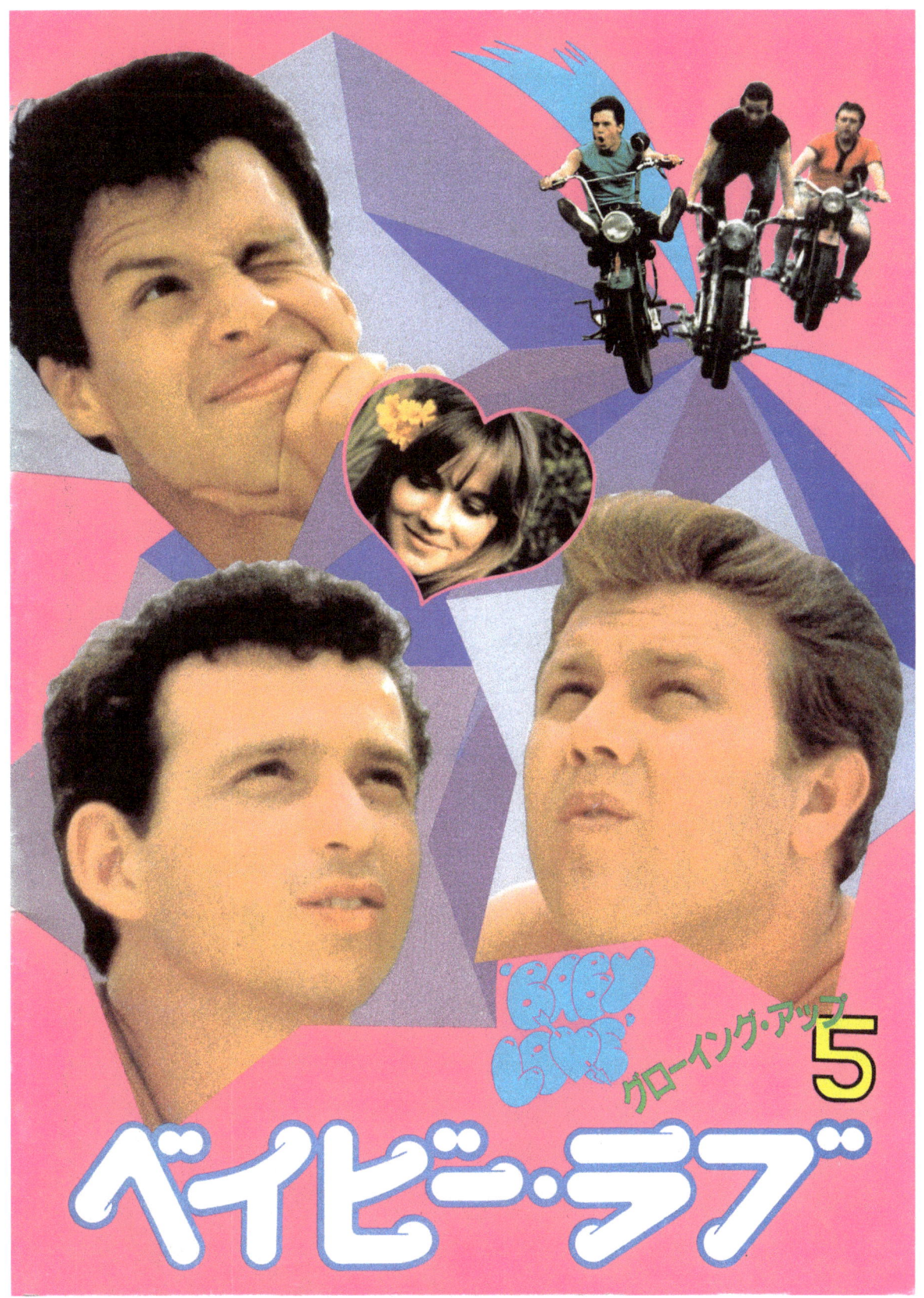

"BABY LOVE" (Lemon Popsicle 5) (18)   Released by Cannon Film Distributors (UK) Ltd.

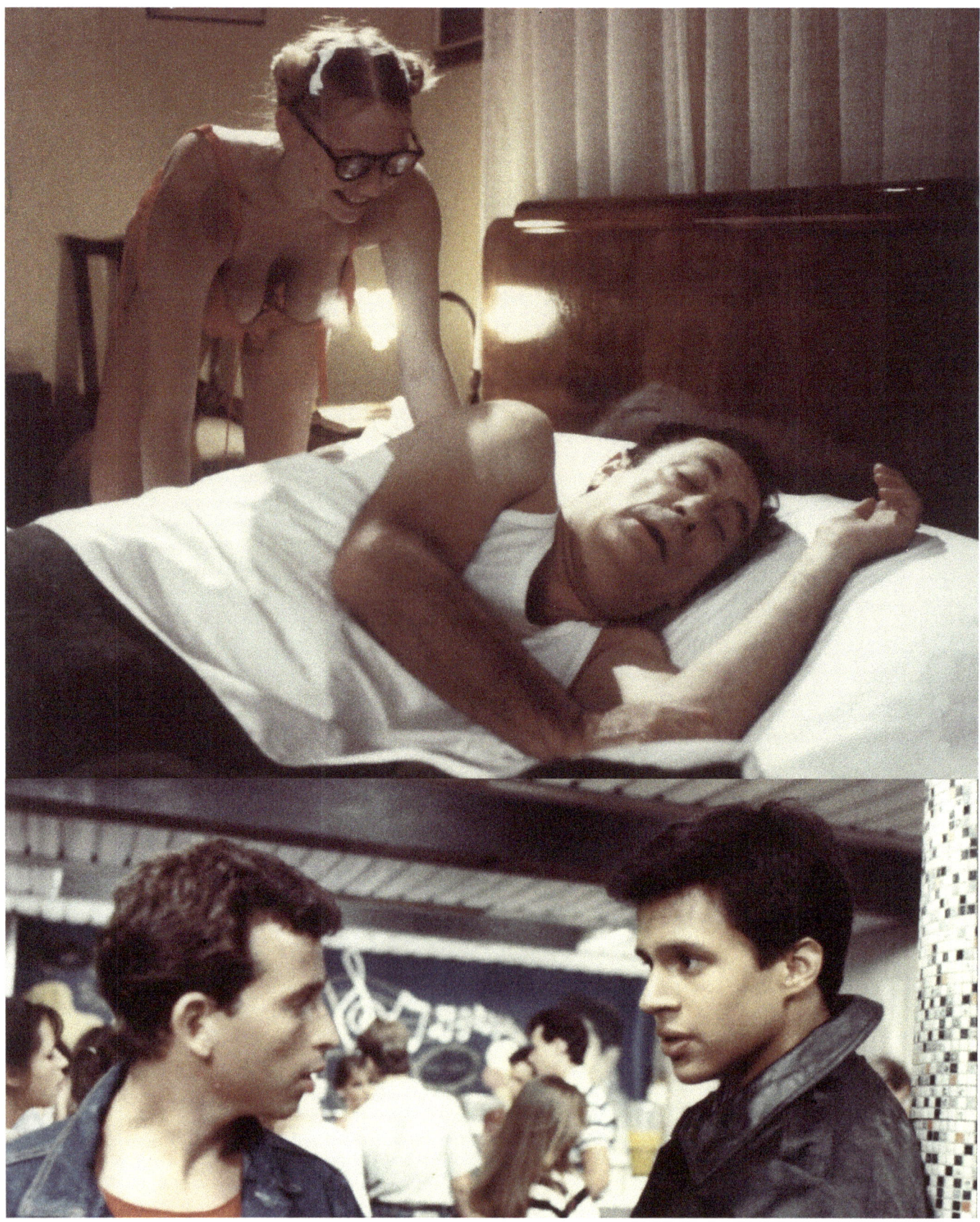

Stefanie Petsch

Up Your Anchor

Harimu Ogen

Eis am Stiel 6 - Ferienliebe

1985

Up Your Anchor

The boys are riding along in a glorious vintage open-topped car and they drive towards a car full of girls that has broken down and is parked by the roadside with its bonnet open. As they drive past, Huey grabs at the backside of one of the girls bent over looking at the car's troubled engine, and her skirt comes off in his hands. He and the boys roar with laughter and Huey holds the skirt aloft like a trophy as they carry on driving down the road. If you involuntarily laughed out loud when the skirt came away in his hand (I nearly fell off my chair) you will have a good time watching this film, for all its strangeness. And it is a strange film. There's an over-extended interlude when the boys sit down to watch the commercially released Super 8mm film of themselves having sex with the nympho in *Lemon Popsicle*, a superb idea when handled with elán, and one that could have pulled the film into the post-modernist style made famous by the French masters, Claude Lelouch and Alain Resnais. There was no fourth person there, in the rooms with them at the nympho's apartment in the first film, except of course the camera crew making the fictional film. So we are watching real-life actors watching themselves playing fictional characters, characters that they are simultaneously playing again many years later. Except that we are not. It's a lazy cheat that turns into a lot of time filling. The Super 8mm film is soon replaced by the 35mm 'movie' and the curious 'homage' becomes a near seven-minute re-run, i.e. a filler, a cheat, and the film as art is critically wounded. The scene comes to an end when Benny copies the penis in the popcorn stunt from *Diner* (1982), except that the staging and the playing are poor. In fact, the staging throughout is mostly poorly done. Very few scenes are allowed to run the right dramatic length. This failing is particularly noticeable at the film's finale with its ineptly staged re-run of the diamonds in the broken glass gag from *Indiana Jones*.

The English title is clearly an attempt to summon the spirit of Frankie Howerd. It fails. The German title translates as *Holiday Love* and the boys do go on a sort of holiday to Venice, and one of them (guess who) falls in love. The film starts badly with a narrator introducing us to the main staff and passengers of a cruise ship, including a diamond smuggling Baron (who copies the poodle-mule joke from the Donald Sutherland-Elliott Gould film, *Spys*). The footage used in this narration is used again as filler later in the film. The Chief Petty Officer is played by Joseph Shiloach playing a different but very similar character to the Sergeant Ramires of his two *Private* films. That the Popsicle boys make no reference at all to his similarity adds to the film's falling credibility. After this introduction, the narrative moves away from the ship for twenty minutes to do re-runs of beach gags from the previous films: spying at a woman in a changing booth leads to Huey being peed on by a naked infant, although here we have a gang of nude peeing infants, etc. Huey arrives at the ship laden down with many bags, of course. Benji moaps around having fallen in love with the Captain's daughter (his reason for being on the ship, having met her at the beach). The soundtrack fills with hits of the era, none of which are properly integrated into the film, and none are used to sing the characters' thoughts. But we do get Benji and Huey wearing sailor suits and running round Venice. Boys running round Venice in sailor suits makes me think of Dirk Bogarde sitting in a deckchair with mascara running down his face. Thankfully the film doesn't go down that route. Our heroes run into the Hotel Villa Mabapa (with the interiors shot in Germany). All leads to a very poorly staged costume party at which Zachi Noy turns up in black drag and gets a big laugh from viewers not too beaten down by political correctness. This is a bad film but it made me laugh more than many 'good' comedy films.

Petra Morzè with Katzur in Venice.

Zachi Noy on a bed of nails! Alas, the scene was deleted.

YFTACH KATZUR

イフタク・カツール（ベンジー）

今回「恋のネイビーブルー」のベンジーは，船長の娘に一目ぼれ。厳しい監視の目をぬすんで，C体験までこぎつけるだろうか……。

イスラエルのテルアビブ出身のイフタク・カツールが俳優を志したのは，13才の時。テルアビブ随一のカメリー・シアターのオーディションを受けて合格し，俳優としての第一歩が始まる。

17才の時，ピーター・シェイファーの「エクウス」の主役として初舞台を踏み，批評家から絶賛される。またたく間に，イスラエルでトップクラスの舞台俳優になり，ハイスクール卒業後も舞台で修業を積み，やがてボアズ・デビッドソン監督に認められ，「グローイング・アップ」でデビューする。この作品でイスラエル版オスカーをはじめ，主演男優賞をほとんど受賞している。

83年6月初来日，"イスラエルのジェームス・ディーン"と女の子たちの熱狂的な歓迎をうけた。

'This time, Benji falls in love at first sight for the Captain's daughter Donna. He tries desperately to sleep with her while trying to stay out of the Captain's gaze. Born in Israel's Tel Aviv, Katzur had wanted to be an actor since he was thirteen. He auditioned in Tel Aviv's Cameri Theatre and was accepted. This was the first step to his acting career. When he was seventeen, he starred in Peter Shaffer's *Equus*. He received good reviews from the critics and soon became a top class actor. When he graduated from high school, and was training to be an actor, he was discovered by Boaz Davidson. He debuted in the *Lemon Popsicle* series. For his work there, he received Israeli's version of the Oscar.'

164

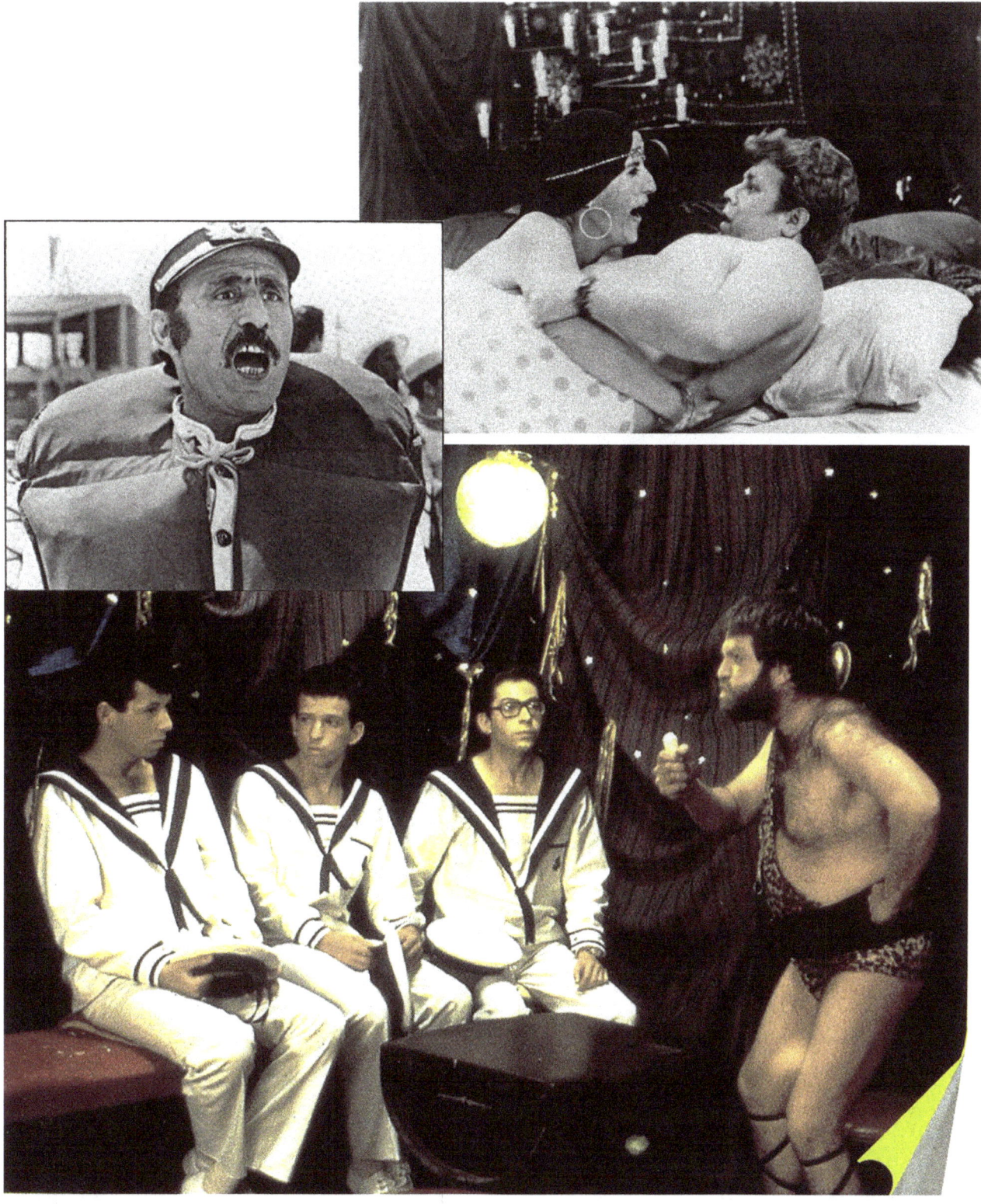

On the 27th August 1985, *Up Your Anchor* was classified as strictly For Adults Only by the UK censor. It was released in British cinemas in December 1985 with *Hot Bubblegum* as the support film. In Britain it was not a box-office success, so the next film, *Young Love,* was released there only on video.

Zachi goes to sea to escape a marriage forced by Joseph Shiloach, but the plot-line is dropped at sea.

Songs used in *Up Your Anchor*

Brook Benton, Baby *You've Got What It Takes*
Brook Benton, *It's Just a Matter of Time*
Chubby Checker, *Slow Twistin'*
Dave Cortez, *Green Onions*
Joey Dee, *Peppermint Twist* and *Shout*
Duane Eddy, *Because They're Young* and *Forty Miles*
Aurelio Fierro, *Io Sono Il Vento*
Frankie Ford, *Sea Cruise*
George Hamilton, *Why Don't They Understand*
Jan and Dean, *Surf City*
Jerry Lee Lewis, *Great Balls of Fire*
Little Richard, *Tutti Frutti* and *Bama Lam Bama Lou*
Domenico Modugno, *Ciao Ciao Bambina*
Sandy Nelson, *Teen Beat*
Dee Dee Sharp, *Mashed Potato Time*
Swinging Blue Jeans, *Hippy Hippy Shake*
The Yardbirds, *For Your Love* and *I'm Still Sad*
Tony Dallara, *Come Prima*

'We have only just reached our peak'

Young Love

Ahava Tzeira

Eis am Stiel 7:
Verliebte Jungs

1987

Young Love

This eighty-three minute film starts with a two-and-a-half minute long (long) shot of a big man (Igor Borisov) trying to put up a deckchair. Can you guess how he gets on? Of course you can. Then with that very poor and over-extended scene over with, the new director, Walter Bannert, intercuts good shots of the boys at the beach looking at the girls, with more shots of the fat man failing to sit in the deckchair again, and again, and again. If it wasn't for the welcome presence of Jonathan Sagall, restored to the series after a disagreement with the producers kept him out of the last one, and the fact that Hanus Polak's multi-layered photography is very good indeed, then you'd think you were watching a turkey. That feeling doesn't go away when the film then moves to the stunt we know will end with Huey being slapped and chased. Benji drops the keys to Huey's borrowed car down the cleavage of a young woman dozing in a deckchair. She doesn't feel the keys at all but takes instant umbrage at Huey each time he gently tries to retrieve them. Comedy fails fastest the further it falls from truthfulness.

The film perks interest with the car itself, a spectacular Ford Mercury convertible. Huey drives it to the Montana and an original idea, one that doesn't make sense because it has no connection to reality. He has taken to loaning out the boot of the car to courting teenagers to make out in. Better luck is had with the soundtrack. We've had Chubby Checker's *The Hucklebuck*; Bobby Freeman singing *C'mon an' Swim*, and there's been a burst of *Volare*. When there's nothing else to engage the mind or tickle the funny bone, the *Popsicle* films always give us great music to listen to.

A big dance party choreographed to Sam The Sham & The Pharaohs takes place at Huey's modern apartment and, despite the continuing low-level of writing (Bobby and a girl would *not* be hiding statue-still and completely hidden beneath a blanket), the film starts to improve. An impressively photographed car cruising scene gets the story rolling. The boys decide to get a job for two weeks to pay for the car's repair. They become odd-job workers at a five-star hotel to which come the friends of the upwardly mobile female proprietor. Among them is a doe-eyed beautiful girl wearing too much lipstick. Can you guess who spends the rest of the film smitten by her? She's played by Sonja Martin, who played a different character in *Private Popsicle* and who will turn up again, in a different role, in *Summertime Blues* (the lack of fidelity to a set universe is a weakness of the series). In *Young Love*, it turns out that Benji had abandoned her after getting her pregnant, a sort of false or forced drama plotting point that goes against the whole character of the films and which turns out to be a red herring.

The cook at the hotel turns out to be the deckchair man, and though he is a formidable presence he plays his two scenes much too large and much too camp.

In compensation there is a lot of attractive nudity, and a lovely striptease appearance from Sibylle Rauch, to complement the attractive Israeli locations, but these move the series further from Israeli memories to South German soft-porn. All nearly drowns in shouted overplaying by the support cast in the film's mistaken identities long final third, as Huey and Bobby conspire to help Benji's romance along. The rather over-violent slap-slap-push-push way of resolving differences sees Bobby and Huey repeatedly ducking a bad girl in the sea as a prelude to breaking all known laws regarding airport safety.

This German VHS cover conveys the popularity of local star, Sibylle Rauch.

Sissi Pitz, actress

I was modelling at the time. The producers of *Lemon Popsicle* saw some of my pictures and invited me over. At first I said no as I didn't want to be an actress, I'd wanted to be a dancer, but I said, "Okay, let's try it!". So I read some lines for them and they liked me and I got the part. Then they sent me to acting school in Athens, where I was coached for fourteen days by Mirka Zakis. We had to shoot the scenes twice. Once in German and again in Hebrew. The Israeli actors did their lines in Hebrew and the German actors did their lines in German. It was difficult because we wouldn't know when to speak because we didn't know when they had finished their lines! But I did learn a few words of Hebrew. It was fun. We worked with a very nice team. They were nice people and they looked after us. The makeup artists, costume designers and producers were all nice people.

Sonja Martin and Sissi Pitz

Songs used in *Young Love*

Brook Benton, *A Rockin' Good Way* and *Kiddio*
Al Bunny, *Eros*
Chubbie Checker, *Hucklebuck*
Dan Dare, *Skyride*
Bill Doggett, *Honky Tonk*
Fingers, *Shakin' In My Shoes*
Bobby Freeman, *C'mon an' Swim*
Bobby Freeman, *Do You Wanna Dance*
The Globe Trotters, *It's a Funny World*

Johnny Hill, *Young Love*
Roy Orbison, *Ooby Dooby*
Carl Perkins, *Gone, Gone, Gone*
Lloyd Price, *Personality*
Little Richard, *Slippin' an' Slidin'*
Platoon, *Private's Progress*
Sam The Sham and The Pharoahs, *Woolly Bully*
Rufus Thomas, *Do The Funky Chicken*
The Tremeloes, *Here Comes My Baby*

Hi-jinks and multi-level photography with a lovely classic car, bettered in appeal only by an artful variation on the Popsicle spy-hole scene featuring Sibylle Rauch herself.

Alle Drei wieder vereint
Eis am Stiel 7. Teil
Verliebte Jungs

Alle Drei wieder vereint
Eis am Stiel 7. Teil
Verliebte Jungs

177

YOUNG LOVE
Lemon Popsicle 7

キャスト CAST

ベンジー/イフタク・カツール BENJI/YFTACH KATZUR
ヒューイ/ツァッチ・ノイ HUGHIE/ZACHI NOY
ボビー/ジョナサン・シーガル BOBBY/JONATHAN SEGAL
ソーニャ・マーチン SONJA MARTIN ■ シシー・リーボルド SISSY LIEBOLD ■ シビル・ローチ SYBILLE RAUCH

スタッフ STAFF

製作総指揮メナハム・ゴーラン&ヨーラム・グローバス MENAHEM GOLAN&YORAM GLOBUS
監督ウォルター・ベネート WALTER BENNERT
撮影ハノス・ポラック HANOS POLLACK ■ 製作サム・ウェインバーグ SAM WAYNBERG
脚本アントン・モーホー&イーザン・エヴァン ANTON MOHO&EYTAN EVAN

Summertime Blues

Blues Ba-Kayitz

Eis am Stiel, 8. Teil

1988

Summertime Blues

Based on an original story by Zachi Noy, and made by the husband and wife team, Reinhard Schwabenitzky and Elfi Escke, this, the final film in the original Popsicle saga, has something that has been missing since the third film, a good sense of pace. Scenes are allowed to find the drama and the laughs. Having said that, there aren't many laughs and they tend to come via a new character, Benji's bratty pre-teen cousin (played by Yaron Shilon, who grew up to be a TV director) but the boy's scenes are too abrupt to achieve their comedy potential. For once, the 'humiliation of Zachi' scene contributes to a narrative-character arc. The Popsicle gang bed down for the night with attractive women - Katzur with Sibylle Rauch, Sagall with Escke - but Zachi has nowhere to sleep but the room of the brat. From this comedy low, Noy's situation rises to the dramatic heights as he gets to build a nightclub of his own, until it's brought crashing down by a gang of villainous bikers (is there not a police force?), only for his luck to rise again in a winning and unexpected finale as he finally gets the girl. This rise and fall and rise arc amounts to the first attempt at character development since the first film. It shifts the series' focus away from the sensitive-selfish Benji to the generous-humorous Huey. The young man who started out with a pocket book of spends and debts becomes a business man, bartering deals, smoking cigars, interviewing staff, and being the first of the boys to find what could turn out to be true love.

The performances are strongly directed for the first time since Davidson left the series. There is no mugging and gooning (except for a bit with Escke in the ugly duckling role). Jack Cohen brings a welcome gravitas to the first quarter of the film as the Escke's father. Other pluses are some excellent photography and a strong sense of location - there can be no doubt that we are in the ancient and modern sea city of Tel Aviv. There is also a welcome return to Fifties culture in the set dressing. Naming the club the *West of Eden* is the first fifties wink for a while. Posters of Fifties movie heroes grace its walls.

Summertime Blues was filmed in German and in Hebrew, and is the only one of the films without an English dub. It wasn't released in English-speaking territories. In fact, it didn't get English subtitles until the Israeli DVD boxset released on 27th February 2006.

Sissi Pitz, actress

In *Summertime Blues* we had to go for job interviews at the nightclub. As I was leaving the club Zachi Noy was supposed to touch my bottom and I had to slap him in the face. It had been a long day and we were all tired. When I slapped him, his cigar fell out of his mouth and we were all laughing! I didn't keep in contact with the other actors. No, not really. I saw Zachi Noy once in Munich and we said "Hi" and had a coffee. I was a TV presenter for six years in Munich. At the moment I am training people in the art of public speaking.

Songs used in *Summertime Blues*

Eddie Cochran, *Summertime Blues*
Little Richard, *Long Tall Sally*
Fats Domino, *Blueberry Hill*
Paul Anka, *Dance On Little Girl*
Mitch Miller, *The Yellow Rose Of Texas*
Guy Mitchell, *Heartaches By The Number*
Fats Domino, *My Girl Josephine*
Johnny and The Hurricanes, *Crossfire*
Paul Anka, *Diana*
Albert West, *Ginny Come Lately*
Paul Anka, *You Are My Destiny*
Bobby Vinton, *Roses Are Red*
Jerry Lee Lewis, *What'd I Say*

Johnny Nash, *Cupid*
Chris Montez, *Let's Dance*
Bobby Vinton, *Blue Velvet*
Caravelli, *La Cumparsita*
Paul Anka, *Lonely Boy*
Doris Day, *Que, Sera Sera*
Doris Day, *Everybody Takes a Lover*
Chubby Checker, *Lets Twist Again*
Percy Faith, *Delicado*
The Palais All Stars, *Mambo No.1*
Charly Rich, *I Feel Like Going Home*
Bobby Vinton, *To Know You is To Love You*

Dan Turgeman plays the leader of the biker gang (centre). He's the real life husband of Anat Atzmon. In 1996, he appeared with Jonathan Sagall and Yehuda Efroni (the ship's captain in *Up Your Anchor*) in *Deadly Outbreak*. With Atzmon co-starring, he co-wrote and produced *Minotaur* (1997). Jack Cohen carries flowers (below).

Eis am Stiel
8.TEIL
SUMMERTIME BLUES
SCOTIA CANNON

Eis am Stiel
8.TEIL
SUMMERTIME BLUES
SCOTIA CANNON

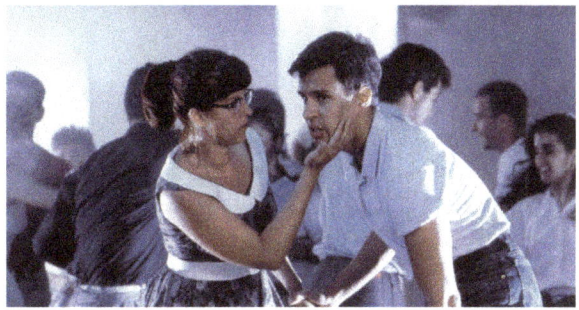

Hungarian DVD

The Last American Virgin

Die letzte amerikanische Jungfrau

1982

The Last American Virgin

The film of the misadventures of fifties Israeli teenagers fits unsurprisingly easily into a remake set in eighties America. Both were decades of innovation in music and teen fashion and both were times when teenagers were social. Imagine a remake set in the selfie generation of ipad-reared teenagers grown and locked in safe home environments? or one that takes place in the nineties when teenagers used pills to disappear inside themselves as they jumped up and down to dance noise that sounded like a car alarm? *The Last American Virgin* is an always enjoyable, always interesting, film that has the power to captivate and astonish viewers, particularly those who haven't seen the original film. It could be said that the downbeat bite at the film's resolution is more powerful than the finale of *Lemon Popsicle* itself, because the American teen film is not the natural home for downbeat endings. That said, the second most popular American high school film, *Carrie,* didn't end with a lot of laughter… Actually it did. When I saw *Carrie* in the cinema, the audience screamed as one and then laughed as one with relief. So the tag-line for *The Last American Virgin* could be 'The ending has less laughs than *Carrie!*'.

For viewers raised on The Original Popsicles, the pleasures of *The Last American Virgin* are muted. Disappointingly, for the most part, Davidson takes the facsimile approach. Many scenes are staged using the exact same camera angles from *Lemon Popsicle,* and the exact same camera-actor choreography (notably so in Bobby's undressing of the nympho) but, because the actors are not the same and the locations are not the same, the truths of the scenes as found in the first film are lost in the photocopies of the scenes in this remake. This is particularly true of the 'new' scene put in place of the dropped trip-to-the-cinema scene. It's the three-girl house-party from *Hot Bubblegum*. The scene ends with the fat guy in bed with 'Benji's' mother (too briefly for the drama or comedy to bite). Placing the scene here is a mistake because it affects the truthfulness of the relationship between the Benji character and his parents. Gone too are many of the little but important scenes of Benji at home with his misunderstanding but supportive and funny and memorable parents. By Benji I mean, of course, Monoson's 'Gary'.

The Americanisations are mostly cosmetic and they work well. Instead of bicycles there are cars. The ice seller of Tel Aviv is now a Californian pizza delivery boy who drives his gay boss's big pink car with its ridiculous cocked-leg caricature of the proprietor mounted to the roof (impressively in times that weren't quite so gay friendly, no attention is paid to this by any character in the film). The one major Americana change, major in that it could be said to be satirical and political, is the abortion-break being switched from a National Service military camp to a Christmas skiing holiday! It's during the abortion scene that the film makes its biggest musical mistake. Playing U2's upbeat rock song, *I Will Follow* over scenes of the preparation for the abortion, and playing it so loudly that it almost drowns out the dialogue, is a *Mistake Royale*. Lyrically the song has some chime with the theme but aurally it is quite unsuitable. The music score does have more hits than misses, with good uses of Devo and power ballads that convey the time and the place, but two more songs fail big and badly because they also come at very important times. The first song failure comes during the first big set-piece, that three-girl party down at Gary's house. The song is *I Know What Boys Like* and it is crushingly dull musically, vocally, lyrically. It kills the party mood. The final song failure comes during the finale and is a failure from over-use. Lionel Ritchie singing *Oh No* (I want you) is used sweetly and aptly as Karen's Theme. It's a fine song, but it is repeated four or five times in the film's last quarter and that's two or three too many.

Lawrence Monoson is a spectacular find for the Yftach Katzur 'Gary' role. He has absolutely the right amount of innocence and apprehension and wonder and so is able to convey the right emotional highs and lows. He's the right age. At twenty-four, Steve Antin is too old and too short (too lacking in visual contrast with Monoson) for the Rick (Bobby) role. Joe Rubbo is no more than adequate as an American Zachi Noy. His is a nervous performance. He often seems to be looking at his fellow players for guidance. He lacks Zachi's stardust but Golan and Globus gave him a second chance with the Noy-styled starring role in the *Popsicle*-esque *Hot Chilli* in 1985. He's better in that but the film isn't nearly as good as this.

The only real improvements from the original film to this increasingly popular remake are technical. The sound recording is clearer (though less realistic). Some of the photography, particularly of the Hollywood landscape, is more impressively cinematic. Mel Welles cameos as the crabs pharmacist and brings a welcome verve that almost makes up for the dubbing he did on *Private Popsicle*.

**Written and Directed by
BOAZ DAVIDSON**

**Producers
MENAHEM GOLAN -
YORAM GLOBUS**

Boaz Davidson - writer, director

Lemon Popsicle was never released in the USA because I wouldn't change the ending of the film. At that time the American audience did not like foreign movies, they are still not crazy about them today, so we decided to bring the story up to date as an American movie. This was not an ordinary remake. I had to Americanize the characters and adapt the Israeli/European atmosphere to an American city's lifestyle in the eighties. In addition to the original film, we used some scenes from *Lemon Popsicle 3*, and we invented some new scenes. The major element that was cut out is the nostalgia. *Lemon Popsicle* was nostalgic. *Last American Virgin* was current.

Lawrence Monoson

I always wanted to be an actor. My family moved from California to New York when I was young and I appeared in an early episode of *Diff'rent Strokes!* That was before *The Last American Virgin*. It was exciting. I was a young kid who had dreams of being an actor and I was in a big TV show! Sitcoms are filmed in front of a live studio audience so, as an experience, it was great.

The Last American Virgin was my first big role. The part of Gary was cast already to someone else but they were having trouble finding a big guy to play the part of David. So they opened up auditions and were seeing lots of different people and I went along and met Boaz. I did a reading and he went and got Golan and Globus and they went bananas over me! They thought I looked like the guy from *Lemon Popsicle*. But you had to be over eighteen to work in those days and I was only seventeen so they needed a driver's licence, which I obviously didn't have!

I had already lost some roles because of the eighteen-year-old labour rule, so my Mom helped me get a phoney drivers licence and I got the part! I think they knew it was phoney but it covered them. It was tough on the guy who got it first but great for me! It was a life-propelling experience. I had just turned seventeen, was still living at home and had the lead in a big movie. Maybe it was a silly teen movie but it also has depth. I wasn't playing someone very far away from myself. I was naive with no experience with women, but Gary was a little sweeter than I was. Gary is a sweet, soulful guy. The shooting schedule was long but everyone was at the start of their careers and it was very exciting.

Diane Franklin

I wanted to be an actress from the age of four, but I started acting professionally in New York at the age of ten. I got the part of Karen by auditioning in New York and then later screen testing in Los Angeles. It was my first lead in a movie, so I was very excited was also nervous because I was supposed to ride a moped, but I couldn't even ride a bike (I am deaf in my right ear which affects my balance). I chose not to mention it because I was afraid if I told them it might prevent me from keeping the part. So, when the time came to shoot the scenes with the moped, I had to tell them. Boaz Davidson was really nice about it and that is why you see me walking in and out of shots with the moped. I was very different from my role as Karen. Karen was simple, innocent and indifferent. I was out-going, funny and passionate. I really had to tone down my personality. Boaz Davidson told me about the *Lemon Popsicle* films but I had no idea how popular they were. I only saw one scene of *Lemon Popsicle* and that was when the boy takes Nikki to the house and she breaks down. I think that scene was directed in a similar style in *The Last American Virgin*. I loved everyone I worked with on *The Last American Virgin*. The cast was very sweet. My best friend, who played the part of Rose (Kimmy Robertson) actually came to my wedding! I've seen Steve Antin occasionally. It was a wonderful experience working on the film.

Joe Rubbo

I got into acting at the age of eight. I was at a premiere of a Joe Namath movie called *The Last Rebel* where Joe Namath was making a personal appearance. When I asked him for his autograph, he wouldn't stop talking to me. He thought I was really funny and talented so he told my mom that she should contact the agencies and he gave her the names! Through the years I did numerous commercials and photographic print work. My first role in a movie was in *The World According to Garp* where I played a wrestler. I auditioned for the role of David in *The Last American Virgin* first in New York and then I had a screen test in L.A. After the screen test I got the part and stayed in L.A. to shoot the film. I loved the part of David (basically he's the same character as Huey in *Lemon Popsicle*). He had all the funny parts in the movie and he got all the chicks. We watched the original film over and over. It was the same director, Boaz Davidson, and his goal was for *The Last American Virgin* to be better and more hip with the times. The movie was a blast to make! It was really like being in school and we all became close friends. I did a lot of ad-libbing and I just tried to make David more cool. A lot of times I was not acting I was just being me! John Belushi was an inspiration and that's who everyone was calling me on the set of *Last American Virgin*. I would love to do a *Last American Virgin* reunion. As a matter a fact, I was kicking around the idea of a remake and me playing David's Dad and putting in a lot of flashback scenes.

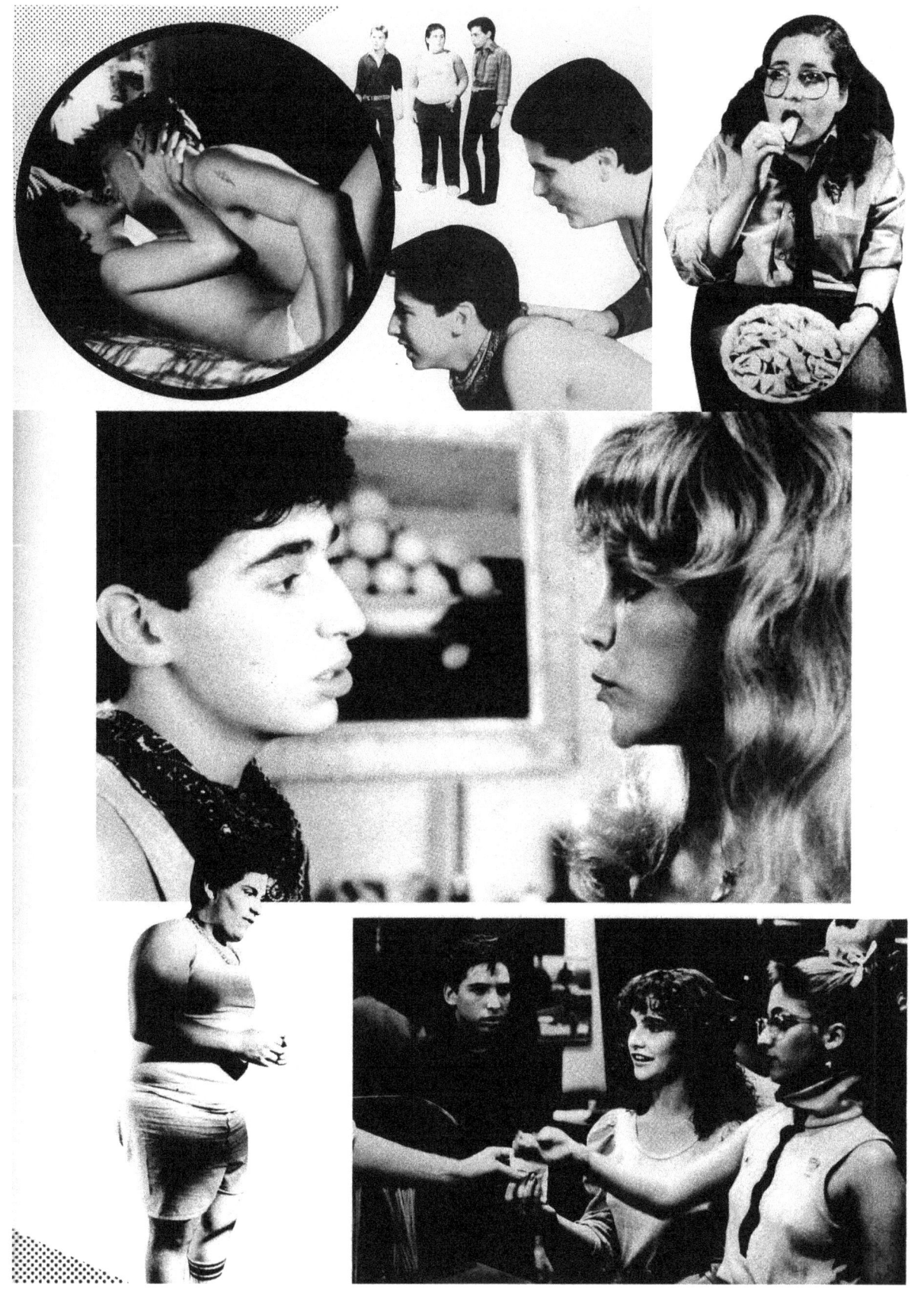

Kimmy Robertson

I was a ballet dancer, one hundred percent classical ballet. I fell in love with ballet when I saw *Romeo and Juliet* starring Rudolf Nureyev and Margot Fonteyn. I had never seen such perfect expression of emotion through dance. I was smitten with Nureyev in particular. The first time I went to New York, I went to catch the Diaghilev Festival at the Lincoln Center. Plus to see Devo in concert too. Both events changed my life for the better.

I took a brand new job with a dance company called American Folk Ballet, wonderful fun company that paid well too. When I was hired, the company was on tour in Israel or China or The Falkland Islands or somewhere, so they put me to work in their office answering phones and being a receptionist. I had no idea what I was doing so I just made stuff up. The talent agent there, Helen Barken, thought I was hysterical and that I should be acting. I said, "No.". I didn't like actors. She said, "Just do it for me. Just go to one audition and see how you like it". She asked me if I knew anyone at all in the business and I said that I had worked for John Thompson for a while doing the Devo fan club. I helped him to cast one of their videos and I had heard he was working at a place called Cannon Films. She got a weird look on her face and held up an envelope with my picture in it addressed to John Thompson c/o Cannon Films 6464 Sunset Blvd. I went, "Wooooo eerie!". So he arranged for me to audition for Boaz Davidson but made it VERY clear before I did, that he had no way of helping me after that. I had never had any acting training but it came pretty naturally, except my knees were shaking. I got the part. I went to a taping Devo was doing for American Bandstand and saw my friend Robin Antin there, we danced together. She told me her brother just got a movie at Cannon and I said so did I!

So cut to months later.... to the inside of a van at three in the morning on Hollywood Boulevard. All the actors were kind of complaining about it being cold and dark and boring. Steve Antin looked up at me and said, "Why are you so happy? What are you smiling about? How come you never complain?" I said, "Hey, I'm making 3,000 dollars a week and nothin's bleeding. I'm HAPPY!"

Diane was lovely and open. Joe was happy and grateful. Steve was funny and handsome and a good dancer too. Lawrence was intense and full of energy. At first no one would talk to me because I was dressed in my Rose wardrobe with glasses and a retainer and stuff, so I hung out with Brian Peck, Victor. He was dressed like a nerd too so he was being avoided as well. He and I spent tons of time making each other laugh. Eventually the people on the set got to know us and liked us for who we are instead of what we were wearing. That happens a lot on sets, people get you confused with your costume. I particularly liked Boaz and how he said 'okay' to using all those great bands. We even used some Devo fan club hats and t-shirts and there were cool posters on the set as well.

We had been told about the *Lemon Popsicle* movies. They talked about them in a very reverent way, as though there were Holy movies about Holy kids in a Holy land. We didn't understand at all. There was nothing on earth to compare them to. Boaz kept tugging on his beard and saying, "You mussssst see the *Lemon Popsicles*... The *Popsicles* would explain everything". Well, we never did and I still have no idea what he was talking about. I would love to though.

My favourite day on the *Virgin* movie was the day before Christmas Eve. We were in Malibu shooting the scene at The Point. It was cold and we had to get in the car after it went into the water. We had to lie down for a minute until they called action, but the waves were crashing over the hood of the car and pulling it further out into the breakline. Soon the waves were going over the windshield and landing right on us in the front seat! It was so bizarre to be lying down in the front seat of a car listening to the ocean all around you. It was so cold and frightening too. I loved that scene because Gary helps Rose jump off the car. It was sweet. That was the last day of shooting the movie. Good thing because I lost my custom-made retainer in the sand.

WERBERATSCHLAG

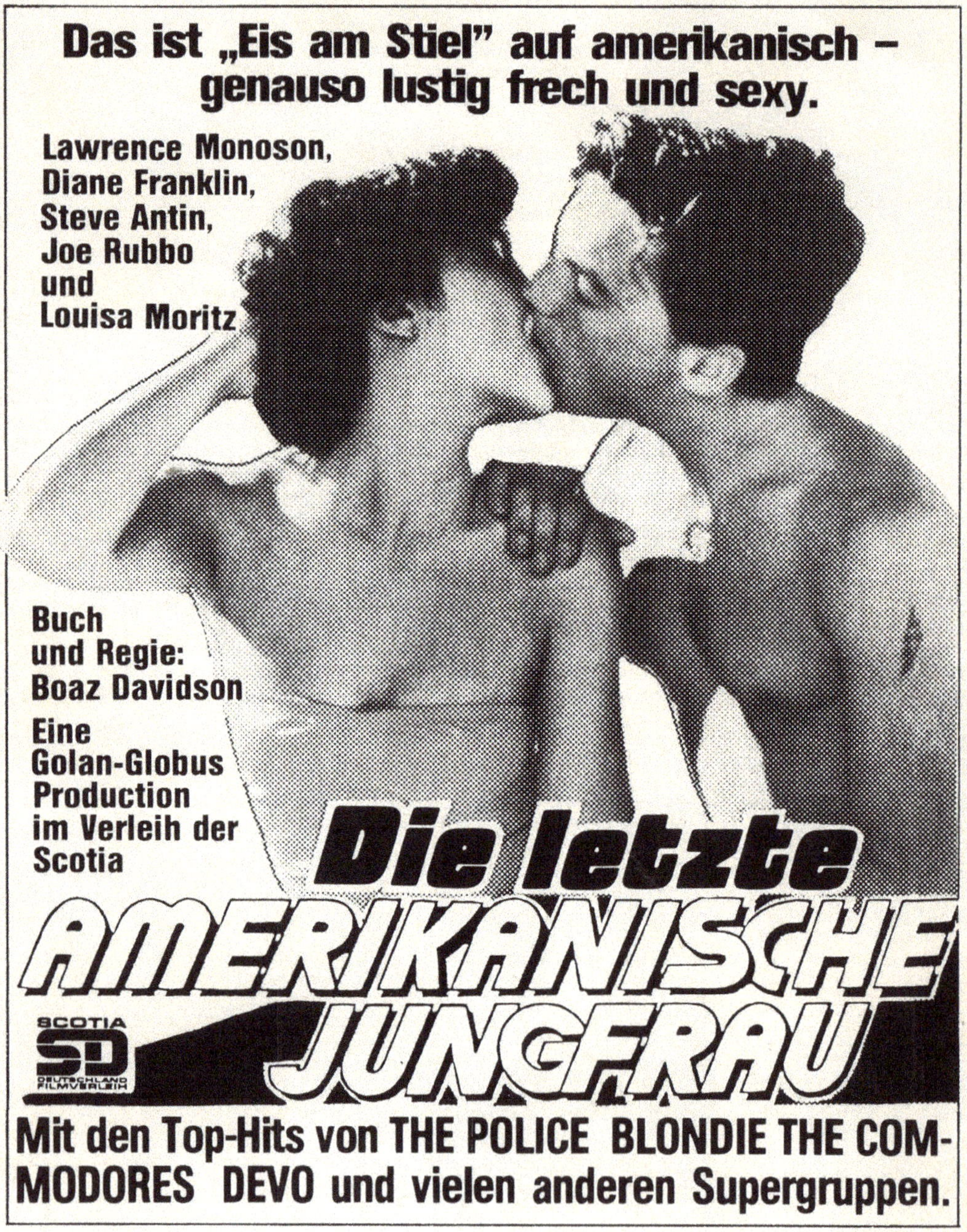

SCOTIA FILMVERLEIH GMBH DEUTSCHLAND

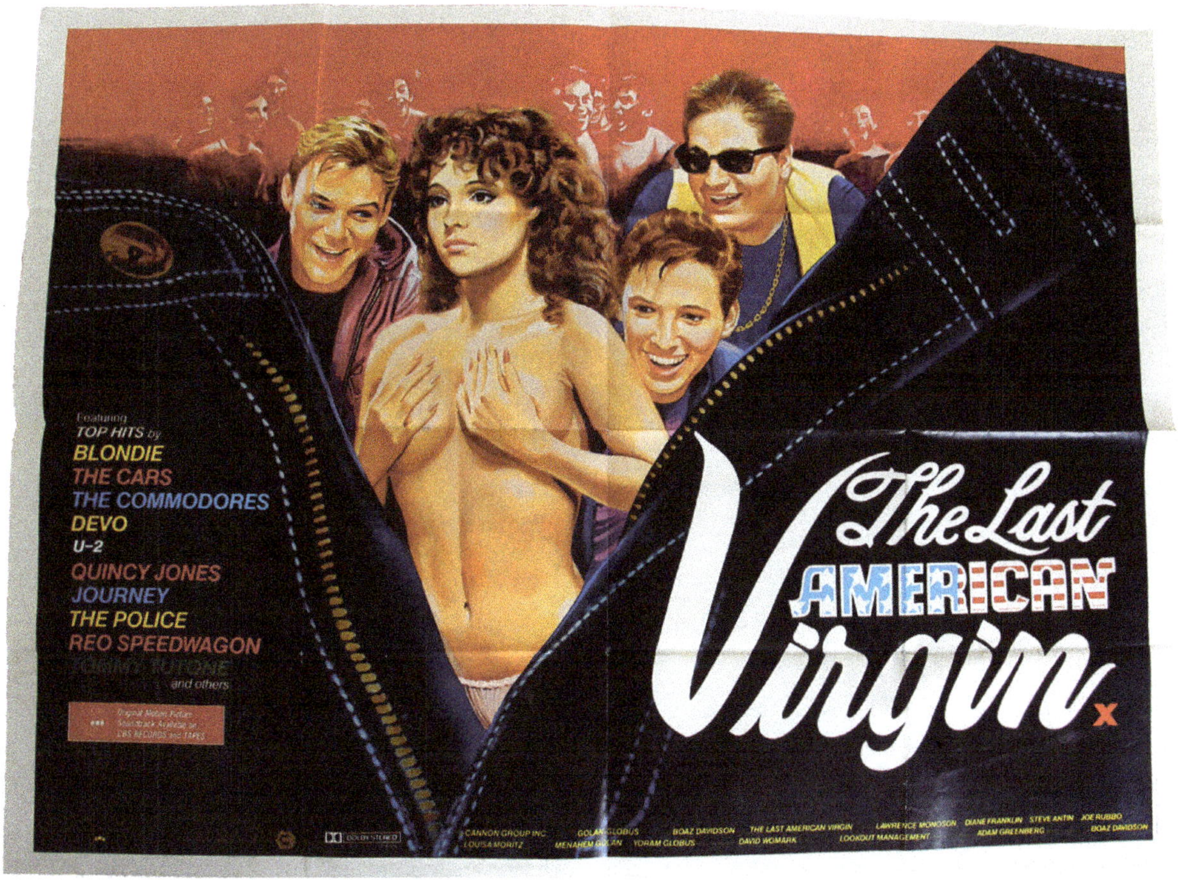
featuring
TOP HITS by
BLONDIE
THE CARS
THE COMMODORES
DEVO
U-2
QUINCY JONES
JOURNEY
THE POLICE
REO SPEEDWAGON
TOMMY TUTONE
and others
The Last
AMERICAN
Virgin
X

She's all over
London from
Sunday Sept 5
SEE LOCAL PRESS FOR DETAILS
The Last
AMERICAN
Virgin
X
featuring
TOP HITS by
BLONDIE
THE CARS
THE COMMODORES
DEVO
U-2
QUINCY JONES
JOURNEY
THE POLICE
REO SPEEDWAGON
TOMMY TUTONE
and others
A VERY FUNNY MOVIE ABOUT THE VERY FIRST TIME...
CANNON FILM DISTRIBUTORS
CANNON GROUP INC. GOLAN-GLOBUS BOAZ DAVIDSON THE LAST AMERICAN VIRGIN LAWRENCE MONOSON DIANE FRANKLIN STEVE ANTIN JOE RUBBO
LOUISA MORITZ MENAHEM GOLAN YORAM GLOBUS DAVID WOMARK LOOKOUT MANAGEMEN ADAM GREENBERG BOAZ DAVIDSON
DOLBY STEREO
IN SELECTED THEATRES
Still in the
WEST END at
CLASSIC
SHAFTESBURY AVE
(formerly Columbia)
Progs. 2.00; 4.10; 6.25; 8.40,
Late Shows Fri. & Sat. at 11.15pm.
CLASSIC
HAYMARKET
Progs. 2.00 (not Sun)
4.05; 6.15; 8.30.
Late Shows Fri. Sat.
at 11.00 pm.
CLASSIC
TOTTENHAM
COURT RD
Progs. 2.00 (not Sun) 3.45;
6.00; 8.20 Late Shows
Fri. & Sat. at 11.00 pm.
CLASSIC
CHELSEA
Sep. Perfs. 2.45; 6.20; 8.50.
CLASSIC
OXFORD ST
Progs. 2.00; 4.10; 6.25; 8.40.
Late Shows Fri. Sat.
at 11.15pm.

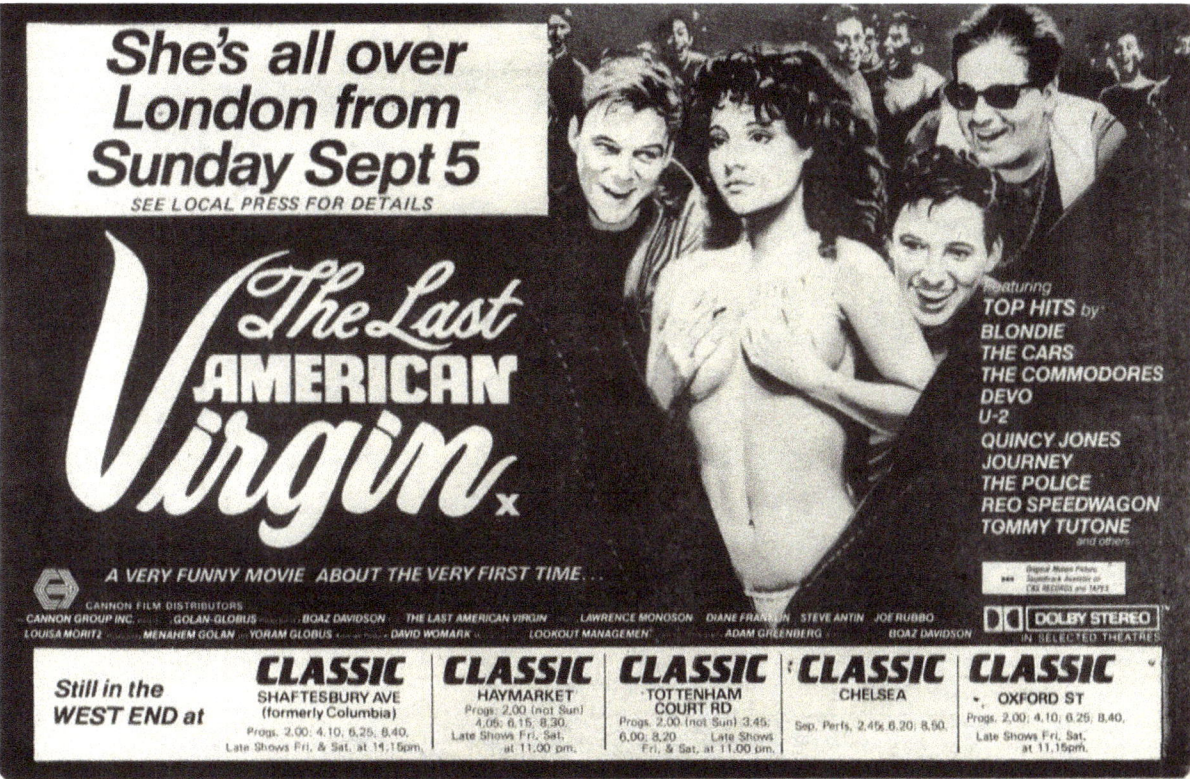

August 1982 — „NEUES FILMPROGRAMM" — Preis öS 3,— / DM —,50

Eigentümer, Herausgeber, Verleger und Druck: FILMPROGRAMM Verlagsgesellschaft m.b.H., Chefredakteur und für den Inhalt verantwortlich: Rudolf J. Maly, alle 1070 Wien, Lindengasse 43, Telefon (0222) 93 64 53. Für die Bundesrepublik Deutschland (nur für Filmtheater) FILMPROGRAMM Verlagsgesellschaft m.b.H., 8000 München, Landshuter Allee 33, Telefon (089) 16 12 91 — Anschrift für Einzelbestellungen und Abonnenten für Österreich, die BRD und das übrige Ausland nur: Filmprogrammdienst, Postfach 126, A- 1071 Wien, Abonnementpreis für Österreich S 50,— inkl. Porto für jeweils 20 Nummern, für die BRD DM 9,—, Einzelpreis für Österreich S 3,—, für Deutschland DM —,50. Für Sammler sind im Einzelverkauf derzeit etwa 2500 Titel vorrätig. Gesamtverzeichnis dieser Titel inklusive Zusendung S 20,— / DM 3,—.

Američka komedija **POSLJEDNJA AMERIČKA DJEVICA**

Američka komedija **POSLJEDNJA AMERIČKA DJEVICA**

Yugoslavian Lobby Cards

Louisa Moritz as Carmela, "I am starting to feel lonely. Come to me, my big burrito."

Franklin wrote a memoir

Mel Welles, Pharmacist in *Last American Virgin*; English dubbing supervisor on *Private Popsicle*.

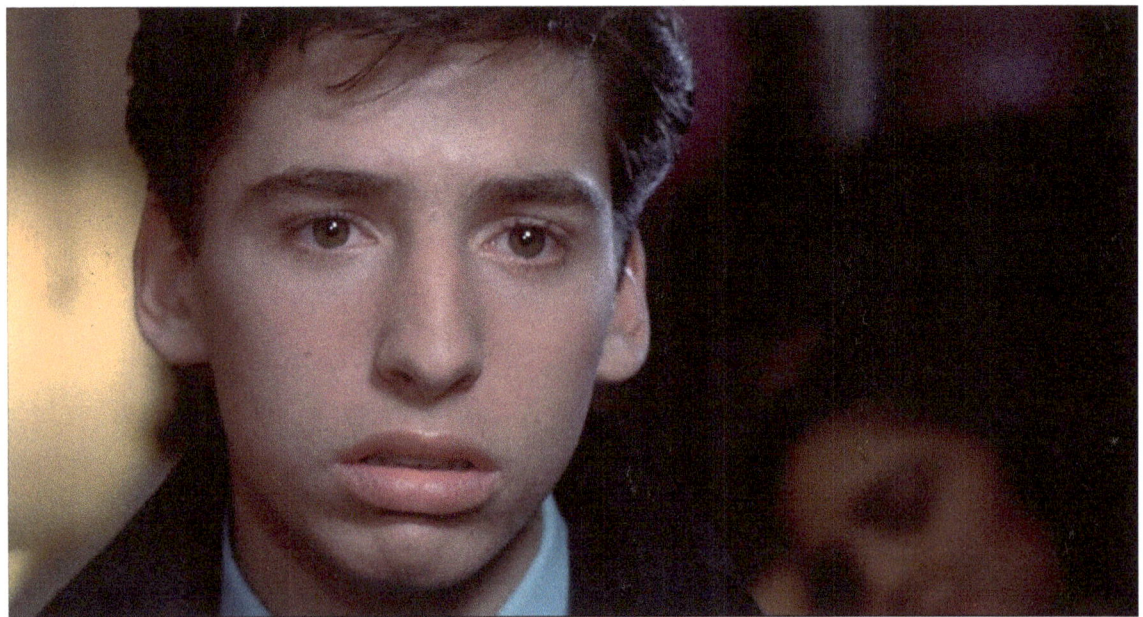

212

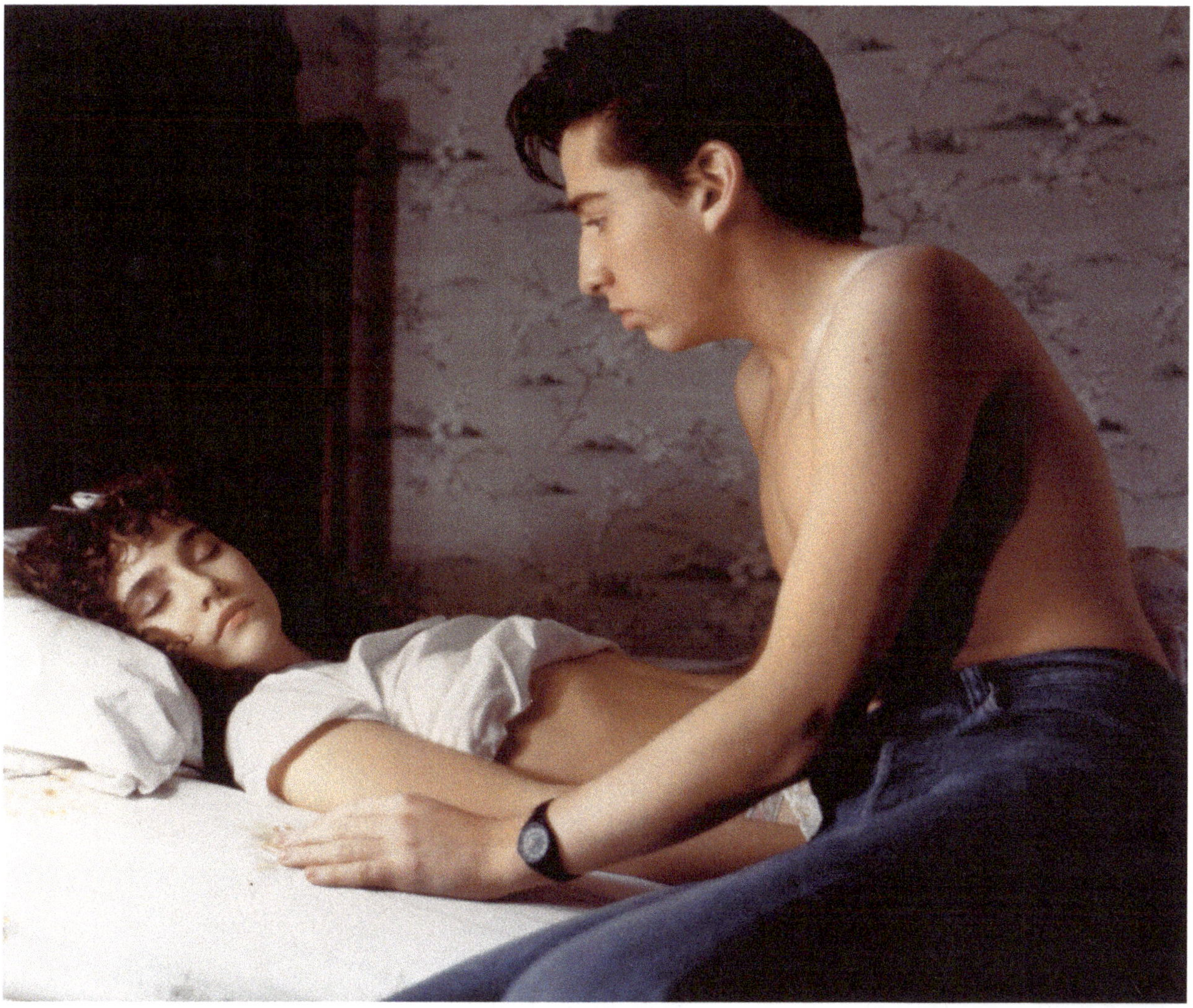

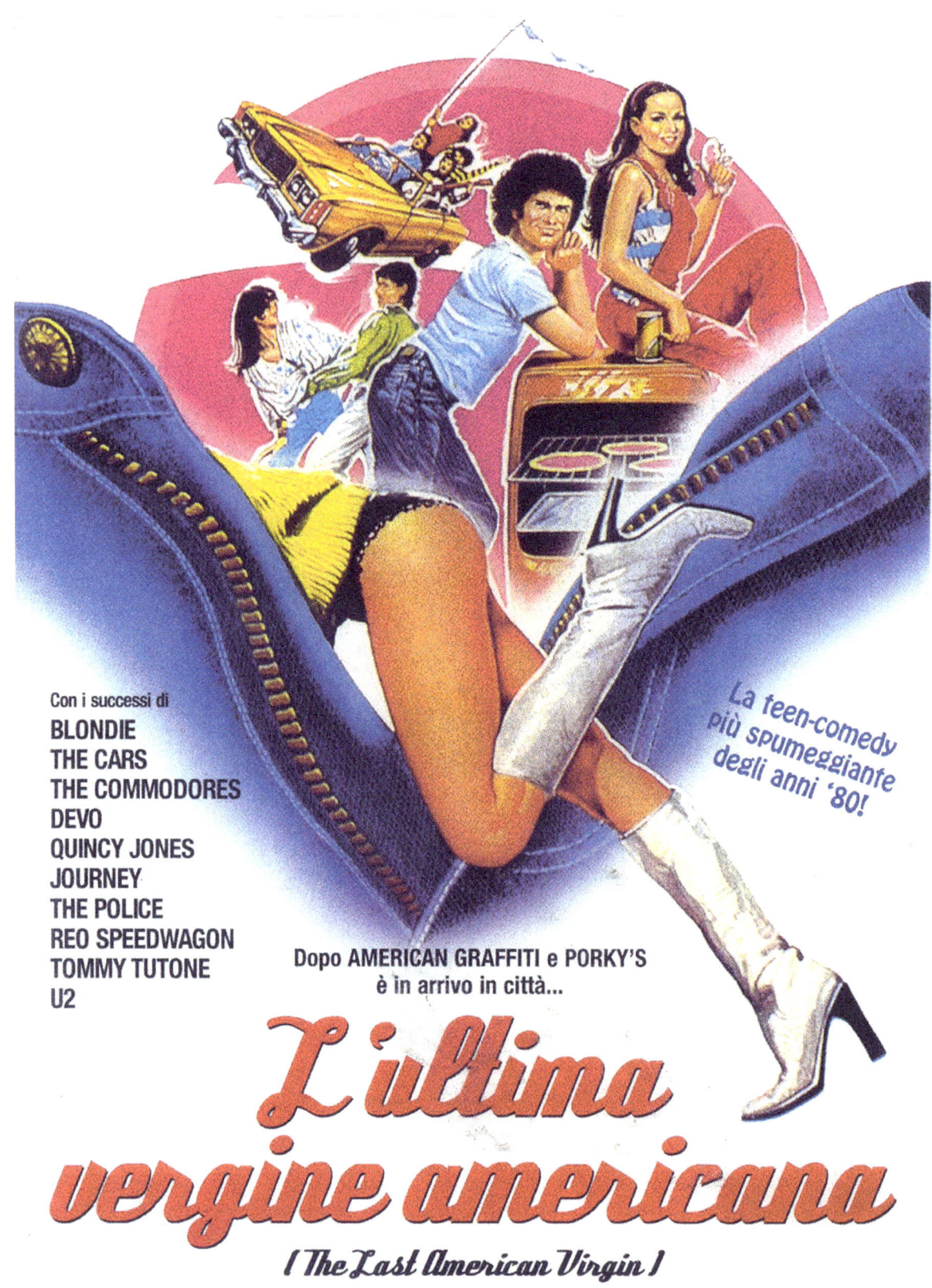

A rare weakness of the film is the casting of the supporting players and the extras. How many teenagers are in this scene? One. Casting mid-twenty somethings as teens can't work visually and it won't work in performance unless the director has time enough to hammer out the overacting. Adults do have a tendency to overact when playing characters younger than themselves because they can't 'be' themselves. The man in the middle with the glasses isn't a school inspector, he's actually meant to be a pupil! He's Brian Peck in the Avi Hadash role. A mid-twenties actor going on forty, he overacts every line and every gesture.

Music in *The Last American Virgin*

The Police, *De do do do de da da da*
Quincy Jones, *Just Once*
Gleaming Spires, *Are You Ready For The Sex Girls?*
Blondie, *In the flesh*
Devo, *Whip it*
The Dancing Brass, *Espana cani*
K.C. & The Sunshine Band, *That's The Way I Like It*
Human League, *Love Action*
The Commodores, *Oh No*
The Cars, *Since You're Gone*
Oingo Boingo, *Better Luck Next Time*
The Waitresses, *I know What Boys Like*
Blondie, *In The Flesh*

Journey, *Open Arms*
REO Speedwagon, *Keep on Loving You*
Las Fabulasasa 3 Paraguayas, *Besame mucho*
Las Fabulasasa 3 Paraguayas, *Granada*
The Dancing Brass, *Espana Cani*
Tommy Tutone, *Teen Angel Eyes*
The Cars, *Shake It Up*
Phil Seymour, *When I Find You*
The Fortune Band, *Airwaves*
Charlene Duncan, *It Ain't Easy Comin' Down*
U2, *I Will Follow*
The Plimsouls, *Zero hour*

The wide gulf between poster images and the film itself has always been a feature of exploitation films, particularly in Italy. I've no idea who the characters on the Italian poster (left) are meant to be (is that David Hasselhoff with a Kevin Keegan haircut?). They're merely images to promote 'sex' and 'cool'.

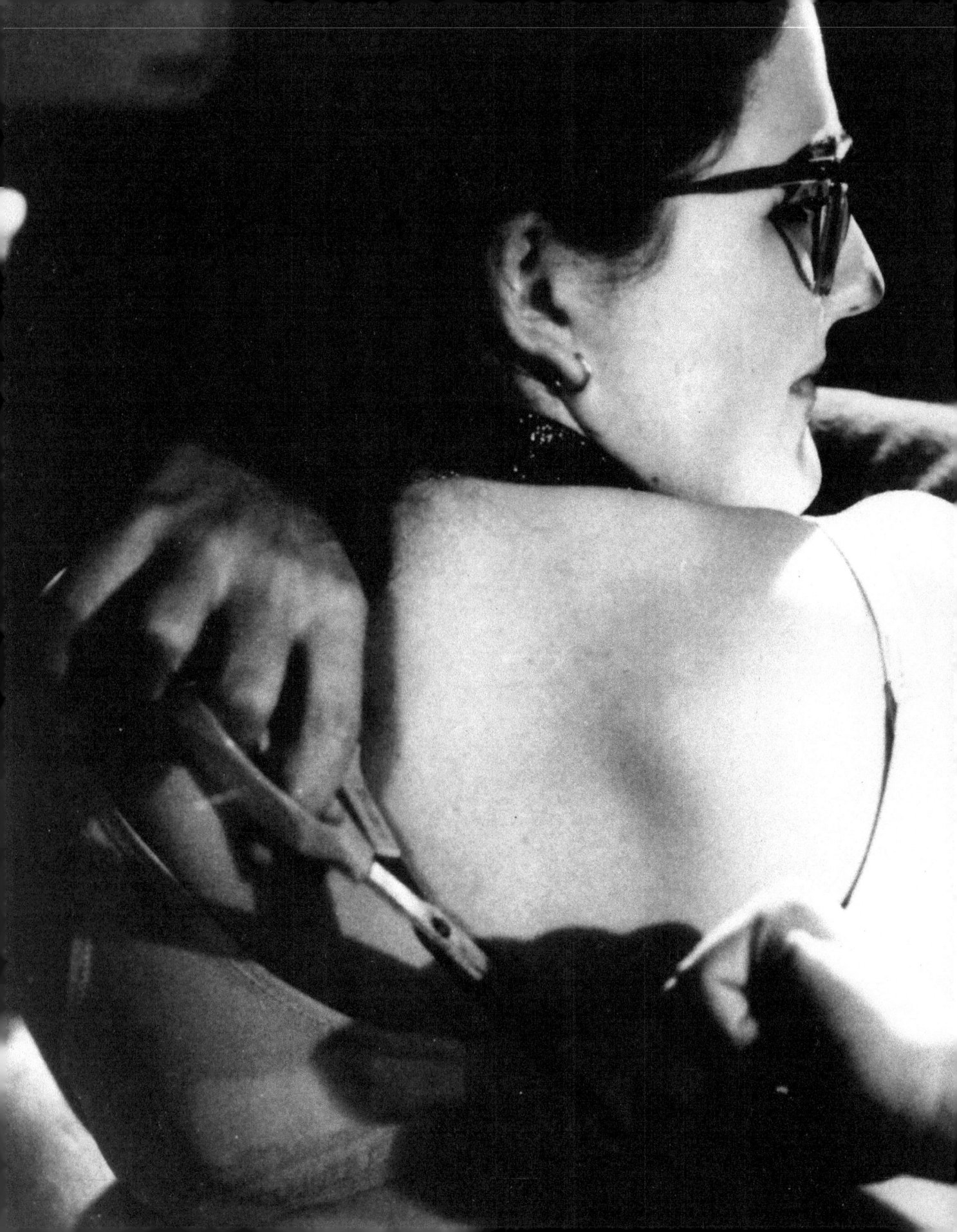

The Party Goes On

Hahagiga Nimshehet

Eis am Stiel 2001, Die neue Generation

2001

The Party Goes On

Made by the director of *Private Manoeuvres*, the first *Popsicle*-cash in, and also containing only Zachi Noy from the original film. In a stroke of genius, he plays the owner of the Montana bar in this tribute-reboot-cash-in. I think there are only three or four original sketches in the film, in one Benji's mother thinks he is gay after seeing him practising the tango in his room with Huey (inexplicably in his underwear of course); in another, which sets up the will-it-end-in-tears-finale, Victor is up a tree spying on courting couples. The rest of the film is mostly variations on well worn scenes, starting with Bobby, Benji, Huey (junior) and Victor hanging out at the Montana and checking out the local talent, including Rina (Miri Buhadana), girlfriend of motorcycle gang leader, Yaki (Dedi Zohar). In a scene right out of *Baby Love*, Huey does his drowning act to distract the lifeguard while Bobby makes a move on the lifeguard's girlfriend. The pyjama party from *Going Steady* is re-created, as is the boating trip and the scene of the trio dressed sheepishly in newspapers following a nude dip, but the scene's effectiveness here is compromised by poor quality TV-style sets (are these painted flats I see before me?). The guys try to sneak in to see a film without paying, only this time it's Huey who climbs in through a window and gets a spanking for his troubles (the newsreel shows Kennedy's inauguration). Huey redoes the penis-in-the-popcorn gag from *Diner* and *Up Your Anchor*. The egg-throwing scene from *Going Steady* now sees Benji being woken up by his next door neighbour playing the trumpet. When the trumpet noise continues through the eggs-for-family-breakfast scene, he lashes out with the eggs to the approval of his mother. The crying trumpet boy appears again to frame the seducing-the-music-teacher scene from *Hot Bubblegum*, now improbably taking place at school (senior Huey overhears Bobby's account of the proceedings and goes knocking at the wrong door with a tuba). The crying trumpet boy is later given a trumpet solo at a school assembly and the guys pelt him with eggs. (If at first you don't succeed with a joke...). Further inspiration from *Hot Bubblegum* comes with a repeat of the end-of-party scene with Benji's mother finding she is sharing her bed with uninvited guests. The first of several peephole scenes is reworked inside a clothes shop. The nympho scene is reworked well as a rumbling launderette romp.

It turned out to be an unlucky thirteen year absence. *The Party* didn't go down well with audiences, the critics, or with Boaz Davidson who sued because he had the rights to the film series. But the film still provides a pleasant diversion, particularly since much of the original music is present and correct, and has been supplemented with some great new tracks. The major flaw is that the cast are ten-years too old and all seem to come from the beautiful people catalogue beloved by trashy soap opera producers. Every girl looks like a supermodel. The film completely lacks the attractiveness of real life. Zachi Noy didn't have anything positive to say about the remake in his interview with *Popsicle Fanzine* (Issue 4 in 2003). He said, "As a person I like Nicky Goldstein very much, he is a great singer, but nothing can be compared with the original films. Could any actor play Rocky as good as Stallone? It was planned as a TV series at the beginning of production and I was sure it had a better chance like this."

p Yoram Globus *d* Tzvi Shissel *sc* Eli Tavor
starring Elad Stefansky (Benji), Nicky Goldstein (Huey), Ido Lev (Bobby), Shani Aloni (Tammy), David Cohen (Froike / Victor), Hagar Tapuchi, Rosina Kambus, Yehuda Efroni, Ilana Avital

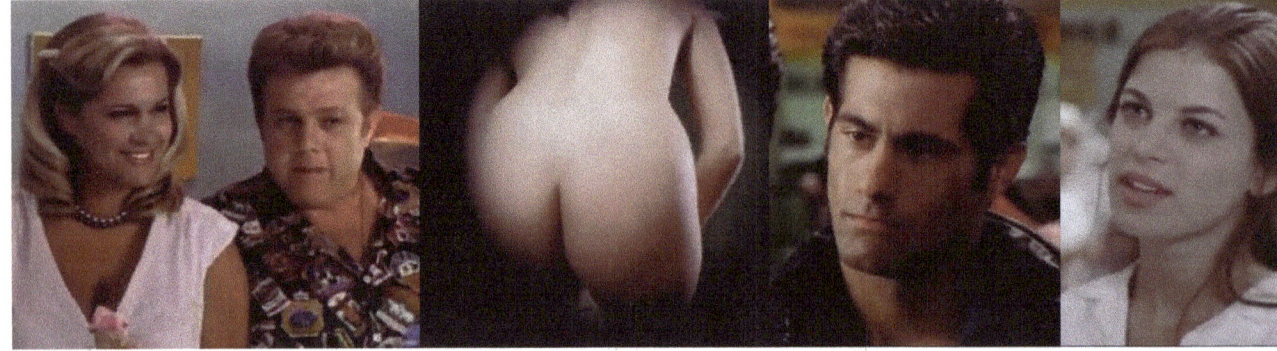

Elad Stefansky

I always had the stage virus, but mostly as a singer. Since I was a kid I performed as a singer. I hadn't trained as an actor but the opportunity came and I took it. As a kid I was an action movie fan, the *American Ninja*, *Rambo,* and all the kitsch movies. My taste improved as I grew up. I like Tim Burton movies and Johnny Depp as an actor, Edward Norton and Seth Rogen and more. There was an ad in the newspaper that the Globus Group were going to film another *Eskimo* movie. A few friends of mine told me I should go because there is a resemblance between the Bentzi (Benji) character and me. Everybody around me grew up on *Eskimo* and other Israeli cult movies, I didn't like those types of movies, I preferred movies from abroad so, only before the auditions, did I start to see *Eskimo*. But I knew them mostly from my friends who always talked and quoted from the films. My favourite one is number three, *Shifshuf Naim* (*Hot Bubblegum*). We had ONE YEAR of auditions because the producer wanted to be sure with the cast. They tried almost every actor in the market so, for a whole year, I didn't know if I'd got it or not. *The Party Goes On* was my first lead role. Before it I did a few bit roles. Zachi is a great man and actor and, during rehearsals and the shooting, he was like a mentor and a friend. We hung out a lot together on and off the set. And, of course, I heard all his stories from the sets of the other *Eskimo* movies. As a teenager, I actually was the Bentzi character myself, the shy guy, who is looking for the one girl to love. So, when I got the part, I gave a lot of myself. Many of my friends told me it reminds them of me. I met Yftach Katzur before the shooting, and it was funny because we discovered we had the same route in life, both were in *Eskimo*, work in advertising, and become businessmen.

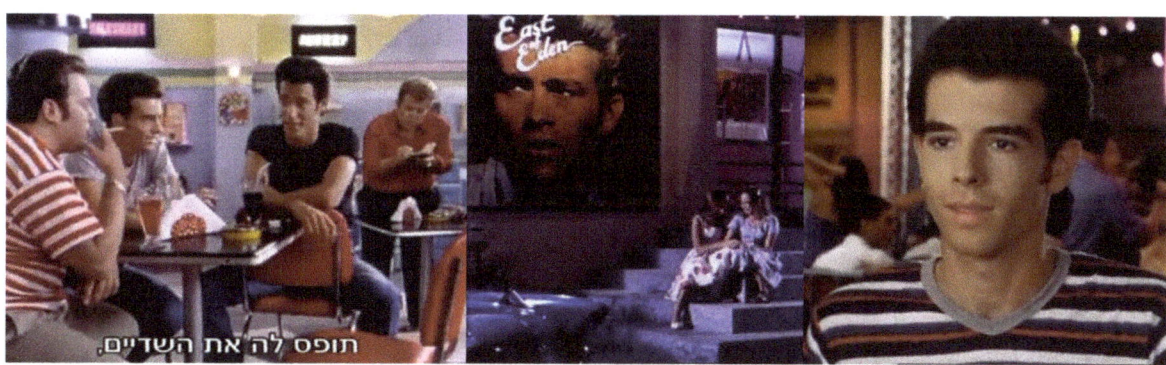

Music in *The Party Goes On*

Chubby Checker, *Let's Twist Again*
Danny & The Juniors, *At the Hop*
Paul Anka, *Put Your Head on My Shoulder*
Paul Anka, *Crazy Love* and *You Are My Destiny*
Paco-Paco, *Takatakata*
Connie Francis, *Stupid Cupid*
The Beach Boys, *Surfin' USA*
The Beach Boys, *Barbara Ann*
Elmer Bernstein, *Theme from Magnificent Seven*
Slave's Chorus from *Aida*
Carmen Miranda, *I Want My Mama*
Bill Haley & The Comets, *Rock Around the Clock* and *See You Later Alligator*
Swinging Blue Jeans, *The Hippy Hippy Shake*
Percy Faith, *Theme from A Summer Place*

Chuck Berry, *Johnny B. Goode*
Los Diablos, *Un rayo de sol*
The Everly Brothers, *All I Have To Do Is Dream*
The Four Aces, *Mr. Sandman*
Jackie Wilson, *She's So Fine* and *Reet Petite*
Neil Sedaka, *Calendar Girls* and *Little Devil*
Andy Williams, *Music to Watch Girls By*
Perez Prado, *Mambo No. 5*
Martin Denny, *The Enchanted Sea*
Peret, *Borriquito*
The Shadows, *FBI*
Surfaris, *Wipeout*
Bobby Vinton, *Mr Lonely*
Ritchie Valens, *Donna*
Norman Greenbaum, *Spirit in the Sky*

Reviewing the Critics

The *Monthly Film Bulletin* was the British Film Institute journal of record until it was merged with *Sight and Sound* magazine in 1992. During the *Popsicle* film era, British film critics had a low tendency to review from the yawning pit of morality. Fun, sex, horror and entertainment were held in low-regard by these Puritans with Pens. They reviewed 70s and 80s films from a 40s and 50s perspective, and often from a high horse. This meant that they were twenty or thirty years behind the films and the public. They also had a desperate need to run with the crowd of fellow critics. Thus an out-and-out masterpiece like Ken Russell's *The Devils*, which didn't pull its punches, was regarded by British film critics as the single worst film ever made. Genuinely innovatory films were completely beyond their ken. Thus Richard Comb wrote of *Star Wars*, now generally accepted to be the most inspiring film ever made (count the number of fan films and events it continues to inspire): "*Star Wars* is monumentally empty, based on not a single idea... the recreation is less than half convincing... Lucas has rather left his audience out in the cold, with only regularly administered shots of special effects to keep them warm." Combs, clearly, was out of his depth, as was his frankly incompetent M.F.B. colleague, Tom Milne, who gave *Rebel Without a Cause* one star out of five when the film was re-released in 1975, and who wrote of *Blade Runner*, released the same month as *The Last American Virgin*, that Ridley Scott's film was "aimless muddle... a narrative so lame that it seems in need of a wheelchair." That is the context in which these reviews were written:

Eskimo Limon (Lemon Popsicle)

Israel, 1977   **Director: Boaz Davidson**

Cert—X. *dist*—Entertainment. *p.c*—Noah Films. *p*—Menahem Golan, Yoram Globus. *sc*—Boaz Davidson, Eli Tabor. *ph*—Adam Greenberg. *col*—Eastman Colour. *ed*—Alain Jakubowicz. *a.d*—Ariel Roshko, Alfred Gershoni. *m. sup*—Jack Fishman. *songs*—"Sealed with a Kiss" by Gary Geld, Peter Udell, performed by Bryan Hyland; "At the Hop" by A. Singer, J. Medora, D. White, performed by Danny & the Juniors; "(We're Gonna) Rock around the Clock" by Max C. Freedman, Jimmy De Knight, "Shake, Rattle 'n' Roll" by Charles Calhoun, performed by Bill Haley; "Tutti Frutti" by Richard Penniman, D. La Bostrie, Joe Lubin, "Long Tall Sally" by Enotris Johnson, Richard Penniman, Robert A. Blackwell, performed by Little Richard; "Chantilly Lace" by J. P. Richardson, performed by Big Bopper; "Put Your Head on My Shoulder", "Puppy Love", "You Are My Destiny", "Diana" by and performed by Paul Anka; "Greenfields" by Terry Gilkyson, Richard Dehr, Frank Miller, performed by The Brothers Four; "My Little One" by D. Sussin, G. Howe, performed by Frankie Lane; "Mr. Lonely" by Bobby Vinton, Gene Allan, performed by Bobby Vinton; "To Know Him Is to Love Him" by Phil Spector, performed by Joe Moss; "Witch Doctor" by Ross Bagdasarian, performed by Jim Morris; "Que Sera, Sera" by Jay Livingstone, Ray Evans, performed by Rosemary Squires; "Hey! Baby!" by Margaret Cobb, Bruce Channel, performed by Bruce Channel; "Hey, Paula!" by Ray Hildebrand, performed by Paul & Paula; "Lollipop" by Beverly Ross, Julius Dixon, performed by The Chordettes; "FBI" by Peter Gormley, performed by The Shadows; "Seven Little Girls Sitting in the Back Seat" by Lee Pockriss, Bob Hilliard, performed by Paul Evans & The Curls; "Ciao, Ciao, Bambina" by Domenico Modugno, Verde, (English lyrics) Mitchell Parish, "Volare" by Domenico Modugno, F. Migliacci, (English lyrics) Mitchell Parish, performed by Domenico Modugno; "Come Prima" by Di Paola, Taccani, (English lyrics) Buck Ram, performed by Marino Marini. *cost*—Tammy Mor. *sd. ed*—(English version) Roy Taylor. *sd. rec*—(English version) Peter Maxwell. *English translation*—Maggie Dickie, Meir Z. Ribalow. *l.p*—Yiftach Katzur (*Benji* [*Benz*]), Anat Atzmon (*Nicki* [*Nili*]), Jonathan Segal (*Bobbie* [*Momo*]), Zacki Noy (*Hughie* [*Yudaleh*]), Deborah Kaydar, Ophelia Shtrel, Menashe Warshavsky, Rachel Steiner, Louis Rosenberg, Yehoshna Luff, Avi Chadash, Dennis Bozaglo. 8,601 ft. 96 mins. *Original running time*—100 mins. *Dubbed*.

Israel, 1957. Benji (short and sensitive), Bobbie (tall and handsome), and Hughie (fat and spivy) are high-school chums who frequent the ice-cream parlour and teen-party circuits. Ditching Hughie for the evening, Bobbie demonstrates his pick-up technique for Benji, fixing them up with dates for the movies. Gaining in confidence, Benji is attracted to Nicki, a new girl in town. She refuses his request for a date, but he pursues her doggedly, even when he becomes drunkenly aware at a friend's party that Bobbie is going steady with her. Benji later takes his two friends to the home of Stella, a middle-aged seductress, but Benji himself remains uninitiated. Benji persuades Bobbie to skip his next date with Nicki, because he needs his friend's moral support when he loses his virginity with a local whore. Bobbie continues to date Nicki, and unthinkingly invites Benji along to provide a partner for Nicki's bespectacled best friend. When Bobbie finally seduces Nicki, he tells Benji to his face. Soon after, discovering that Nicki is pregnant and that Bobbie is unconcerned, Benji undertakes to look after her. He borrows money from his deliveryman boss and helps himself from his mother's purse to pay for an abortion, and nurses her after the operation in his grandmother's old house. Responding at last to his attentions, Nicki tells Benji that she loves him. He has a locket inscribed for her, but when he arrives at Nicki's birthday party with the present, he finds her back in Bobbie's arms.

In the context of recent films designed primarily to promote 'soundtrack' albums, *Lemon Popsicle* is more audacious than most. Unashamedly subordinating its narrative to the music-track, the film allows the songs to tell the story (notably "Put Your Head on My Shoulder", "Puppy Love" and "Mr. Lonely") and relegates itself to visual accompaniment. Apart from one desultory dance, the teenagers never seem to engage with the music or give any indication that they belong to their age. The film's perspective on the period is that of an older generation, and the chronological confusion is emphasised by glimpses of a 1957 Pathé newsreel and a parade of early Sixties cars and fashions—a vagueness underlined by the film's irrelevant but catch-all title. Where *Cooley High* borrowed the formula of *American Graffiti*, but adapted it to its own cultural context, *Lemon Popsicle* merely transports the stock elements of rock'n' roll mythology to an Israeli setting (which could as easily represent any Jewish neighbourhood for all that the film reveals about Israeli youth in the late Fifties) and repackages them, ready dubbed, for second generation rock 'n' roll fans. Significantly, perhaps, the only potentially exciting scene recalls the 'chicken run' in *Rebel Without a Cause*, even though it ends bathetically as the 'borrowed car' in which the four kids are necking careers down the beach and into the sea. Resuming its leaden pace, the movie ends on a rising crane shot of Benji alone on the street, the most uplifting moment in this whole sad, secondhand experience.

MARTYN AUTY

Sapiches (Private Popsicle [Lemon Popsicle IV])

Israel/West Germany, 1982 **Director: Boaz Davidson**

Cert—18(X). *dist*—Cannon. *p.c*—Golan-Globus (Tel Aviv)/KF Kinofilm (Munich). A Cannon Group production. *exec. p*—Amnon Globus. *p*—Menahem Golan, Yoram Globus. *p. co-ordinator*—Henia Mendelbaum. *p. manager*—Haim Idan. *location manager*—Eitan Alon. *post-p. co-ordinator*—Karen Hoenig. *asst. d*—Shaul Dishi, Uri Nusbaum. *sc*—Boaz Davidson. *ph*—Adam Greenberg. In colour. *addit. ph*—Nissan Mofkadi, Avi Koren, Rami Siman Tov. *ed*—Bruria Davidson. *a.d*—Ariel Roshko. *m*—Paul Fishman. *"The Private Popsicle March" by/m. soundtrack sup*—Jack Fishman. *songs*—"Livin' Doll" by Bart, performed by Cliff Richard; "See You Later Alligator" by Guidry, performed by Bill Haley; "My Special Angel" by Duncan, performed by Bobby Helms; "Charlie Brown" by Leiber, Stoller, performed by The Coasters; "I Like It" by Murray, performed by Gerry and the Pacemakers; "Da Doo Ron Ron" by Spector, Greenwich, Barry, performed by The Crystals; "Mr. Sandman" by Ballard, performed by Robin Merrill; "Who Put the Bomp" by Mann, Goffin, performed by Barry Mann; "Rise and Shine" by P. Fishman, "Strictly Private" by J. Fishman, performed by The Rookies; "Whole Lot of Shakin' Goin' On" by David, Williams, performed by Jerry Lee Lewis; "Lucky Lips" by Leiber, Stoller, performed by Cliff Richard and the Shadows; "Silence Is Golden" by Crewe, Gaudio, performed by The Tremeloes; "Speedy Gonzales" by Kaye, Hill, Lee, performed by Pat Boone; "Mr. Blue" by Blackwell, performed by The Fleetwoods; "Bend Me, Shape Me" by Weiss, English, performed by Amen Corner; "I Want My Mama" by Paiva, Paiva, Stillman, performed by The Popsicles; "With All My Heart" by Marcucci, De Angelis, performed by The Tymes; "Let There Be Drums" by Nelson, Podoler, performed by Sandy Nelson; "Soldier Boy" by Green, Dixon, performed by The Shirelles. *cost. design*—Tammy Mor. *cost. sup*—Bernard Stockinger. *wardrobe*—Rina Rimon. *make-up*—Moni Monsono. *titles/opticals*—MGM. *sd. ed*—Susan Dudeck. *sd. rec*—Eli Yarkoni. *post-sync d*—Mel Welles. *sd. re-rec*—Michael J. Kohut, Jay M. Harding, Carlos De Larios. *foley*—Ken Dufva, David Lee Fein, Keith Olsen, Robert Perrisi, Dorothy Wright, Frederico Loaker. *sp. audio consultants*—Kenny Bornstein, Dan Wetherbee. *l.p*—Iftach Katzur (*Benji*), Zachi Noy (*Hughie*), Jonathan Segal (*Rena*), Menache Warshawsky (*Captain Romek*), Bea Fiedler (*Eva*), Dietmar Siegert (*Norwegian General*), Dvora Keidar (*Sonya*), Joseph Shiloah (*1st Sergeant Randit*), Moshe Ish Kassit (*Captain*), Dvora Bakon (*Marshmallow*), Shmuel Eizer (*Boris*), Louis Rosenberg (*Military Psychiatrist*), Anatol Constantin (*Army Barber*), Olga Spandorf (*Mrs. Pomerantz*), Pesach Gotmark (*Mr. Pomerantz*), Arie Shein (*Mr. Klinger*), Noam Aviram (*Draftee*), Hagit Mor (*Girl Soldier*), Mimon Ruth (*Night-club Singer*), Meira Arazi (*Female Norwegian Officer*), Sabich Goldreich (*Impresario*), Rina Levi (*Opera Singer*), Gili Klein (*Nurse*), Jupiter Leonid (*Army Doctor*), Alexander Rotblum (*Accordionist*). 9,004 ft. 100 mins. *Dubbed*.

Israel, the early 1960s. On the eve of their national service, Benji, Hughie and Bobbie attempt to seduce Eva, a German temptress, only to be chased through the streets in various stages of undress by her drunken husband. Escaping from his possessive mother, Benji joins his friends at a boot camp where they incur the displeasure of Sergeant-Major Randit. Hughie quickly organises a black-market confectionery and pornography business, using the profits to invest in counterfeit officers' uniforms. Benji is smitten with Private Rena who, believing him to be a captain, responds to his advances. Rena and two friends agree to meet the trio at a nearby night-club, but are ordered to leave by the female Captain Romek, who is dating Randit. In order to escape, the boys are forced to disguise themselves as an all-girl vocal group. Taken with Hughie's blonde incarnation, Randit ditches Romek and lures the private to his quarters. His attempt at seduction is foiled, however, by the jealous Romek. During an inspection by a Norwegian general, Hughie contrives to fall into a latrine, dragging the visiting officer with him. Benji and Hughie pretend to be gay in order to get psychiatric leave. The army doctor gives Benji a pass but makes a pass at Hughie. After an idyllic weekend at the beach, Rena discovers Benji's true rank and casts him off, leaving him naked in the middle of the camp. In order to pursue Rena off the base, Benji arranges a furlough via Randit, but he has to promise the sergeant-major a date with his 'cousin'—Hughie in drag. Romek surprises them all at the club, and Hughie's sex is revealed. Rena forgives Benji.

Golan and Globus may have gone up-market since their first international success, but this *Lemon Popsicle* carry on is a return to the latrine which is the foundation of their empire. The military setting provides an excuse to parade all the worst jokes from *Carry on Sergeant*, to caricature the Indian sergeant-major beyond belief, and to have various male characters attempt to seduce fat Hughie. The soundtrack's assortment of bygone hits is mercilessly cut, interrupted, and talked through, and the whole ghastly mess dubbed in a variety of weird accents, perhaps understandably since the post-sync work is credited to Mel Welles, best remembered as the incomprehensibly Yiddish florist in Corman's *Little Shop of Horrors*.

KIM NEWMAN

Roman Zair (Baby Love [Lemon Popsicle V])

Israel/West Germany, 1983 **Director: Dan Wolman**

Cert—18. *dist*—Cannon. *p.c*—Golan-Globus Productions (Tel Aviv)/Kinofilm (West Berlin). A Boaz Davidson film. *exec. p*—Sam Waynberg. *p*—Menahem Golan, Yoram Globus. *assoc. p*—Amnon Globus, Rafi Adar. *p. co-ordinator*—Henia Mendelbaum. *p. manager*—David Lifkind. *location manager*—Tal Ron. *post-p. sup*—Karen Hoenig. *asst. d*—Shaul Dishi, Handas Ziv. *sc*—Boaz Davidson, Eli Tabor. *ph*—Ilan Rosenberg. In colour. *2nd Unit ph*—Yachin Hirsh. *ed*—Mark Helfrich. *assoc. ed*—Uri Katoni. *a.d*—Ariel Roshko. *m. sup*—Jack Fishman. *m. ed*—Mark Helfrich. *songs*—"Crazy Love" by and performed by Paul Anka; "Rescue Me" by Smith, Miner, performed by Fontella Bass; "Sweet Little Sixteen" by Chuck Berry, "Maybelline" by Chuck Berry, R. Fratto, A. Freed, performed by Chuck Berry; "Rhythm of the Rain" by Gummoe, performed by The Cascades; "Apache" by Lordan, performed by The Cherokees; "He's So Fine" by Ronnie Mack, performed by The Chiffons; "Summertime Blues" by Cochran, Capehart, performed by Eddie Cochran; "Only Sixteen", "You Send Me" by Sam Cooke, "What a Wonderful World" by Campbell, performed by Sam Cooke; "16 Candles" by L. Dixon, A. R. Khent, performed by The Crests; "Dream Lover", "Multiplication" by Bobby Darin, "Splish Splash" by Bobby Darin, Murray, performed by Bobby Darin; "The End of the World" by Sylvia Dee, Arthur Kent, performed by Skeeter Davis; "The Wanderer" by Ernie Maresca, performed by Dion and the Belmonts; "Locomotion" by Goffin, King, performed by Little Eva; "Tiger" by Ollie Jones, performed by Fabian; "Ginny Come Lately" by Geld, Udell, performed by Brian Hyland; "Raunchy" by Justis, Manker, performed by Bill Justis; "Pretty Little Angel Eyes" by Boyce, Lee, performed by Curtis Lee; "Twilight Time" by B. Ram, M. Nevins, A. Dunn, performed by The Platters; "The Girl Can't Help It" by Troup, "Keep a Knockin'" by Penniman, performed by Little Richard; "Wipeout" by Wilson, Fuller, Benny Hill, Connelly; "Take Good Care of My Baby" by Goffin, King, performed by Bobby Vee. *cost*—Tami Mor. *cost. sup*—Rena Ramon. *wardrobe*—Ruthi Davidson. *make-up*— Moni Mansano (artist), Lili Ben-Yair. *titles/opticals*—MGM. *sd. rec*—Eli Yarkoni. *sd. re-rec*—Jay M. Harding, Gregory H. Watkins, David J. Kimball. *sd. effects/foley*—Studio Anzellotti, Rome. *p. assistant*—Osnat Behiri. *l.p*—Yiftach Katzur (*Benji*), Zachi Noy (*Hughie*), Jonathan Segal (*Bobbie*), Devora Keidar (*Sonya*), Menashe Warshawsky (*Romek*), Stefanie Petsch (*Gili*), Sabrina Cheval (*Ruthi*), Avi Hadash (*Froyke*), Bea Fiedler (*Dentist's Assistant*), Dolly Dollar (*Frieda*), Misha Nathan (*Dolek*), Rachel Shor (*Client at Dentist*), Ruth Davidson (*Risha*), Karol Markovich (*Dentist*), Miri Toledano (*Nurit*), Slaughter Jones (*Life-guard*), Reneta Langer (*Life-guard Assistant*), Orit Cohen (*Judy*), Shmuel Aizer (*Theatre Attendant*), Zinger David (*Doctor*), Marta Levis (*Pianist*), Rachel Tlitman (*Ballet Teacher*). 7,574 ft. 84 mins. *Dubbed*.

Benji, Bobbie and Hughie hang out together, bike-riding on the beach and picking up girls at the Café Montana. Bobbie's sister Gili introduces him to her dance-class friend, Ruthi, and Bobbie asks Benji to occupy his sister so that he can be alone with Ruthi. After making love to her, Bobbie takes the prize money for riding his bike closest to the cliff edge. (Fat Hughie, who organised the event, is left with only a small percentage as usual.) Benji and Gili are mutually attracted but, despite Ruthi's encouragement, Gili is cautious about rushing her shyly reluctant admirer. Bobbie hypocritically admonishes Gili for not doing her homework and for fooling around with the boys. When he then accuses Ruthi of being a bad influence on his sister, she tells him about Gili's affair with Benji. Bobbie beats up his best friend and extracts a promise from Benji not to date Gili again. When Gili subsequently finds Benji paired off with another girl, she takes one of the suicide tablets that Ruthi has kept ever since the break-up of an affair with a married man. In despair, Benji takes off on his bike to commit suicide. But a doctor at the hospital manages to save Gili's life, and informs Bobbie that not only was she not pregnant (as her brother had suspected), but is still a virgin. Bobbie rushes after his friend and just prevents him from riding off the cliff. Gili and Benji are reunited with Bobbie's blessing.

The late 50s/early 60s mythology of surf 'n' rock has fostered a variety of cultural outgrowths. Although *American Graffiti*, made in 1973, spawned the present crop of *Lemon Popsicle* movies—*Baby Love* represents number five—the real progenitor of the musical anthology genre was probably *The Girl Can't Help It* (1957). Nothing, however, could be further from the latter's contemporary zest than this limp piece of nostalgia for a long-lost youth. Instead of attempting to evoke the youth sub-culture of the period, *Baby Love*, like its predecessors, opts for the simpler course of titillating jaded palates. The ugliest hypocrisies of the consumerisation of sex abound. Handsome Bobbie, who has all the fun with the girls, jealously protects his sister from the attentions of his best friend, only to condone their romance when he discovers that she is still a virgin. More to the point, perhaps, the adventures of Benji, Hughie, Bobbie, Gili and Ruthi are about as erotic as those of the Famous Five.

ROBERT BROWN

The Last American Virgin

U.S.A., 1982   **Director: Boaz Davidson**

Cert—X. *dist*—Cannon. *p.c*—Hollywood-European Productions. *p*—Menahem Golan, Yoram Globus. *assoc. p*—David Womark. *location manager*—Gary McNett. *asst. d*—Mark Allan, Eric Jewett, Ken Bornstein. *sc*—Boaz Davidson. *ph*—Adam Greenberg. In colour. *ed*—Bruria Davidson. *a.d*—Jim Dultz. *m. co-ordinator*—Paula Erickson. *m. sup*—Lookout Management. *songs*—"De Do Do Do, De Da Da Da" by Sting, performed by The Police; "Just Once" by B. Mann, C. Weill, performed by Quincy Jones; "Are You Ready for the Sex Girls" by Leslie Bohem, David Kendrick, performed by Gleaming Spires; "That's the Way I Like It" by H. W. Casey, R. Finch, performed by K. C. and the Sunshine Band; "Love Action (I Believe in Love)" by Ian Burden, Philip Oakey, performed by The Human League; "Oh No" by Lionel B. Richie Jnr., performed by The Commodores; "I Know What Boys Like" by Chris Butler, performed by The Waitresses; "In the Flesh" by Chris Stein, Deborah Harry, performed by Blondie; "Open Arms" by S. Perry, J. Cain, performed by Journey; "Since You're Gone", "Shake It Up" by Ric Ocasek, performed by The Cars; "Whip It Up" by Mark Mothersbaugh, Gerald V. Casale, performed by Devo; "It Ain't Easy Coming Down" by Ken Hirsch, Ron Miller, performed by Charlene; "I Will Follow" by and performed by U2; "Better Luck Next Time" performed by Oingo Boingo; "Keep on Loving You" by Kevin Cronin, performed by REO Speedwagon; "Besame Mucho", "Granada" performed by Los Fabulosos 3 Paraguayos; "Espana Cani" performed by The Dancing Brass; "When I Find You" performed by Phil Seymour; "Zero Hour" performed by The Plimsouls. *wardrobe*—Caren Berger. *make-up*—Richard Arrington. *titles/opticals*—MGM. *sd. ed*—Michael Sloan. *sd. rec*—Mark Ulano. Dolby stereo. *sd. transfers*—John Murray, Tom Siiter. *p. assistants*—Kathy McMahon, Dan Wetherbee, Gary Zembow. *l.p*—Lawrence Monoson (*Gary*), Diane Franklin (*Karen*), Steve Antin (*Rick*), Joe Rubbo (*David*), Louisa Moritz (*Carmela*), Brian Peck (*Victor*), Kimmy Robertson (*Rose*), Tessa Richarde (*Brenda*), Winifred Freedman (*Millie*), Gerri Idol (*Roxanne*), Sandy Sprung (*Mother*), Paul Keith (*Father*), Phil Rubenstein (*Gino*), Roberto Rodriquez (*Paco*), Blanche Rubin (*Librarian*), Michael Chieffo (*Soda Jerk*), Leslie Simms (*Mrs. Applebaum*), Harry Bugin (*Doctor*), Julianna McCarthy (*Counsellor*), Mel Welles (*Druggist*), Sylvia Lawler (*Assistant Druggist*), Nancy Brock (*Ruby*), Lyla Graham (*Mrs. Roswell*), Mordo Dana (*Jeweller*), Robert Doran (*Earl*), Noel Scott (*1st Boy*), Peter Ellenstein (*2nd Boy*), Rob Reese (*3rd Boy*). 8,304 ft. 92 mins.

Rick (good-looking and precocious), Gary (naive and impressionable) and David (fat and spivvy) are high-school friends who frequent the local bars and party circuit. Gary holds a small party at his parents' house but, although Rick and David have a good time, he himself is thwarted by his parents' early return home. In the course of his evening job delivering pizzas, Gary is subjected to the amorous attentions of Carmela, a bleached-blonde Mexican bombshell, and flees her aggressive attempts at seduction. Rick and Gary are both set on Karen, the 'catch' of the school; Rick secures the first date, leaving Gary with Karen's best friend Rose, a New Wave devotee. In an attempt to distract Rick from Karen, Gary organises an outing to Carmela's. Once again, Rick and David are able to enjoy themselves before the arrival of Carmela's beefy sailor-admirer breaks up the party. The luckless and uninitiated Gary refuses Rick's request for the keys to his grandmother's vacant flat, and in a further effort to keep Rick from Karen, organises a session for the three of them with a local hooker. Next day, the trio all have crabs. Eventually, however, Rick and Karen get it together, and Karen winds up pregnant. Rick abandons her, but the ever-faithful Gary arranges and pays for her abortion. After convalescing at Gary's, Karen horrifies him by running straight back into Rick's arms.

In a neat and unashamed feat of cultural transportation (not to say vagabondage), the plot and characters of *Lemon Popsicle* are transferred wholesale from Israel in the 1950s to present-day America (where this sorry series finds its origins, of course, in *American Graffiti*). Divested of any nostalgia for a lost era, and of the mythological trappings of rock 'n' roll, this third-hand article is so thin in outline and threadbare in detail that it even betrays the rather dubious under pinnings of George Lucas' original. The mixture of Human League, Quincy Jones and Journey—to mention only the musical content—suggests the lack of any coherent cultural context for the grotesque characterisations and love story. Most irritating, perhaps, is the way these supposedly contemporary characters are encumbered with 50s trappings—rather redundantly, to say the least. In the age of the Pill, for example, there is nothing particularly heart-rending about a pregnant, unmarried girl, nor is there anything intrinsically amusing, at a time of serious mass drug addiction, about coke snorting. And least of all is it possible to rouse any interest in a smooth, self-obsessed young man who always gets what he wants, and in his friend who, while rying to emulate him, comes up empty-handed.
                                         ROBERT BROWN

The Last American Virgin reviewed by Raymond Durgnat

Durgnat was that rarest of breeds, a British film critic and theorist who liked to look beyond the canon and who knew that good taste wasn't the highest virtue of the Seventh Art. This review was first published in *Films on Screen & Video* in November 1982.

THIS IS ONE of a sudden gaggle of movies whose sexual grossness has aroused the ire of feminists, ideologues, and all the other exponents of the New Prudery – or (let's be fair) the New Puritanism. *Porky's* and *Hog Wild* clearly signal that they're unabashedly piggish about every kind of carnal carry-on. *The Last American Virgin* is less consistently rumbustious in its oscillations between caricature and intimism. But it edges a notch or two closer to, not realism exactly, but a kind of rude, ribald populism. It contemplates the discomfitures and ignominies of everyday experience.

It's a mood long familiar in British vulgar culture – from Donald McGill postcards down to the first and freshest of the *Carry Ons* (Sergeant, Nurse). Thereafter the *Carry On* turned to broad parodies of familiar genres, which blurred their 'everyday' focus.

Subsequently, the *Confessions* films suggested, but passed on, an opportunity to work out the line which these American films about outrageous teenagers are doing much better. They're certainly not high art, and even as low art they're pretty hit-and-miss, but their sloppy-go lucky mixture of the familiar, the vulgar, and the absurd does correspond to a type of popular attitude, and makes a good compost for an unsentimental, lively new realism. Certainly the innocence of Donald McGill and the *Carry On* is gone: but how could it not go, in this era of the Kinsey Report, the Hite Report, Gay Lib, sex lessons in schools, and every other incentive to a more intricate kind of knowingness? Essentially *The Last American Virgin* is just a set of teenage escapades, which take our hero (and his friends) from their first, rather callow, sexual breakthroughs to the deeper heartbreak that opens up the ironies of adulthood. Our hero busses pizzas for the Pink Pizza Parlour, and that's a convenient job for cobbling together some typical teenage experiences in comically exaggerated form. Here's the tradition-enshrined litany of pubescence: undersized sex organs, terrifying hookers, getting a look at the girls in the showers, the male panting for petting while the girl crunches the crisps, and getting dope for the girls (a modern issue and comic material like anything else). Frantically but unavailingly our hero longs for a high-status girl who, just as obstinately, prefers his socially slicker buddy. But our boy gets his chance when her birth control precautions slip a gear (even in this brave new world of the pill). He sells his dearly beloved stereo to buy her an abortion. She's grateful for an hour or two, but does it last? As an example of the film's sillier, clumsier moments, there's an encounter with a nympho Mexican spitfire.

And though the voyeurism that then gets involved is highly likely (particularly by certain American norms), it's worked out in a kind of knee-jerk way, where any more sensitive film-maker (let alone a Bunuel) would have sussed out the shades of awe and mystery and scruple which go along with curiosity. Still, the film has its scattering of recognition points and reminiscent situations. The necking buggies lined up along the moonlit beach. The pharmacist bemused by over-devious requests for something to kill lice in pubic hair. The class wimp with perpetually sticking-plastered specs. The unlucky fat boy with wobbly titties. When the film settles into its abortion theme, it makes a pretty good stab at catching that modern casualness which weirdly mixed real relief with a sense of cop-out.

Overall it's an unsubtly shaped story, and prefers a kind of scattergun technique, never passing up the quick laugh or quick sigh for the sake of some overarching dramatic structure. But that's a not uncommon technique these days, and there's some sort of reasoning behind it, insofar as the norms, values and emotions on which drama depends are so often in doubt. Especially among adolescents.

At any rate, it's lively and gaudy and funny as it goes, especially if you take a rather low view of human nature. Its unedifying wildly tolerant attitude to modern manners works in basically the same way as the sharpest pop music has been doing, from *Come Outside* back in the '60s to *The Boiler* recently.

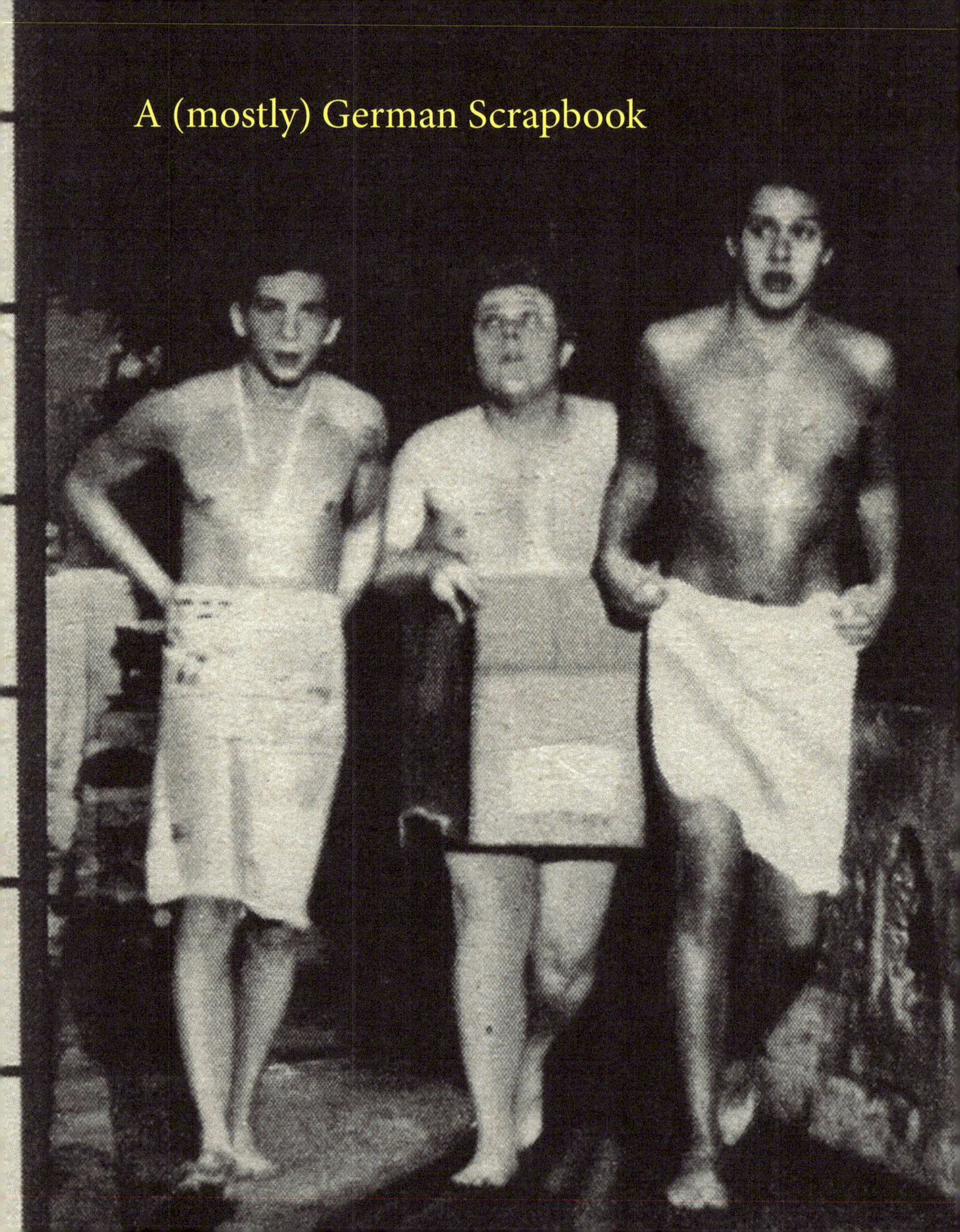
A (mostly) German Scrapbook

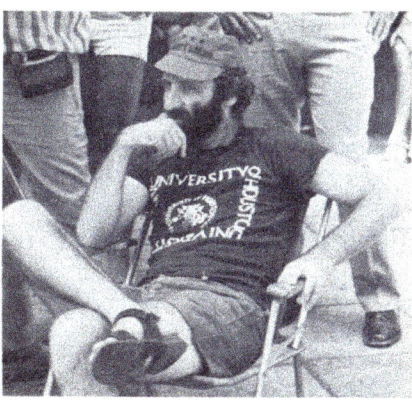

Zweites „Eis am Stiel"

Die „Eishelden" Jesse Katzur (der Junge mit der Eistüte) Jonathan Segal und der dicke Cachie Noy verschwinden noch nicht in der Versenkung. Eine Fortsetzung des Erfolgs-Films „Eis am Stiel" ist fest eingeplant, sie soll nächstes Jahr – „wenn es wärmer wird" – in die Kinos kommen. Viele von Euch haben die Zentrale gefragt, ob die Musik zu „Eis am Stiel" auf Platte erschienen ist. Wir haben uns erkundigt. Leider gibt es das „Stiel-Eis" auf Platten gepreßt noch nicht zu kaufen.

Die drei Stars aus „Eis am Stiel": Cachie (L), Jonathan (M.) und Jesse

BOAZ DAVIDSON

Boaz Davidson wurde am 8. November 1943 in Tel-Aviv geboren. 1967 ging er an die London Film School. 1970 bestand er dort sein Examen als Filmemacher. Ab 1970 begann er, Spielfilme, Dokumentarfilme, Werbefilme, TV-Stücke und Musik-Shows zu inszenieren. Er zählt zu den jüngsten und zugleich produktivsten Regisseuren in Israel. In den letzten sieben Jahren hat er neun Filme gedreht, darunter die Co-Regie von OPERATION THUNDERBOLT. LEMON POPSICLE ist sein jüngster Film.

'He is among the youngest and at the same time the most productive directors in Israel. In the last seven years he has directed nine films, including co-directing *Operation Thunderbolt*. *Lemon Popsicle* is his most recent film.'

it's everything about being seventeen
ENTERTAINMENT
Featuring 25 chart bustin' hits of the 50's
including original tracks by
BRYAN HYLAND
BILL HALEY · LITTLE RICHARD
BIG BOPPER · PAUL ANKA
THE BROTHERS FOUR
FRANKIE LAINE
BOBBY VINTON
BRUCE CHANNEL
PAUL & PAULA
THE CHORDETTES
THE SHADOWS
Original Soundtrack Album available on
WARWICK RECORDS WW5050
THE FABULOUS FLAVOUR OF THE FIFTIES
Lemon Popsicle
X
FROM THURSDAY 8th MARCH:-
classic
OXFORD STREET
636 0310
scene
off LEICESTER SQUARE
439 4470
centa
PICCADILLY CIRCUS
734 1449
ODEON
SWISS COTTAGE
722 5905
ODEON
WESTBOURNE GROVE
229 3369
AT PRINCIPAL ODEON AND OTHER IMPORTANT THEATRES FROM SUNDAY 11th MARCH
SEE LOCAL PRESS FOR DETAILS

이 영화의 주인공은 당신 자신이다!
*영화시작 5분—
서로가 말못할 사건이
연속적으로 펼쳐진다.
Growing
Up
'83
24시간은 너무짧아
DOLBY STEREO
그로잉·업

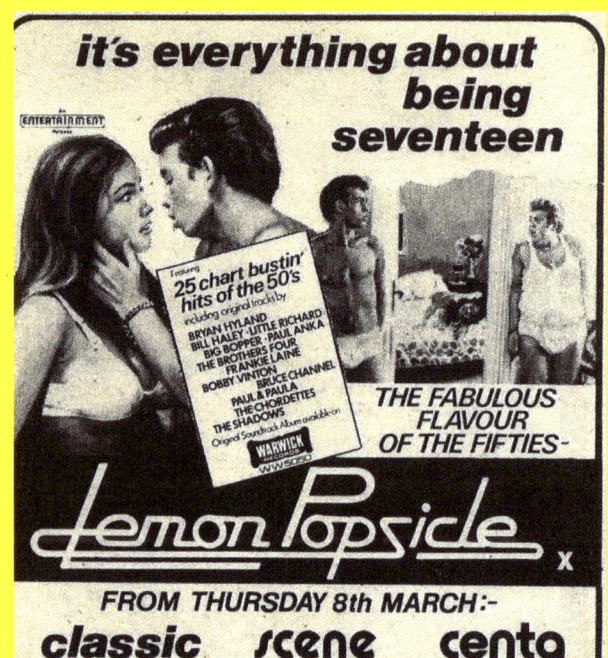

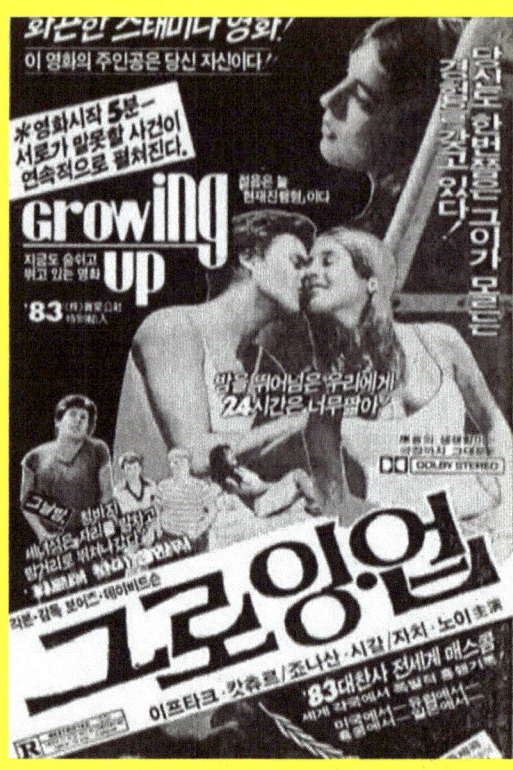

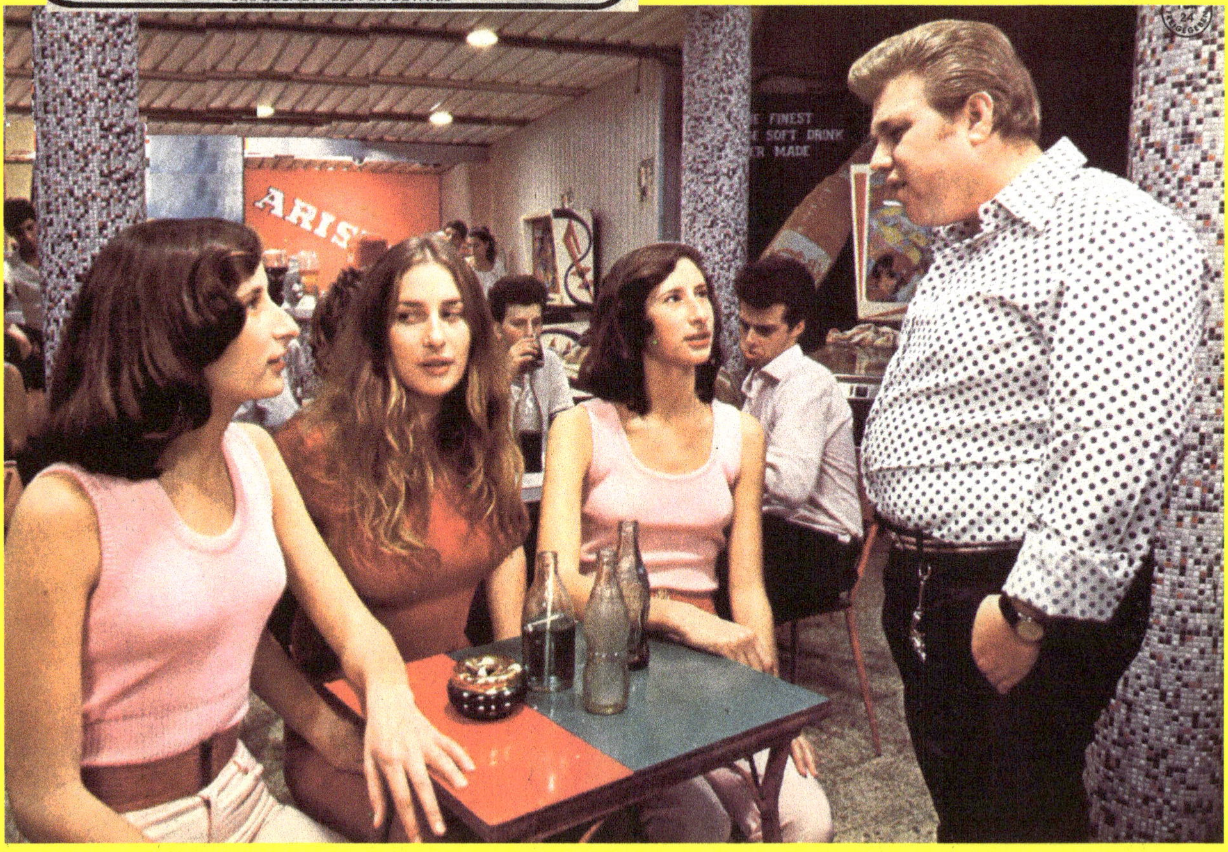

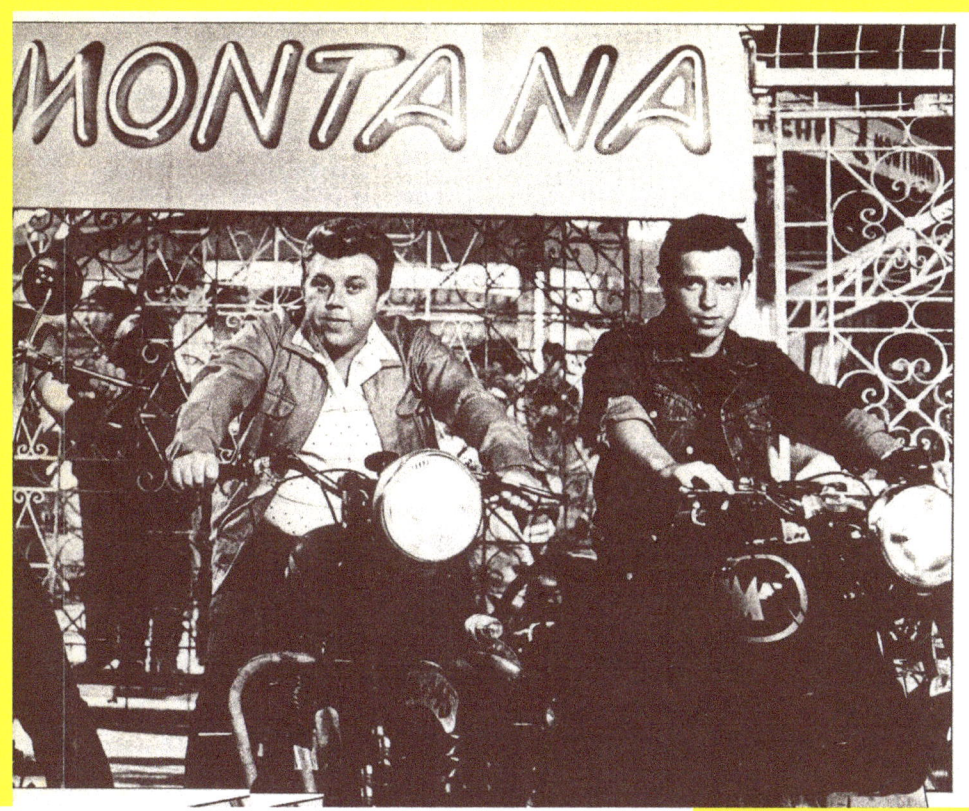

Die Lage ist unverändert positiv. Am Strand hüpfen die Bräute herum, daß den Jungs der Pulsbeschleuniger durchbrennt. Das Quecksilber in den Thermometern schlägt alle Guiness-Rekorde – und das Wasser zischt, wenn sich so hitzige Temperamente wie Benny oder Bobby, Johnny oder Victor ins Meer stürzen. Lebensmüde? Liebesmüde? Keine Spur. Als Bobby, unternehmungslustig wie immer, das Wasser bis zur Unterlippe, um Hilfe schreit, hat er nur ein Ziel: die flotte Mieze des Rettungsschwimmers. Er provoziert eine rasche Mund-zu-Mund-Beatmung und kassiert dafür noch Benny ab, der gegen ihn gewettet hat. Als aber Johnny seinen massigen Körper in die Wellen wirft, um, auf Bobbys feuchten Spuren, auch ein kleines Küßchen zu erhaschen, erntet er stattdessen blaue Flecke – vom Rettungsschwimmer, der viel zu rasch zurückkam.

The situation remains positive. On the beach, the chicks bounce around the guys revving their accelerators.

とをしてい　など，映像とともにそれらのヒット・

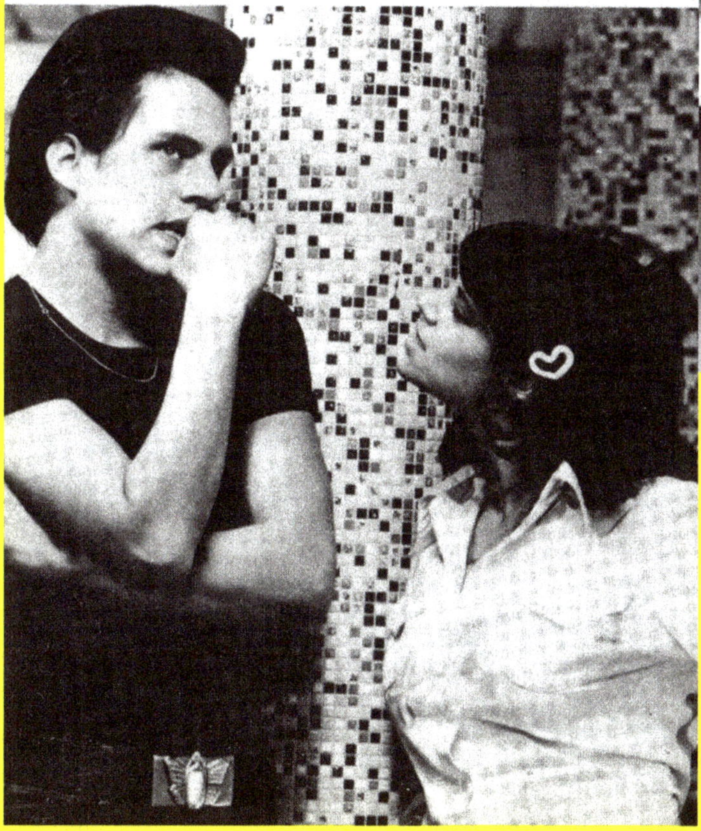

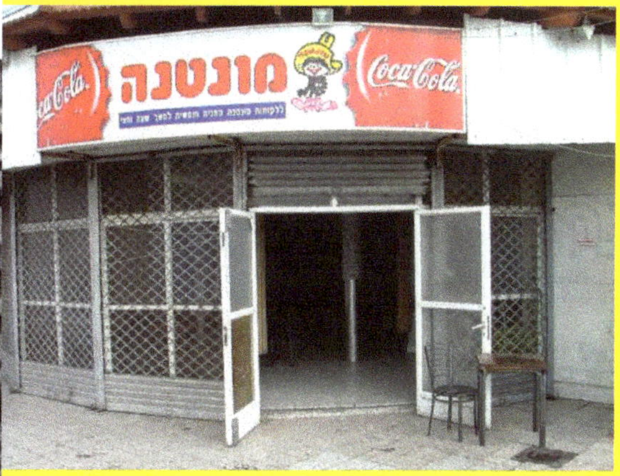

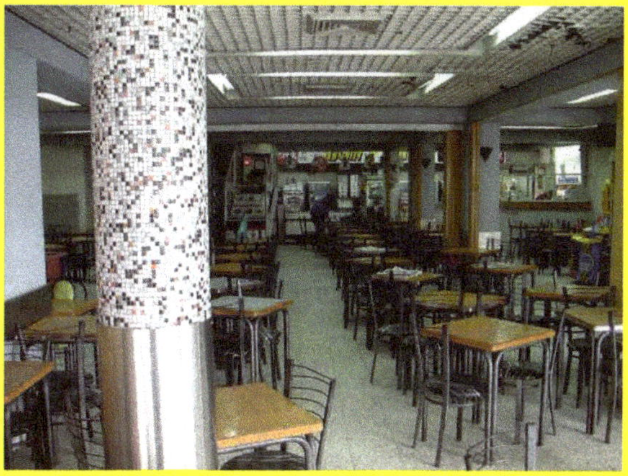

Dieter Stein created a *Lemon Popsicle* comic strip for the German version of MAD magazine: "When I was a teenager, I was an avid MAD reader and the idea of being on the crazy editorial staff was a dream of my youth. Later some cheap imitation of MAD popped up and I contacted the owner of that magazine, who told me to do any artwork like MAD and send it to him. So I finished some drawings in the MAD style and got in touch

with Herbert Feuerstein, the chief editor of MAD himself... and it worked! I often tried to participate in creating the stories or to give some input, but writers (Feuerstein has been one) are a species that don't live on the same planet as artists. After some years I got many liberties to put in as many little jokes as I liked, caricatures of friends or the editor and other hidden allusions."

"To be honest, I hated the film. As an ecologist, political activist and intellectual of the 80's, *Lemon Popsicle* was a torture to me. I've found some original correspondence with H. Feuerstein. He emphasises that this parody is definitely the nastiest we ever did! Much later I realised that *Eis am Stiel* has been a parody itself."

"I drew about two hundred pages for the magazine, even the SPY vs. SPY strips were created by me (without signing it), but drawing film parodies was actually the highlight. Mort Drucker was the American artist who did every big movie spoof, such like Indiana Jones, 007, *Star Wars*, etc. I admired him and his brilliant technique. So it was a great honour for me to work on all the German productions. I took the job very seriously. I collected as much material as

possible, pictures in youth magazines, press kits (if available), film posters and I even took pictures from the cinema screen with extra sensitive films that I developed by myself. It is a pleasure and a great honour that Jonathan Sagall (saw the article re-produced in issue 18 of the UK *Popsicle* fanzine) contacted me and confessed that he likes my art. We've had a nice correspondence. He asked for a signed copy of the original artwork to hang in his study."

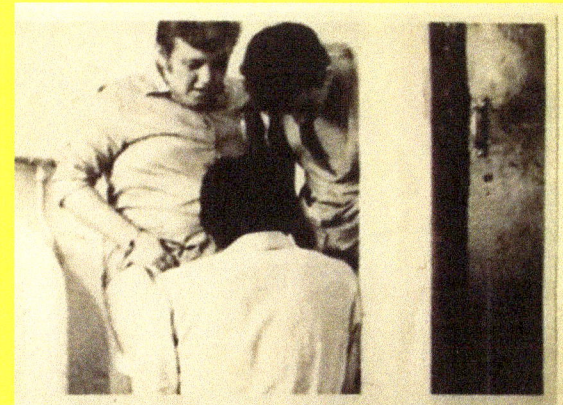
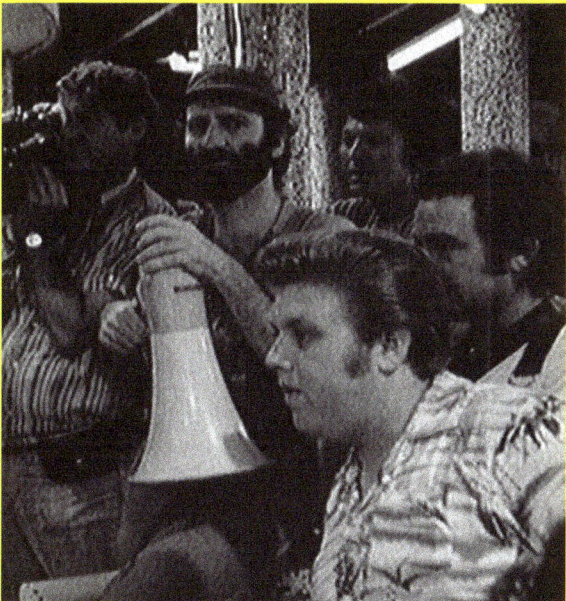

Israeli poster for *Lemon Popsicle*

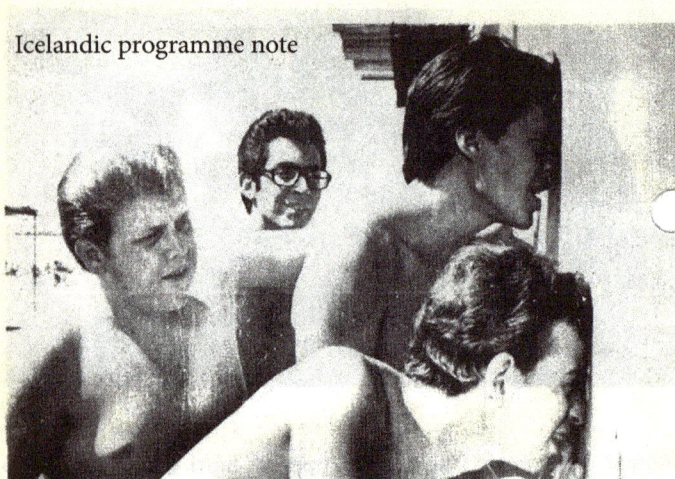
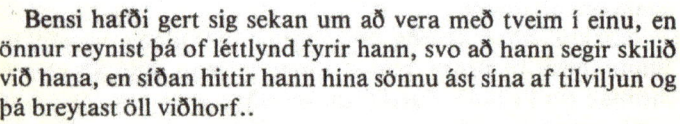

Icelandic programme note

Bensi hafði gert sig sekan um að vera með tveim í einu, en önnur reynist þá of léttlynd fyrir hann, svo að hann segir skilið við hana, en síðan hittir hann hina sönnu ást sína af tilviljun og þá breytast öll viðhorf..

PRIVATE POPSICLE
Fourth in the popular series

● First we met them in *Lemon Popsicle* as a trio of teenagers with little else on their minds but ice cream parlours and girl friends. We renewed our acquaintance with them in *Going Steady*, a sequel to the original in which the chums were then into motorbikes and rock 'n' roll, but still keenly interested in girls, as they were in *Hot Bubblegum*, the third in the series. And now they pop up yet again in *Private Popsicle* where we find them waiting, not without many misgivings, to be drafted into the Israeli Army. They are, of course, Benji (Yftach Katzur), Bobby (Jonathan Segall) and the plump Huey (Zachi Noy). They're pictured below.

The transition from their free-and-easy existence to military life is not going to be easy for the three tearaways — short haircuts, vaccinations, I.D. pictures, picking up army gear and weapons is not quite their scene. However, the proximity of an army girls' camp brightens up the prospect considerably and it's just like Benji to get himself involved with the General's daughter. *Private Popsicle* (Certificate 18 for Cannon Films release) is another jelly popsicle romp but this time with a military background, so it can really be said to go off with a bang!

Now in production is *Popsicle V*, subtitled *Baby Love*. □

Film Review (UK) July 1983

The popular Popsicle pals (Zachi Noy, Jonathan Segall and Yftach Katzur) still have an eye for the girls.

Besonders den dicken Zachy Noy (zweiter v. l.) hat das Publikum ins Herz geschlossen

Eis am Stiel, Teil I, II, III

Wiederaufführung einer der populärsten Kino-Filmserien

Vom munteren Teenager-Trio der „Eis am Stil"-Serie gibt es bereits drei Folgen. Wer sie noch nicht gesehen hat, bekommt nun die Gelegenheit, die Pennäler-Liebesabenteuer der israelischen Jungens zu erleben. Es dreht sich alles um Liebe und Rock'n Roll. Untermalt von fetzigen Songs aus den 50er und 60er Jahren ziehen die drei mit chromblitzenden Ami-Schlitten durch die Gegend, immer auf der Suche nach Mädchen. Schau-

Sibylle Rauch

Benny (Jesse Katzur) hat sich in die hübsche Tammy (Yvonne Michels) verliebt

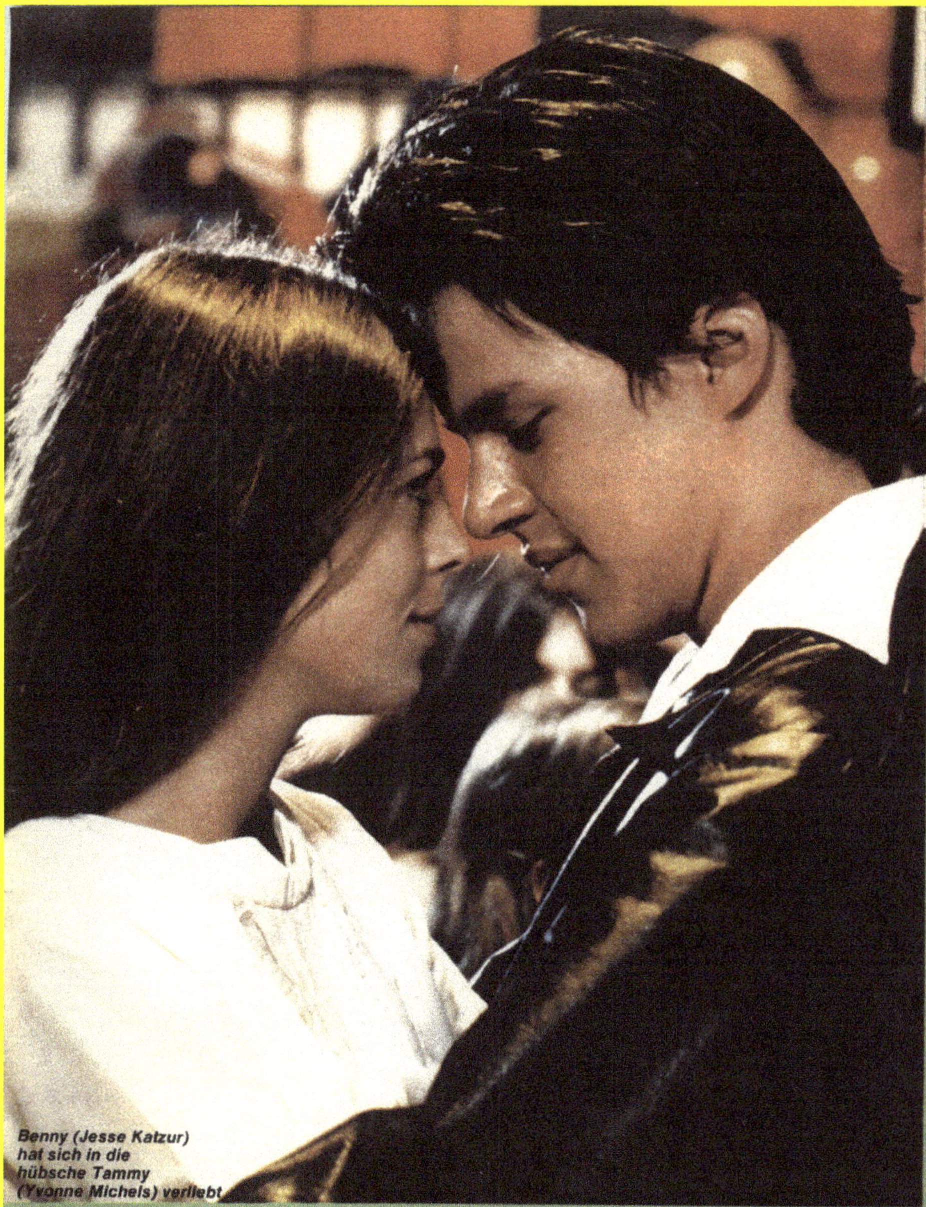

NEU IM KINO

Geldquelle: Sie klauen leere Flaschen auf dem Hinterhof eines Lebensmittelgeschäfts und tragen sie durch die Vordertür wieder herein und kassieren das Flaschenpfand.

Zachi zu BRAVO: „Es gibt sehr viele lustige Situationen. Höhepunkt ist ein großer Krach zwischen uns und den Mädchen in einer Eisdiele und schließlich der Abschlußball, bei dem es dann drunter und drüber geht."

Für Zachi Noy ist „Eis am Stiel II" bereits sein 14. Film. Der Schauspieler: „Die meisten Filme wurden aber nur in meinem Heimatland Israel gezeigt."

Die Musik in diesem Film stammt unter anderem von Little Richard, Jerry Lee Lewis, Chubby Checker und Ray Charles.

Peter Raschner

Fotos: Scotia International

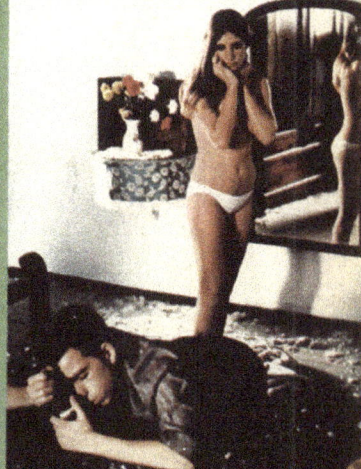

Tammy ist entsetzt: Ihr Freund hat zuviel getrunken

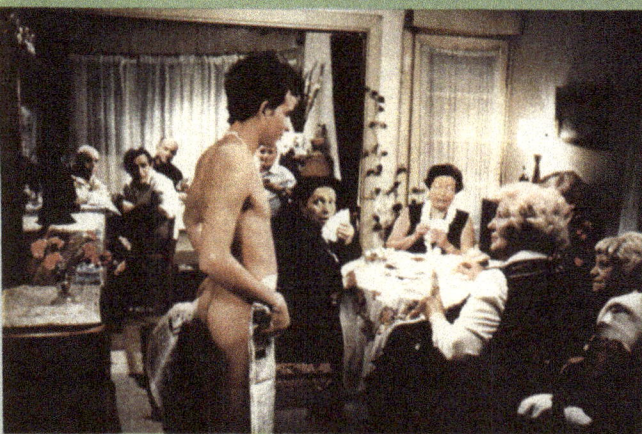

Nackt muß Momo durchs Hotel. Seine Kleider wurden ihm gestohlen

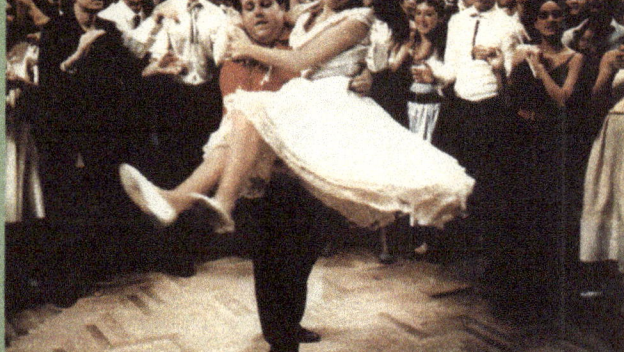

Der dicke Johnny rockt beim Abschluß-Ball wie ein Verrückter

Film Magazin

Ein heißer Film über das Treiben der Jugend der fünfziger Jahre wurde im vorigen Jahr zum Superhit. Jetzt gibt es einen Nachfolger

Es geht weiter wie gehabt: Teenager „flippen" zu alten Number-one-Hits, in der Eisdiele ist der Teufel los, und dazu gibt es natürlich wieder jede Menge kesse Sprüche. Regisseur Boaz Davidson hat soeben den zweiten Teil seines Erfolgsstreifens „Eis am Stiel" fertiggestellt. Mit diesem neuen Film, dem er den Untertitel „Feste Freundin" verpaßt hat, knüpft der israelische Filmemacher genau da an, wo er mit seinem ersten Werk aufgehört hat. Die Probleme der Jugend der fünfziger Jahre haben es ihm angetan, und wenn hier auch von Problemen die Rede ist, so sollte man das Ganze doch nicht allzu ernst sehen: Auch der zweite Teil von „Eis am Stiel" ist wieder ein ausgesprochener „Juxfilm" – mit gelegentlichem ernstem Hintergrund zwar, aber doch zum Schmunzeln.

Auch die Schauspieler sind dieselben geblieben. Jeremy Katzur als Benny, Zachi Noi als Johnny und Jonathan Segal als Momo. Natürlich ist auch wieder Rachel Steiner dabei, und als einzige neue die hübsche Yvonne Michaels. Schwierigkeiten gab es in dieser eine Million teuren Verfilmung nur mit den israelischen Behörden: Alle drei männlichen Hauptdarsteller leisten nämlich zur Zeit ihren Militärdienst ab. Erst nach einigem Hin und Her bekamen die Helden einen Sonderurlaub für die Dreharbeiten. Dafür zeigte sich Boaz Davidson dann nicht kleinlich: Er verschickte tausend Freikarten an die Militärbehörde...

Eis am Stiel 2. Teil

In den alten Zeiten des Rock'n'Roll war eine ganze Menge los. Unsere Freunde trugen natürlich auch ihren Teil dazu bei

Die Liebe ist natürlich das Thema Nummer eins. Damals wie heute. Und superheiße Feuerstühle gab es in den fünfziger Jahren auch schon. Beides zusammen wirft im zweiten Teil von „Eis am Stiel" einige Probleme auf

Nun schlecken sie wieder!

Eis am Stiel
3. Teil

Hau Ruck!

I love you!

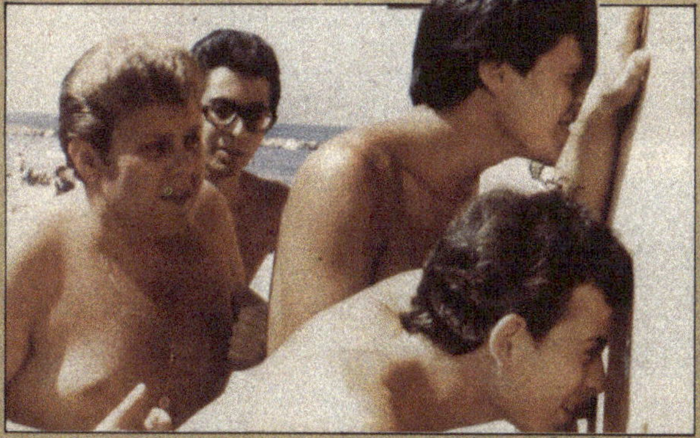

Ein Riesenspaß, die Mädchen beim Ausziehen zu beobachten

Mit der langbeinigen Cousine gehen die vier auf Radtour

Herstellungsland:	Israel, Regie: Boaz Davidson, Buch: Davidson/Tabor, Kamera: Adam Greenberg, Produktion: Golan/Sam Waynberg, Verleih: Scotia

Darsteller:

Benny	Jesse Katzur
Nellie	Anat Atzmon
Momo	Jonathan Segal
Johnny	Zachi Noy

Start ab: 10.4.1981

Wenn Zachi sich verliebt, tappt er besonders häufig ins Fettnäpfchen

Hey, was soll das?

Die munteren Teenager von „Eis am Stiel" sind wieder am Rumoren! Auch im dritten Teil dieser erfolgreichen Serie sorgen Johnny, dargestellt von Zachi Noy, der schüchterne Benny (Jesse Katzur) und Mädchenheld Momo (Jonathan Segal) für quietschvergnügte Kinofans. Reifer sind die Jungen natürlich nicht geworden, im Gegenteil: Unermüdlich schliddern sie von einer Romanze in die andere. Logisch, daß da heftige Eifersuchtsszenen nicht ausbleiben. Im Mittelpunkt der Geschichte steht diesmal langbeiniger Besuch aus Europa: Die 15-jährige Cousine macht ihre Aufwartung. Wider aller Erwartung ist sie tausendmal hübscher als angekündigt. Es vergehen keine drei Minuten, und die Freunde haben sich in das Mädchen verliebt. Das allerschlimmste: Die Kleine spielt das böse Spiel von der ersten Liebe mit. Schließlich glaubt jeder der Jungs, er habe sie für sich alleine und bereitet das größte Abenteuer seines Lebens vor: Jenes erste Schäferstündchen. Blauäugig balzen sie auf Betten und Balkonen, nicht ahnend, daß gerade der beste Freund im Anmarsch ist. Bis der dicke Johnny dann noch von der Mutter bei etwas „ganz Schlimmen" erwischt wird und erbärmlich Prügel bezieht ... *L.K.*

Sibylle Rauch aus dem Film „Eis am Stiel":

Szenen aus „Eis am Stiel III": Sibylle spielt ein Mädchen, das gern mit Jungen flirtet

„Ich finde nichts dabei, mich so zur Schau zu stellen", sagt Sibylle Rauch, die am 14. Juni 1960 in München geboren wurde und richtig Erika heißt. Ihre Maße: 93–65–90

Beifall auf offener Szene kriegt Sibylle im Kino, wenn ihr in dem Juxfilm rein zufällig der Busen aus der Bluse hüpft

„MICH KENNEN ALLE NACKT"

Vor zwei Jahren war sie noch eine brave Rechtsanwalts-Gehilfin und trug eine Brille. Jetzt ist sie Spezialistin für Busenrollen. BRAVO schildert, wie es dazu kam...

München, Fußgängerzone, Winter 1979: Ein gutaussehender junger Mann geht auf Sibylle zu und spricht sie an. Sie kommt gerade aus einem Kaufhaus, vollbepackt mit Schreibmaterial für die Rechtsanwalts-Kanzlei, in der sie arbeitet. Sie starrt den Mann, der sich als Fotograf ausgibt, ungläubig an. Er sagt: „Sie sind ein sehr hübsches Mädchen. Ich würde sehr gern mit Ihnen Fotoaufnahmen machen."

Sibylle: „Ich fühlte mich echt greislich, hatte auch eine Brille. Kein Mensch hatte vorher jemals zu mir gesagt, daß ich gut ausschaue. Natürlich habe ich das nicht ernst genommen und sagte ihm das auch. Der Fotograf gab mir trotzdem seine Visitenkarte und meinte: ‚Sie können sich vergewissern, daß ich ein Studio habe. Ich bin einer der besten Fotografen Deutschlands.' Da bin ich neugierig geworden..."

Wir sitzen mit Sibylle in einem Café. Sie ist total ungeschminkt, ihre blonden, gewellten Haare fallen ihr unterbrochen ins Gesicht. Sie spricht hektisch, verhaspelt sich. Sie ist viel natürlicher, als man sich bei ihren erotischen Fotos vorstellen kann. „Die Höhenflug-Phase habe ich längst hinter mir", sagt sie.

Als Sibylle vor zwei Jahren angesprochen wurde, arbeitete sie als Anwaltsgehilfin bei einem bekannten Rechtsanwalt. Eigentlich hatte sie nach der mittleren Reife Krankenschwester werden wollen, aber das hat ihr der Vater, ein Computer-Fachmann, ausgeredet.

Über ihre Kindheit erzählt Sibylle: „Die war sehr glücklich, bis zu dem Zeitpunkt, als sich meine Eltern getrennt

Ihre graue Slamkatze „Mausi" liebt sie fast so wie Freund Michael

Gut für die Figur: jeden Tag mindestens eine halbe Stunde Gymnastik

Kurz nach ihrer Entdeckung zum Fotomodell: Sibylle, damals noch schwarzhaarig, siegte bei einer Miß-Wahl im italienischen Ort Belvedere

Rechts oben: Sibylle mit einem Foto aus dem „Playboy". Darunter: Ihr Paß verrät ihren echten Namen

haben. Das hat sich auf mich und meine zwei Jahre jüngere Schwester Silvia sehr negativ ausgewirkt. Wir mußten nun allein zurechtkommen, haben aus der Büchse gekocht, in der Schule habe ich auch ziemlich nachgelassen. Mein Selbstbewußtsein, ohnehin nie das größte, wurde immer kleiner. Und schön fand ich mich sowieso nie. Mein Äußeres war mir auch ziemlich wurscht. Ich lief meistens in weiten Herrenhemden herum."

Zu jenem Zeitpunkt also tauchte der Fotograf auf.

Sibylle: „Nach der Arbeit bin ich eines Tages dann doch ins Studio gefahren. Da hab' ich gesehen, daß es ein echter Fotograf war mit Maskenbildnerin und so. Und dann fing der Fotograf an, mich total umzukrempeln. ‚Deinen Typ müssen wir grundlegend ändern. Dein Pony ist gar nichts. Und das mit der Brille... Mußt du

denn die tragen?' Na ja, eigentlich schon, weil ich auf dem linken Auge schlecht sehe', sagte ich.

‚Und die schwarzen Haare (ich hatte sie mir so gefärbt) sind auch nichts. Ich könnte aus dir was machen. Du könntest vielleicht sogar ein Playmate (Mädchen des Monats) für den ‚Playboy' werden. Da würden 5000 Mark rausspringen.'

Er kam mit diesem Herren-Magazin an, zeigte mir die Mädchen – die waren alle nackt. ‚Muß ich mich da auch ausziehen?' fragte ich ganz zaghaft. ‚Na ja, das wäre schon notwendig', antwortete er. Ich habe mich da schon irgendwie geschämt. So was habe ich noch nie gemacht.

Wir vereinbarten einen Fototermin für nächste Woche. Ich kam, die Maskenbildnerin war auch da, und ich hab' mich ausgezogen. Hinter ein paar Möbelstücken, total nackt. Das war ein verdammt ungutes Gefühl.

Erst recht, als der Fotograf mich genau anschaute und verschiedenes auszusetzen hatte. Dann wurden die Aufnahmen gemacht. Verschiedenste Posen. Ich konnte das überhaupt nicht, hab' mich irrsinnig blöde angestellt. Bei den erotischen Szenen hab' ich nur einen hilflosen Blick zustande gebracht.

,Ich mache das nicht', gingen mir plötzlich die Nerven durch. ,So kann ich nicht weiterarbeiten. Lieber mache ich meine Lehre zu Ende, da liegt mir viel mehr daran.'"

Nun, die Fotos wurden ein voller Erfolg. Sogar Sibylles Chef, der Rechtsanwalt, war stolz auf sie, als er sie im „Playboy" sah. Ebenso ihr Vater, der sich die Fotos in seiner Firma an die Wand hängte.

Sibylle war das alles nicht gewohnt. Sie wurde plötzlich Mittelpunkt, auch in den Discotheken. In der Kanzlei wurde sie unkonzentriert, verlor die Lust an der Arbeit. Ihre Lehre machte sie dennoch mit der Anwaltsgehilfenprüfung zu Ende – dann kündigte sie. In der Hoffnung, es werde schon weiterlaufen.

Sibylle: „Am Anfang ging's auch ganz gut. Ich kriegte weitere Fotoaufträge. Das Ausziehen hat mir nun nichts mehr ausgemacht. Ich wurde immer routinierter, habe mehr Körperbewußtsein bekommen."

Dann kam die ganz große Krise: „Ich hatte einen neuen Freund mit Geld, mit dem zog ich in Discotheken herum; jede Nacht haben wir Rum getrunken. Und das hat man mir bald angesehen. Ich war aufgeschwemmt, sah nicht mehr so gut aus.

Von dem Zeitpunkt an wurde ich von den Fotografen nicht mehr vermittelt. Ich war ziemlich fertig, deprimiert. Hab' mich gehen lassen, weinte, es ging steil bergab."

In dieser Situation kam Regisseur Franz Marischka und versprach mir 2000 Mark für eine kleine, freizügige Rolle in dem Film „Der Kurpfuscher und seine fixen Töchter". Seine Bedingung: Ich müsse innerhalb von 14 Tagen wieder so gut aussehen, wie auf den Fotos.

Mein Freund schrie mich an: ‚Nackt aufzutreten, das ist unter deinem Niveau.' Ich antwortete: ‚Soll ich warten, bis Hollywood anläutet?' Ich hatte kein Angebot, keinen Pfennig Geld und wohnte bei meinem Freund, lebe von ihm.

Der große Krach mit dem Freund

Danach kam ‚Drei Lederhosen aus St. Tropez' (Gage DM 2500), und dann meldete sich die Scolla-Film mit ‚Eis am Stiel'. Dafür bekam ich 7000 Mark. Ich überlegte mir, daß ich so schlecht nicht sein könne, wenn ich unter so vielen Mädchen ausgesucht werde. Die Discotheken-Rennerei ging mir plötzlich auf den Wecker. Ich habe mit meinem Freund Schluß gemacht. Jetzt bin ich mit Michael befreundet, der nicht mit mir angeben will, der lieb zu mir ist und mich versteht."

Würdest du das Risiko wieder eingehen, einen festen Job wie deine Kanzleistelle für eine ungewisse Zukunft aufzugeben?

„Ja, mein Risiko war groß. Vor allem muß man sehr aufpassen, von wem man sich auf der Straße ansprechen läßt. Und auf alle Fälle sollte man einen Beruf erlernt haben, in den man zurückkann, wenn es mit der Filmerei aus ist."

Christa Schechtl

Zachi als Soldat

Der Dicke aus „Eis am Stiel“, Zachi Noy, kommt diesmal als Soldat in die Kinos. In dem Lustspiel „Meine Mutter, der General“ spielt Zachi einen jungen Offizier beim Panzercorps. Als sich seine Mutter auf die Suche nach ihm macht, kommt es in der Kompanie natürlich zu den tollsten Verwechslungen.

Zachi Noy

My Mother, The General (*Imi Hageneralit*, 1979) was a Golan and Globus precursor to *Private Popsicle* minus the slapstick and the sex. It was written by Eli Tabor. Joel Silberg directed.

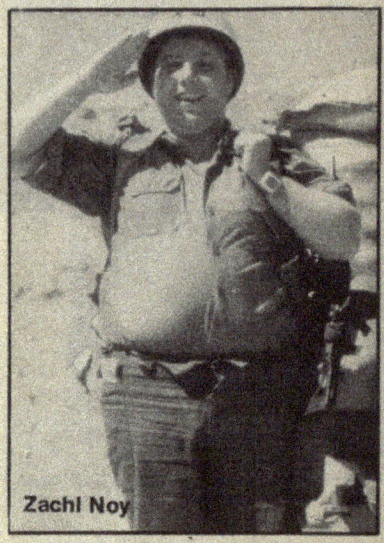

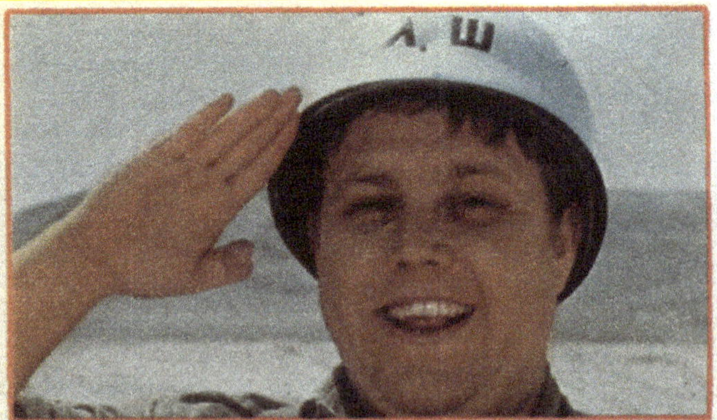

ZACHI NOY Der gemütliche Dicke aus „Eis am Stiel“ kommt jetzt als Soldat in „Meine Mutter, der General“. Ob er wieder die Lacher auf seiner Seite hat?

In Unterhosen und Unterhemd halten der dicke Johnny (Zachi Noy) und der dunkelhaarige Benny (Jesse Katzur) einen Ehemann im Wohnzimmer fest. Nebenan vergnügt sich namlich Memo (Jonathan Segal) mit der Ehefrau . . .

Dies ist eine der komischsten Szenen aus dem vierten Teil der Erfolgs-Serie „Eis am Stiel“. Wieder geht es um verzwickte Situationen, erste heiße Liebesschwüre, verrockte Partys und viel, viel Musik von Cliff Richard, Jerry Lee Lewis, Bill Haley und den Platters.

Die drei Freunde erleben diesmal allerdings keine unbeschwerten Sommerferien, sondern müssen eine harte militärische Ausbildung von einigen Wochen hinter sich bringen. Kein Wunder, daß in dem Soldaten-Laden bald alles schiefläuft. Und als sich des Generals Töchterlein Betty (lieb die Neuentdeckung Sonja Martin), in Benny verliebt, laufen die Militärs Amok. Bei einem großen Militär-Fußball-Turnier renkt sich alles wieder ein. Und Benny wird vor lauter Liebe sogar Torschützen-König.

„Eis am Stiel“ ist immer für zwei vergnügliche Kino-Stunden gut. Und der fünfte Teil ist auch schon in Vorbereitung . . .

Texte: Peter Raschner

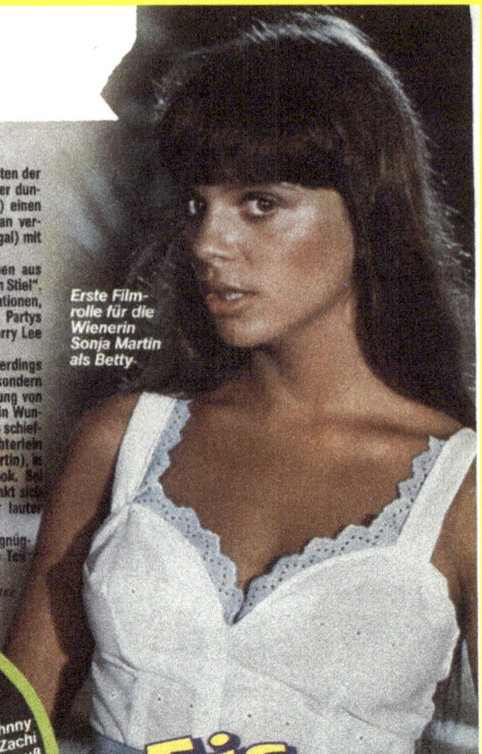

Erste Filmrolle für die Wienerin Sonja Martin als Betty

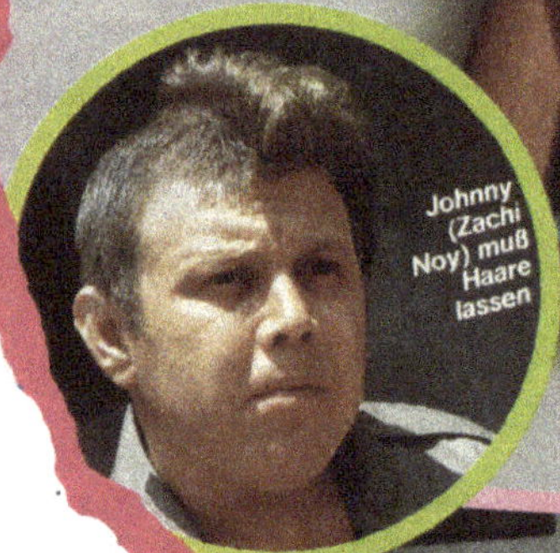

Johnny (Zachi Noy) muß Haare lassen

Eis am Stiel

4. Teil

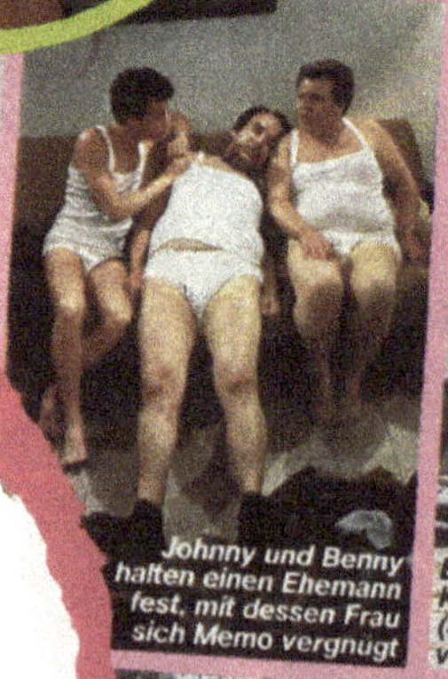

Johnny und Benny halten einen Ehemann fest, mit dessen Frau sich Memo vergnügt

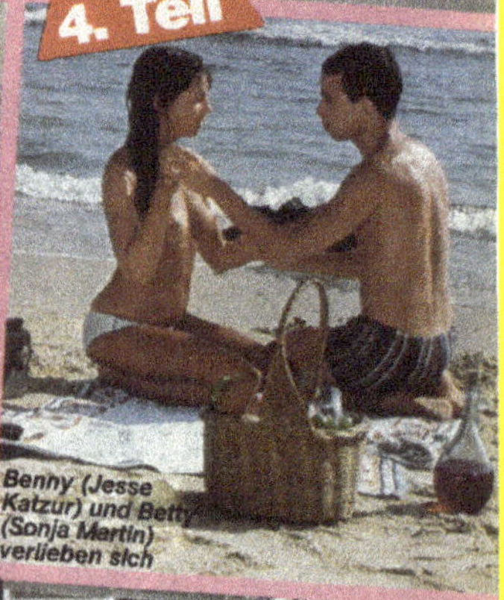

Benny (Jesse Katzur) und Betty (Sonja Martin) verlieben sich

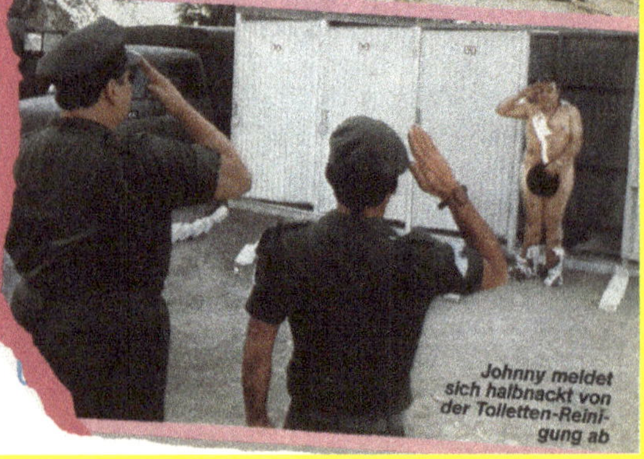

Johnny meldet sich halbnackt von der Toiletten-Reinigung ab

Derbe Schönheiten

Fernab des militärischen Drills startet Benny ein eigenes Manöver...

Eis am Stiel, 4. Teil - Hasenjagd

Nachdem sich „Eis am Stiel" in unseren Breitengraden unabhängig von Temperaturen so gut verkaufen ließ, produzierte der israelische Regisseur Boaz Davidson eine vierte Version seines Teenie-Spektakels

After the good sales of *Lemon Popsicle,* regardless of the temperatures in our latitudes, a fourth version of the teen spectacle has been produced by the Israeli director. Boaz Davidson.

George Lucas versetzte 1973 die damalige Teenager-Generation zurück in die frühen sechziger Jahre. In „American Graffiti" läßt er Jugendliche einer amerikanischen Kleinstadt im Jahre 1962 in einer Nacht den Schwebezustand zwischen Jugend und Erwachsenwerden erleben, das Ganze eingängig unterlegt mit der Musik aus jener Zeit. Der Erfolg dieser heiteren Reminiszenz nicht zuletzt auch an ein heiles Amerika rief einige mehr oder weniger begnadete Epigonen auf den Plan.

Einer von ihnen ist der israelische Autor und Regisseur Boaz Davidson. 1977 eröffnete er mit „Eis am Stiel" eine für ihn wahrlich „fröhliche Eiszeit". Während die Kritik sein Produkt mit Kostverächtung strafte, ihm allenfalls Übelkeitsgefühle nach Genuß attestierte, schleckte das Publikum es begierig. Die Geschichte der drei pubertären Freunde, die in Tel Aviv erste Erfahrungen in Sachen Sex, Liebe und dem dazugehörigen Kummer sammeln, wurde ein Renner. Die Folge: Davidson produzierte weiter, überzog den Handlungsschmelz mit Hits aus den fünfziger Jahren.

Inzwischen ist er bei Teil 4 angelangt: Auf die drei Teenies wartet diesmal das Jugendlager, militärischer Drill ist angesagt. Benny und Johnny kommen in Begleitung ihrer Eltern ins Camp. Bobby nimmt derweil Abschied von seinen diversen Freundinnen.

Ihr Einstieg ins militärische Dasein beginnt mit einem neuen Styling: Kurzhaarschnitt, Uniform, Bewaffnung. Bei ihren angestrengten Überlegungen, wie sie den Drill schnellstens umgehen können, kommt ihnen die Fußball-Begeisterung ihres Generals gelegen. Sie treten der Fußballmannschaft bei, von dem Irrglauben geleitet, dadurch das Streßvolumen verringern zu können. Das Training schluckt sogar noch die Freizeit.

Im benachbarten Camp tummelt sich das begehrte andere Geschlecht. Eine Tatsache, die dem Film die notwendigen Verwicklungen garantiert. Benny verliebt sich ausgerechnet in die Tochter des Generals, ohne es jedoch zu wissen. In ihrem ersten Urlaub lädt das Offizierstöchterchen Betty Benny und seine Freunde zu sich nach Hause ein. Trotz eines gerade laufenden Disziplinarverfahrens gelingt es ihnen, aus dem Camp zu entwischen. Als Vater General die Entlaufenen erblickt, ist die Fete für sie auch schon beendet. Er schickt sie zurück, und er verbietet Benny, Betty wiederzusehen.

Nach weiteren Verwicklungen ist schließlich mit dem Happy-End auch das Filmende in Sicht. König Fußball führt die Liebenden zusammen...

...mit großem Erfolg

„Hut ab" vor dem Sergeant

Originaltitel: Eis am Stiel, 4. Teil — Hasenjagd
Herstellungsland: Israel; **Buch und Regie:** Boaz Davidson; **Kamera:** Adam Greenberg; **Gesamtleitung:** Amnon Globus; **Produktion:** Golan-Globus-Productions, Tel Aviv, KF Kinofilm, München;
Besetzung:
Benny . . . . Jesse Katzur
Johnny . . . . Zachi Noy
Momo . . . . Jonathan Segal
Rina . . . . Sonja Martin
Eva . . . . Bea Fiedler
Vater . . . . . Menashe Warschewski

Start ab: 18.3.1983

Rachel Steiner

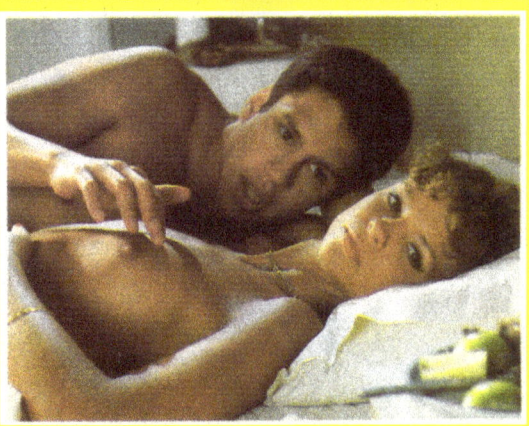

The new Playboy generation is alive again. In the tried and trusted way, the 'infernal trio' enjoy music and chicks.

Bulliger Schutzpatron

Eis am Stiel
5. Teil – Die große Liebe

Der Playboy-Nachwuchs wird wieder aktiv. In bewährter Manier genießt das „Trio Infernal" Musik und Miezen

Possierliche Spiele im Pool

Bewegte Blickpunkte

Zwar fördert manch ein Kinobesuch die Erkenntnis, daß der größte Genuß durchs Eiskonfekt kam. Diese Erfahrung scheint jedoch zumindest den Besuchern der „Eis am Stiel"-Filme fremd zu sein. Hier fällt eher das Eiskonfekt vor lauter Lachen aus der Hand. Der anhaltende Erfolg dieser seit 1978 schwappenden Welle zeigt, daß noch nach über fünf Jahren Fans von Benny, Bobby und Johnny nicht genug von den Abenteuern der Nachwuchs-Playboys kriegen.

Was hinter dem Erfolg dieser Serie steckt, kann man nur ahnen. Wesentlich ist aber ohne Zweifel die bunte Mischung aus flapsigen Sprüchen, heißem Rock aus Petticoat-Zeiten und Klamauk beim Pirsch auf die Girls — sowie natürlich die vielen Bräute, mal kratzbürstig, mal BH-sprengend, mal mit kräftig ohrfeigender Hand. Oft endet, zu unserem Vergnügen, die flotte Jagd nach der Frau der Träume auch beim bärbeißigen Vater. Sitzt man dann im Kinosessel, die Stimmung vom Rocksound angeheizt,

Waidmannsgerechte Beute- und Bräuteschau

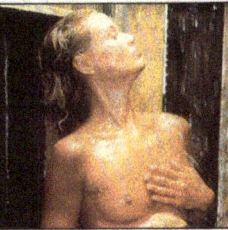
Unverhüllte Reizesfülle

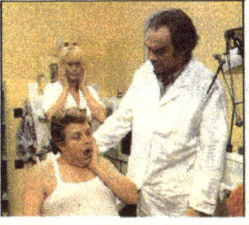
Zum „Geheimtip der Saison" nur über den Zahnarztstuhl

fällt es auch älteren Semestern gar nicht so schwer, sich mit dem „Trio Infernal" auf der Jagd nach einem ausgefüllten Liebesleben zu identifizieren. Gern lacht, leidet oder fühlt man mit dem Helden — sei es nun der forsche Gewinner Bobby, der Romantiker Benny oder der Pechvogel Johnny. Nicht zuletzt diese Rolle des ewigen Verlierers macht Zachi Noy zum großen Gewinner beim Publikum.

Bis schließlich die „große" Liebe zum Happy End führt, müssen die drei wieder einmal manches Abenteuer durchstehen und etliche Ohrfeigen einstecken. Alles beginnt ganz locker, Sonne, Meer und Strand — was will man mehr? Doch da entdeckt Bobby, daß die Freundin des Rettungsschwimmers so hübsch ist, daß man ruhig eine Mund-zu-Mund-Beatmung riskieren kann. „Wetten, daß...", sagt er den anderen beiden — und ein Hilferuf bringt ihn ans Ziel. Johnnys Versuch, ebenso clever bei der Kleinen anzukommen, endet freilich in den Armen ihres Freundes. Das Pech bleibt ihm treu, denn während Bobby der Zahnarzthelferin Inga auf den Zahn fühlt, stimmt bei Johnny schon wieder das Timing nicht. Nur ein Spurt rettet ihn vor den Marterwerkzeugen des echten Zahnarztes, der ihm die Liebeslust ein für allemal austreiben will. Frieda (Dolly Dollar spielt Bennys Cousine) scheint ihm zwar gewogen, doch dieses Techtelmechtel führt direkt in eine mittlere Katastrophe...

Teens & Twens sind treue Fans

71,5 Mio. DM spielten bisher die ersten vier „Eis am Stiel"-Folgen in den deutschen Kinos ein

Eis am Stiel (1978)	19,5
Eis am Stiel, 2. Teil – Feste Freundin (1979)	15,9
Eis am Stiel, 3. Teil – Liebeleien (1981)	21,2
Eis am Stiel, 4. Teil – Hasenjagd (1983)	14,9

Allein der romantische Benny scheint diesmal das große Liebesglück zu haben. Doch auch bei ihm steht vor der Freud das Leid. Schließlich ist seine Angebetete, das Rollschuhgirl Ginny, Bobbys kleine Schwester. Und da Bobby von sich auf Benny schließt, will er Ginny vor dem „Schlimmsten" bewahren...

Aber keine Angst: Nach turbulenter Action gibt es auch für Ginny und Benny das ersehnte Glück zu zweit. Vorher gibt es jedoch jede Menge heißer Sprüche und Musik von Little Richard, Bill Haley und den Shadows satt.

Herstellungsland: BRD/Israel 1983; Regie: Dan Wolman; Buch: Boaz Davidson und Eli Tavor; Kamera: Ilan Rosenberg; Gesamtleitung: Sam Waynberg und Amnon Globus; Produktion: KF Kinofilm, München, und Golan-Globus Productions, Tel Aviv
Besetzung:
Johnny . . . . Zachi Noy
Benny . . . . Jesse Katzur
Bobby . . . . . . .Jonathan Segal
Ginny . . . . Stefanie Petsch
Frieda . . . . Dolly Dollar
sowie Sabrina Cheval, Bea Fiedler, Menasche Warschewski, Deborah Kedar, Renate Langer

Start ab: 9.3.1984

Eis am Stiel – 5. Teil

Neu im Kino!!!

Blick durch den Bretterzaun: Das Girl (rechts) ist aber auch eine Augenweide

Kraftprotz-Gehabe am Strand. So versuchen die Boys die Mädchen in diesem fünften Teil der „Eis am Stiel"-Filmserie anzumachen

Benny läßt sich in der Mittagspause im Zahnarzt-Behandlungsstuhl verwöhnen. Ginny (Steffi Petsch) verliebt sich in den Casanova Benny

DIE GROSSE LIEBE

Bobby (Jonathan Segal) schreit und tut, als würde er absaufen. Dabei kann er schwimmen wie ein Fisch. Doch Bobby wartet auf die flotte Mieze, die als Rettungsschwimmerin am Strand tätig ist. Er provoziert eine rasche Mund-zu-Mund-Beatmung. Und er hat Glück. Die Rettungsküsse dauern immer länger...

Benny (Jesse Katzur) sitzt im Behandlungsstuhl eines Zahnarztes und grinst glücklich vor sich hin. Pervers? Keineswegs! Der Zahnarzt ist gerade in der Mittagspause, und die niedliche Assistentin Inga treibt mit dem zufriedenen Patienten im Behandlungsstuhl frivole Spielchen...

Johnny (der dicke Zachi Noy) hat ein Auge auf die vollbusige Frieda (Dolly Dollar) geworfen. Als er sie aber nach Hause bringt, schlägt Friedas Familie Alarm. Und Johnny ist plötzlich der ganz große Sündenbock...

Im fünften Teil der „Eis am Stiel"-Serie treiben die drei Freunde wieder ihre Späßchen. Wie immer geht es um Mädchen, Mädchen und noch einmal Mädchen. Der Untertitel dieses Streifens lautet „Die große Liebe". Sie trifft Benny wie ein Blitzschlag. Er verknallt sich Hals über Kopf in Ginny (zum erstenmal auf der Kinoleinwand: Steffi Petsch, eine 17jährige Gymnasiastin aus Wolfratshausen bei München), die im Film die Schwester von Bobby ist.

Bobby sieht es gar nicht gern, wie sich der Casanova Benny an seine noch unschuldige Schwester heranmacht.

Es kommt sogar zu Prügeleien zwischen den beiden Freunden. Bobby schleppt sein Schwesterchen schließlich sogar zum Arzt, um festzustellen zu lassen, ob sie noch Jungfrau ist. Natürlich kriegen sich die beiden schließlich doch.

Auch dieser fünfte Teil der Erfolgs-Filmserie lebt von witzigen Dialogen und heißer Musik. Filme, die einfach nicht totzukriegen sind...

Peter Raschner

Abgeschlossener BRAVO Film-Foto ROMAN

NEU! Eis am Stiel 6. Teil

FERIENLIEBE

Am Strand tummeln sich Teenager, Jungen und Mädchen. Sie machen Tauziehen. Sie haben das Seil durch die Umkleidekabine gespannt. Plötzlich ein kräftiger Ruck und die Bretterwand der Umkleidekabine stürzt ein. Die Nackten stehen alle im Freien...

Sie haben wirklich fast nur Blödsinn im Kopf, die jungen Leute um Johnny, Benny und Bobby, die sich in den Ferien täglich am Strand treffen. Herrliche Sonne, fetzende Musik, hübsche Girls, das Leben scheint ein Vergnügen zu sein.

Doch dann trifft Benny ein Mädchen mit braunen Kulleraugen. Um ihn ist es geschehen. Der dicke Johnny wird von einem wütenden Vater mit der Tochter erwischt. Nun soll Johnny gleich zum Standesamt rennen...

Ziemlich verrückt geht es im sechsten Teil des erfolgreichen „Eis am Stiel"-Films mit dem Untertitel „Ferienliebe" zu. Wir haben Euch diesen Ulkstreifen mit Zacchi Noy, Jesse Katzur und Yehuda Afroni als neuen Bobby bereits vorgestellt...

Johnny, Benny, Bobby und ihre Clique vergnügen sich täglich am Strand. Sie haben meist nur Blödsinn im Kopf. Dann verknallt sich Benny in die hübsche Dana. Der dicke Johnny hat auch eine „Braut" gefunden

Pech für Johnny: Der Vater des Girls, ein Schiffsoffizier, will, daß sie heiraten. Die drei Kumpels heuern auf dem Schiff „Orion" an, denn der Vater von Dana ist der Kapitän. Auch die Offiziere haben nichts gegen sexy Girls.

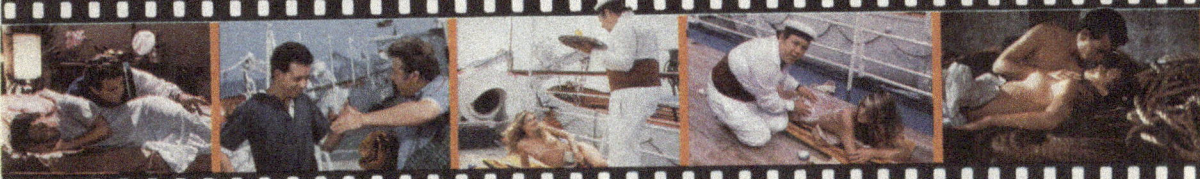

Johnny will die Frau des Kapitäns verführen. Als es nicht klappt, versucht er bei anderen Schönheiten zu landen. Benny und Dana vergnügen sich im Lagerraum des Schiffs

ENDE

Der dicke Johnny wird schließlich „gefoltert" und in die Küche zur Strafarbeit abkommandiert. Bei der Ankunft in Venedig unternehmen Benny und Dana eine Gondelfahrt

Eis am Stiel – 6. Teil

– FERIENLIEBE –

Die Möchtegern-Playboys aus den Fünfzigern gehen auf Kreuzfahrt. Als Leichtmatrosen der Liebe zieht mancher Sturm über sie hinweg.

Der Erfolg der „Eis am Stiel"-Komödien scheint ungebremst. Der sechste Teil legt diesem Trend nichts in den Weg. Im Gegenteil, er wird der Seriennummer mehr als gerecht. Wie nicht anders zu erwarten, dreht es sich bei den Boys aus den wilden Fünfzigern wiedermal um Girls, Girls, Girls. Und das Zuschauerhoch zeigt, daß Thema Nr. 1 auch in den Achtzigern nichts an Popularität verloren hat, zumal der Kino-Spaß von heißem Rock'n Roll angetrieben wird, der damals wie heute das Eis zum Schmelzen bringt. Mit von der Partie sind wieder Zacki Noy als liebestoller Johnny, der kein Fettnäpfchen ausläßt, und Jesse Katzur entdeckt als Benny seine große Liebe.

Wie gefährlich es sein kann, eine Braut aufzureißen, kriegt Johnny gleich zu Anfang zu spüren. Kaum ist er bei einem neuen Hasen ins Bett gehüpft, als auch schon der aufgebrachte Vater vor ihm mit dem Messer herumfuchtelt. Johnny, vor die Alternative gestellt, entweder zu Schaschlik verarbeitet zu werden oder die Ehre der Kleinen mit der Heirat zu retten, wählt einen dritten Weg: Die Flucht.

Mit Benny zusammen verdingt er sich auf einem Kreuzfahrtschiff, Ziel Venedig. Vom Regen kommt er dort allerdings in die Traufe. Ihr Boß ist ausgerechnet der wilde Messerschwinger, und der nimmt seinen Schwiegersohn in spe gehörig unter die Fittiche. Aus dem Playboy-

---

'The success of the *Lemon Popsicle* comedies seems unstoppable. The sixth part puts nothing in the way of this trend. On the contrary, it more than meets the standard of the series. As to be expected, it revolves around the boys from the wild 1950's again, around girls, girls, girls. And the high number of spectators shows that the number one topic

Leben an Bord soll vorerst nichts werden, Maloche ist angesagt und die heißen Käfer, die sich auf dem Sonnendeck knusprig braun braten lassen, sind für sie off limits.
Clever wie die beiden sind, finden sie genügend Wege um dem Galeeren-Sklaven-Dasein zu entfliehen. Während Johnny von einem Dilemma ins nächste tappt und aus lauter Jagdfieber gar das Bett einer Nonne mit dem einer willigen Schwedin verwechselt, verliebt sich Benny ausgerechnet in die Tochter des Kapitäns. Und das bringt nicht weniger Komplikationen mit sich. Ganz nebenbei werden die beiden auch noch in einen Diamanten-Coup der Unterwelt verwickelt und dürfen sich in Venedig als Detektive und Gondoliere betätigen. Und alles nur wegen der Liebe.
Neu an Bord ist die Wienerin Petra Kogelnig als Tochter des Kapitäns. Wenn alles gut geht, könnte „Ferienliebe" ihr Start für eine Kino-Karriere sein. Seit Dan Wolman im fünften Teil die Regie für die Serie übernahm, kam neuer Pfiff hinein, die Späße scheinen runder und schneller zu laufen. Diese Frischzellen-Behandlung hat „Eis am Stiel" gut getan.

Darsteller: Zachi Noy, Jesse Katzur, Petra Kogelnik, Yossi Shiloach, Bea Fiedler
Regie: Dan Wolman
Produzent: Dietmar Siegert
Kamera: Ilan Rosenberg
Herstellungsland: Deutschland/Israel
Start: 10. Mai 1985

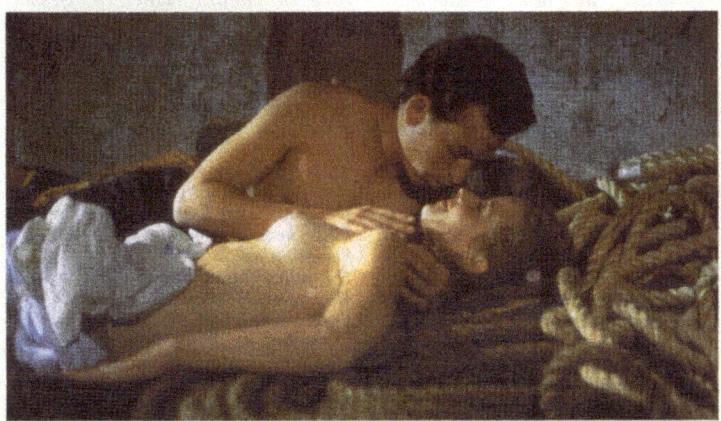

has lost nothing in popularity in the 80's. The cinema hit of the rock n' roll era still causes the 'Eis' to melt today... Since Dan Wolman took over directing the series for the fifth film, a new style came in, the jokes seem to be running thick and fast. This unforgettable treatment has served *Lemon Popsicle* well.'

BRÄUTE Stiel

„HABEN WIR SCHON DIE STARTPOSITION ERREICHT?"

Während es in der Kajüte des Kapitäns sehr heiß hergeht, ist die Crew auf Landgang

Johnny glaubt die Englein singen zu hören

„EI SCHAU MAL DA! DER DICKE HAT JA EINEN GANZ SCHÖNEN UMFANG!"

Der Besuch bei einer Wahrsagerin stürzt Johnny in höchste Nöte

Im nächsten POP/Rocky:
Eis am Stiel — Verliebte Jungs

FIEDLER: DER BUSEN DER NATION

Ist er Vater von Beas Sohn? Prinz Albert von Monaco traf Bea in München...

Ob Busenstar oder Skandalnudel – Bea Fiedler (32) wußte schon immer ihre körperlichen Reize (Brustumfang 105, Taille 68, Hüfte 96) gewinnbringend und effektvoll in Szene zu setzen. Die gebürtige Duisburgerin brach mit 17 eine Friseurlehre ab, posierte als „Model" für Bikinis und Margarine, bevor sie mit 20 als „Playmate" im Playboy landete. Bis zur Geburt ihres Sohnes Daniel-Werner am 28. Juli 1987 absolvierte Bea 25 Auftritte in Sex-Filmen wie „Die Insel der 1000 Freuden". Seitdem hofft sie auf den Anruf von „Danys" Vater. Prinz Albert von Monaco soll 1986 in München eine heiße Nacht mit Bea verbracht haben.

1987 gibt's wieder «Eis am Stiel»

Zurzeit wird wieder gedreht. Regisseur Walter Bannert und seine Crew drehen in Israel die 7. Runde des Klamauk-Dauerbrenners «Eis am Stiel». Untertitel: Verliebte Jungs. Wieder dabei: Zachi Noi, Jesse Katzur und Jonathan Segal. Auch Sybille Rauch mischt wieder mit.

Auch in der siebten Runde von «Eis am Stiel» laufen Zachi Noi, Jesse Katzur und Jonathan Segal wieder zur Höchstform auf

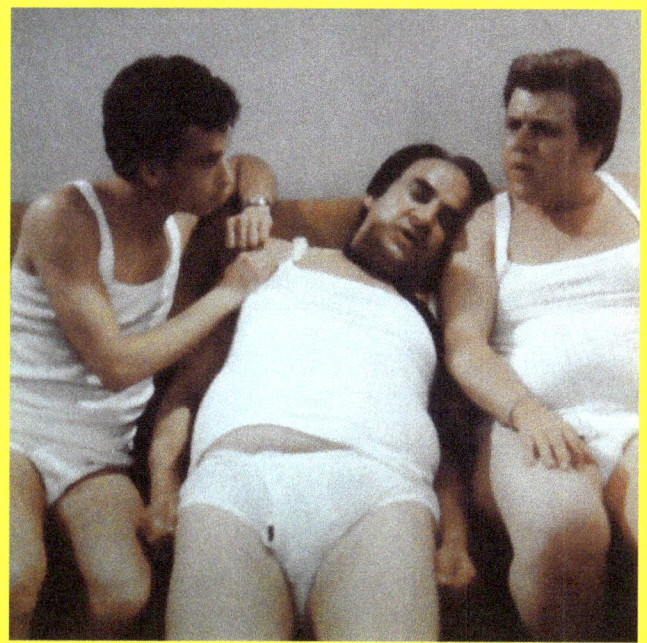

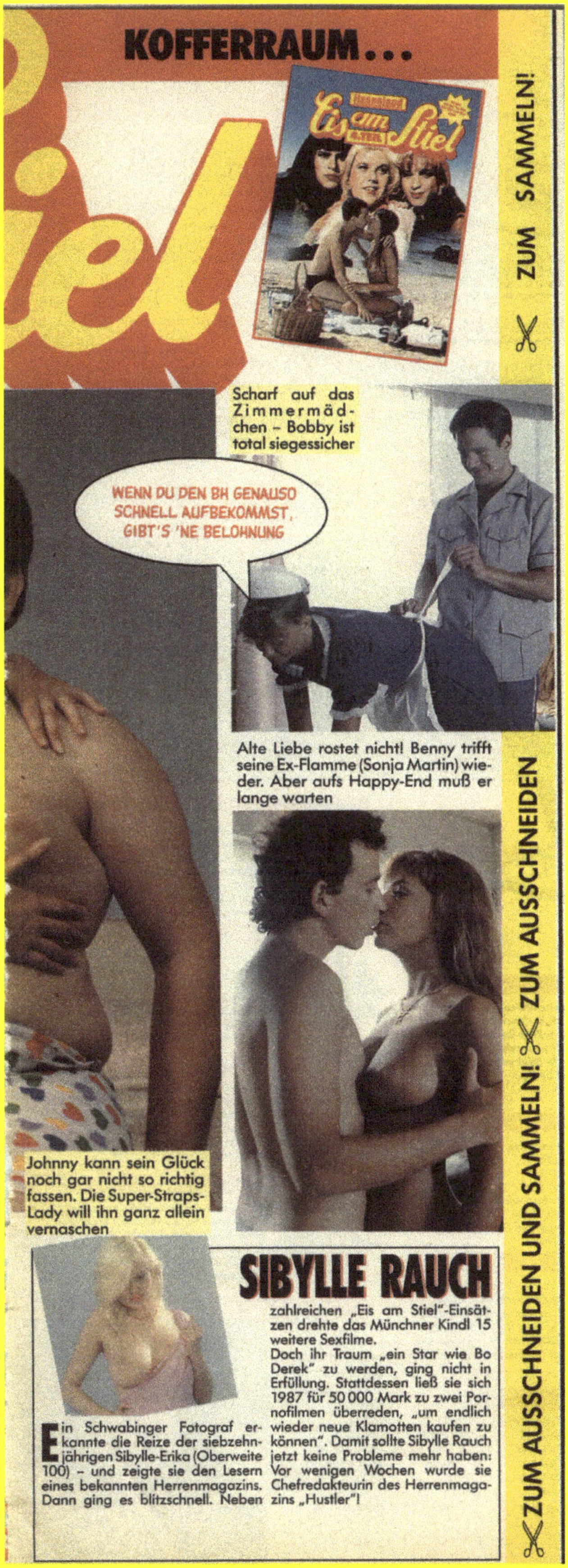
KOFFERRAUM...

Scharf auf das Zimmermädchen – Bobby ist total siegessicher

Alte Liebe rostet nicht! Benny trifft seine Ex-Flamme (Sonja Martin) wieder. Aber aufs Happy-End muß er lange warten

Johnny kann sein Glück noch gar nicht so richtig fassen. Die Super-Straps-Lady will ihn ganz allein vernaschen

SIBYLLE RAUCH

Ein Schwabinger Fotograf erkannte die Reize der siebzehnjährigen Sibylle-Erika (Oberweite 100) – und zeigte sie den Lesern eines bekannten Herrenmagazins. Dann ging es blitzschnell. Neben zahlreichen „Eis am Stiel"-Einsätzen drehte das Münchner Kindl 15 weitere Sexfilme.

Doch ihr Traum „ein Star wie Bo Derek" zu werden, ging nicht in Erfüllung. Stattdessen ließ sie sich 1987 für 50 000 Mark zu zwei Pornofilmen überreden, „um endlich wieder neue Klamotten kaufen zu können". Damit sollte Sibylle Rauch jetzt keine Probleme mehr haben: Vor wenigen Wochen wurde sie Chefredakteurin des Herrenmagazins „Hustler"!

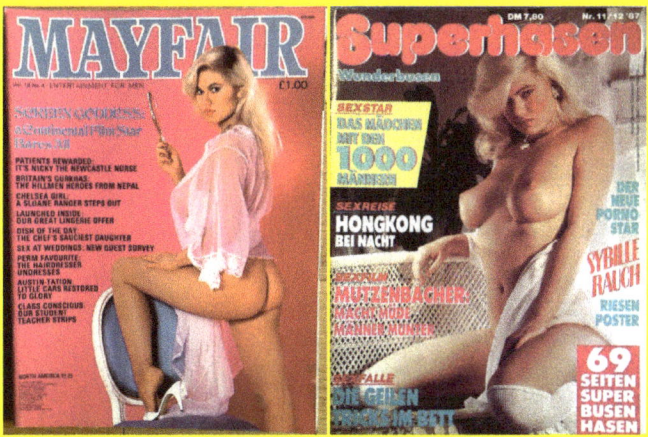

Sybille Rauch's life story is told in the TV film *Das sündige Mädchen* (2001).

'Zachi Noy, the lovable fat man from the *Lemon Popsicle* films is looking for a double. At the turn of the new year, Zachi will be making the adventure comedy *The Fat Brothers.* If you think you look like Zachi send a photo to the following address...'

BRAVO FILM HOT NEWS

Zachi Noy, der liebenswerte Dicke aus den „Eis am Stiel"-Filmen, sucht ein Double. Im neuen Jahr dreht Zachi die Abenteuer-Komödie „The fat Brothers." Wer von Euch glaubt, wie Zachi auszusehen, der kann ein Foto an folgende Adresse schicken: Imagimotion, Osterwaldstr. 9-10, 8000 München 40. Zu Händen von Herstellungsleiter Joschi N. Arpa...

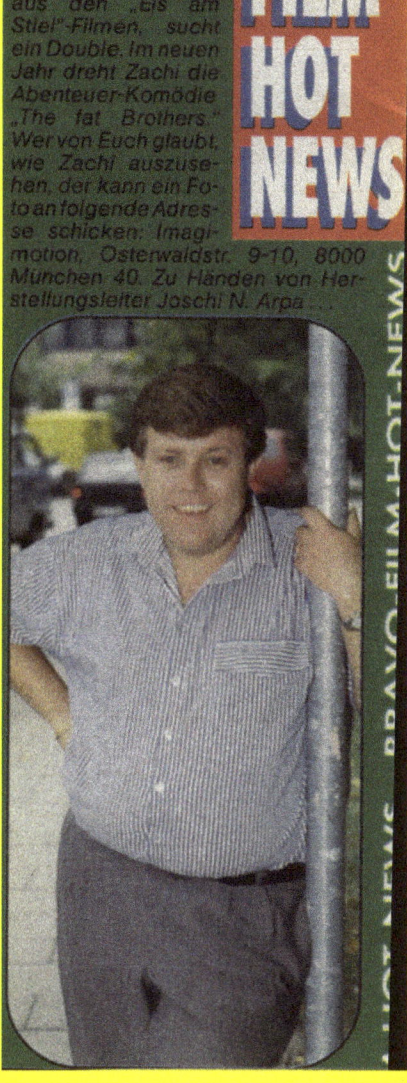

VIDEO

Eis am Stiel – VERLIEBTE
7. TEIL

„Eis am Stiel" schmeckt offenbar auch noch nach dem 7. Aufwärmen. Dafür, daß es nicht im Hals steckenbleibt, sorgen drei in den Jungbrunnen gefallene Darsteller und ständig nachwachsende Publikumsgenerationen

Der komische Dicke, Zachi Noy, kann sich mit seinen Freunden mal wieder so manchen Ausrutscher leisten — kein Wunder, wenn man ständig ins Fettnäpfchen tritt. Bei verheirateten Frauen ist oft allerdings Vorsicht geboten — wegen der Ehemänner, natürlich

Auf ein Neues: die Chaoten von der Sexfront sind wieder im pausenlosen Einsatz

Das hätten sich die Macher dieser beliebten Serie vor zehn Jahren nicht träumen lassen. Eine kleine, frische Sommerkomödie wollten sie drehen über die Probleme von drei durchschnittlichen Jugendlichen mit dem Thema Nummer eins. Bis heute ist daraus einer der größten Serienerfolge der Filmgeschichte geworden. Und das Erstaunliche: die drei Hauptdarsteller sind immer noch mit von der Partie!

Was macht die Filme der „Eis am Stiel"-Serie wohl so populär? Es ist die gelungene Mischung aus flotter Unterhaltung, lockeren Sprüchen und fetzigen Hits der 50er und 60er Jahre. Außerdem kann sich der Zuschauer mit den Figuren identifizieren, die da auf der Leinwand oder dem Bildschirm auftreten. Es sind keine Supermänner und -frauen, sie haben Schwächen und Fehler wie wir alle. Johnny (Zachi Noy) zum Beispiel, ist alles andere als ein attraktives Mannsbild, aber ein fröhlicher Kerl, der jeder auch noch so unmöglichen Situation immer das Beste abzugewinnen weiß. Bobby (Jonathan Segal)

'Funny fat guy Zachi Noy can afford some slip-ups with his friends time and again – no wonder, if you are always making bluders. However, caution is advised with married women – because of the husbands, of course. Bobby gets lucky first and has intensive training from a chambermaid on how to make a bed. Johnny comes by the lady with

JUNGS

Was gibt's denn da wohl zu sehen? Die Vermutung liegt nahe, unsere Freunde haben einmal mehr das Ziel ihre pubertären Träume gesichtet: Mädchen, Frauen, schnelle Autos, am besten alles zusammen. Doch nachdem das Auto kaputt ist, heißt es erst einmal jobben. Mal sehen, wie das Trio mit der Doppelbelastung, Arbeit und Frauen, fertig wird

heiten restlos beseitigt sind, geschehen die abenteuerlichsten und unglaublichsten Dinge, stets nach dem Motto: Kein Fettnäpfchen ist zu groß für uns.

Eis am Stiel, 7. Teil — Verliebte Jungs
Cannon Screen Entertainment, BRD/Israel 1986. Unterhaltung, ca. 90 Min. Regie: Walter Bannert, FSK: ab 16 Jahren. Hauptdarsteller: Zachi Noy, Jesse Katzur, Sibylle Rauch. Kinostart: 21.5.1987

Videostart: 9.11.1987

dagegen ist der Sexprotz, der allerdings mit seiner Masche gar nicht so gut ankommt, wie er erhofft. Ja und dann ist da natürlich noch der hoffnungslose Romantiker Benny (Jesse Katzur), ständig auf der Suche nach der großen, wahren Liebe.

In diesem Sommer soll es wieder richtig losgehen. Die Voraussetzungen dafür sind überaus günstig. Johnnys Eltern sind für drei Wochen verreist, das bedeutet: sturmfreie Bude! Fast noch schöner: Vatis Cadillac ist dagegeblieben und langweilt sich in der Garage. Es fehlt also nur noch das Salz in der Suppe, sprich: die Mädchen. Doch so gut ausgerüstet, dürfte das ja kein Problem sein. Die drei Freunde schwingen sich in das Cabrio, und ab geht's. Doch bei ihrem Spähen vernachlässigen sie leider den Blick auf die Straße, und schon hat's gekracht. 600 Dollar, sagt der Mann in der Werkstatt, und damit ist es aus mit dem vergnüglichen Sommer. Jetzt heißt es arbeiten!

Doch unsere Stehaufmännchen haben natürlich Glück im Unglück und bekommen Aushilfsjobs in einem Strandhotel, und wo ein Strand ist, da sind auch Mädchen. Bobby hat als erster Glück und läßt sich von einem Zimmermädchen intensiv erklären, wie man Betten macht. Johnny kommt bei der Dame mit dem Hund (Sibylle Rauch) gut an, bei ihrem zu früh heimkehrenden Ehemann allerdings gar nicht. Und der arme Benny muß hier ausgerechnet auf seine alte, einzig wahre Liebe treffen, die er doch schon (fast) vergessen hatte. Bis nun alle drei auf ihre Kosten kommen können und alle Klar-

EIS!

Angesichts des ausgefallenen Sommers und des bereits im August begonnenen Herbstes hat die Eisindustrie erhebliche Umsatzeinbußen erlebt. Wir helfen, denn zum Videostart von „Eis am Stiel 7" verlosen wir zusammen mit VMP Video dreimal ein Eis essen, zu dem Sie maximal 10 Freunde mitbringen dürfen. Vorher allerdings noch eine kleine Aufgabe: Nennen Sie uns bitte drei weibliche Hauptdarstellerinnen aus der erfolgreichen „Eis am Stiel"-Serie. Senden Sie die Namen auf einer ausreichend frankierten Postkarte bitte bis zum 17.11.1987 an VIDEOPLAY, Stichwort: „Eis", Karlstr. 26, 2000 Hamburg 76, der Rechtsweg ist ausgeschlossen und nun cool ans Werk.

the dog (Sibylle Rauch), but her husband returns home early. And poor Benny meets his old true love that he had (almost) forgotten. Until now, all three can count to their cost without explanation, the most adventurous and most incredible things that always happen according to the motto: No blunder is too big for us.'

Eis am 8's Total normal

Die verrückten Abenteuer der nimmermüden Drei

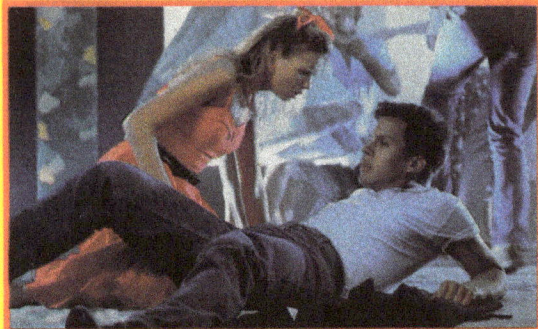

Auch in diesem Sommer können Freunde leichter und lockerer Kinounterhaltung sich an „Eis am Stiel" delektieren. Zum achten und sicher nicht letzten Mal gehen die drei Old-Boys Johnny (Zachi Noy), Benny (Yiftach Katzur) und Bobby (Jonathan Segal) auf Brautschau. Aber weil die Jagd auf die netten Girls auf Dauer die Nerven strapaziert, gibt's nur eine Möglichkeit, die Mädchen müssen selbst kommen. Und was wäre als zärtliche Falle besser geeignet als eine Bar.

Ein entsprechendes Lokal – ideal am Strand gelegen – ist bald gefunden. Jetzt muß nur noch der Besitzer überredet werden, sein okay zu geben. Wozu der gute Mann auch bereit ist, nur muß der Barbesitzer in spe auch sein Schwiegersohn werden, und die Tochter ist leider nicht gerade ein Wonnemäuschen.

Es kommt zu vielen Mißverständnissen, Hektik, Trubel und Liebeleien, bis schließlich jeder die „Richtige" hat und einem Happyend nichts im Weg steht... wenn es da nicht eine wilde Rokkerbande gäbe, die auf die neuen Barbesitzer gar nicht gut zu sprechen ist.
Unsere drei Freunde haben alle Mühe, aus diesem chaotischen Abenteuer unbeschadet herauszukommen, denn es geht wieder einmal rund, am Strand und bei den schönen Mädchen.

EIS AM STIEL VIII
(Lemon Popsicle 8) BRD/Israel 1988 (ca. 90 Min.) Regie: Reinhard Schwabenitzky/Kamera: Karl Kases
Mit: Sissi Liebold, Sonja Martin, Sibylle Rauch, Sally Cooke, Elfi Eschke, uam.
Kinostart: 18. August 1988

'This summer, fans of lighter and looser cinema entertainment can enjoy *Lemon Popsicle*. For the eighth and surely not the last time, the three old boys go looking for girls. But hunting indefinitely for nice girls strains the nerves, so there's only one way, the girl must come herself. And what would be better suited to do this than a bar...

'There are many misunderstandings, hustle, bustle and flirtations... Our three friends all have trouble coming out of this chaotic adventure unscathed, as once again it revolves around the beach and beautiful girls.'

STRAND Stiel

ZUM AUSSCHNEIDEN UND SAMMELN!

ICH RETTE POLLY – UND DU KÜMMERST DICH UM DIE JUNGS MIT DEN MOFAS DA VORNE...

Benny übt mit der heißesten Bewerberin den Klammerblues (l.) und ahnt noch nicht, daß schon die Rockergang anrückt, um die Bar einzuäschern

O JOHNNY, MEIN DICKER, KLEINER WONNEPROPPEN – LIEBST DU MICH WIRKLICH?

Johnny ist der verschreckten Polly nachgerannt, um sie vor dem Sturz von den Klippen zu bewahren – Er kommt spät – aber nicht zu spät

15 x EIS AM STIEL FÜRS OHR!

POP/Rocky verlost Super-Soundtracks zur Serie: Schreibt unter dem Stichwort „Lollipop" an POP/Rocky, Werinherstr. 71, D-8000 München 90. Es gibt zehn Alben und zehn Cassetten zu gewinnen. Der Rechtsweg ist ausgeschlossen. Leser in Österreich können aus rechtlichen Gründen nicht teilnehmen! Wer kein Glück hat, kann LP oder MC bei der edel Company, Postfach 520151, D-2000 Hamburg 52 bestellen. Viel Glück!

SUMMERTIME-BLUES — 8. TEIL

Johnny (Zachi Noy), Bobby (Jonathan Sagall), Benny (Jesse Katzur)

NEUES Film-PROGRAMM Nr. 8867

EIS AM STIEL 8. TEIL SUMMERTIME BLUES

Liebe, Leiden, Lollipop
Eis am Stiel

1978 lief auf der Berlinale ein Beitrag, welcher der bis dato erfolgreichste israelische Film werden sollte. Er bildete den Auftakt zu einer mehrteiligen Kinoreihe in deutsch-israelischer Gemeinschaftsproduktion. Heiße Musik und nackte Haut, kongenial auf Partys und am Strand in Szene gesetzt, waren auch in den 80er Jahren angesagte, aber weitgehend unter der Decke gehaltene Themen. Noch Jahre später lockten sie Jugendliche klammheimlich vor die Fernseher. „Das ‚erste Mal' war nie witziger als mit ‚Eis am Stiel'", stellt dann auch der Begleittext in den Inlays der DVD-Edition fest.

Zu den ungewöhnlich melancholischen Klängen von Bobby Vintons „Mr. Lonely" verlässt ein enttäuschter Teenager eine Party, auf der ihm das Schwofen nicht vergönnt gewesen ist, und geht die Straße hinunter. Der „einsame Soldat" hat seiner Traumfrau auf ihrer Geburtsparty ein Geschenk samt Gravur ihres Namens machen wollen, sie aber in der Küche in inniger Umklammerung mit seinem besten Freund erwischt, der sie erst geschwängert und danach fallengelassen hat, wohingegen er sich um sie kümmerte und ihr geliehenes Geld zur Abwicklung einer Abtreibung zur Verfügung stellte. Diese Schlussszene muss bekannt sein, um aus heutiger Sicht verstehen zu können, warum der Trailer zu „Eis am Stiel" den Film als „Lustspiel" beschreibt, bei dem sowohl gelacht als auch geweint werden könne. Die meisten Zuschauer haben die Reihe vermutlich als eher lustig denn traurig in Erinnerung. Des Rätsels Lösung führt letztlich zum Regisseur.

Der Erfinder von „Eis am Stiel" ist Boaz Davidson, geboren in Tel-Aviv im November 1943. Laut seiner Aussage basieren die Filme auf seinen persönlichen Erfahrungen, die er als Teenager im Israel der späten 50er Jahre gemacht hat. Bis Teil vier führte er Regie und betätigte sich zudem als Co-Autor, für Teil fünf steuerte er lediglich das Drehbuch bei. Der traurige Schluss von Teil eins sei „im Film, weil er sich so ereignet hat", gab er 1978 in einem Interview an.

Die Handlungen der Filme drehen sich auch in den weiteren Teilen von „Eis am Stiel" meistens um komplizierte Liebschaften des empfindsamen und notorisch klammen Benny (Jesse Katzur). Ihm zur Seite steht seine resolute Mutter Sonya (Dvora Kedar), die ihrem Sohn schon mal ohne Wissen ihres Mannes Romek Geld zusteckt – aber auch das Nachbarkind mit Eiern bewerfen kann, wenn ihr dessen Geigengefiedel auf die Nerven geht. Mehrere Szenen spielen in Bennys Elternhaus in oftmals geselliger Verwandtenrunde.

Das Aushängeschild und Gesicht der Reihe ist aber eindeutig „der kleine, clevere Dicke". Das dürfte daran liegen, dass Johnny (Zachi Noy) in den Filmen eine ähnlich sympathische Rolle des Pechvogels wie Donald Duck in Entenhausen zufällt: Alles, was er in Sachen Amore anpackt, geht schief, und irgendwann erwartet dies das Publikum auch: So landet er in zahlreichen Verwechslungsszenen in Erwartung seiner Freundin im Bett von Bennys Mutter oder gerät beim Klavierunterricht unter den strengen Augen einer Beethoven-Büste nicht etwa an die nymphomanische Lehrerin, sondern an ihre Schwester. Klar, dass er bei Versuchen dieser Art viel einstecken muss.

Dabei ist der korpulente Johnny aber eigentlich immer perfekt vorbereitet, wenn er das andere Geschlecht in Angriff nimmt: Er hat stets

Pariser bei sich, kämmt sich die Haare, bevor er ein Mädchen anspricht, und verfügt über ein ansehnliches Repertoire an flotten Sprüchen (à la „Ich hab mit meinem schon Preise gewonnen, da hast du noch beidhändig gepullert"). Darüber hinaus entwickelt er als einziger der Jungs frühzeitig Geschäftssinn, indem er minutiös die Schulden seiner Freunde bei ihm protokolliert, eine „Datenbank" an Damen für gewisse Stunden führt, Motorradrennen inklusive eigenen Wettbüros veranstaltet und den Kofferraum seines Autos als Liebeslaube vermietet. In „Summertime Blues" schwingt er sich im Kampf gegen eine Motorrad-Gang zum Geschäftsführer einer Bar auf, um das schöne Geschlecht gewissermaßen in die eigenen vier Wände zu locken. Dass sich dabei „Bayerns hügeligster Exportartikel" Sybille Rauch als Eva erfolgreich um einen Personalposten ausgerechnet bei Bennys und Johnnys Freund bewirbt, dem Schönling Bobby, überrascht nicht. Am Ende findet Johnny möglicherweise sein persönliches Happy End mit dem einstigen „hässlichen Vogel mit Brille" und Opern-Fan Polly Braun, die eigentlich die zentrale Person des achten und letzten Films darstellt. Gespielt wird sie von Elfi Eschke, die mit Regisseur Reinhard Schwabenitzky, ihrem heutigen Ehemann, auch in zwei Didi-Hallervorden-Filmen zusammenarbeitete. Dass „Summertime Blues" der „Eis am Stiel"-Reihe zugeschlagen wurde, erfuhr Schwabenitzky nebenbei erst am Abend der Deutschland-Premiere, als er durchs Fenster seiner Limousine erstmalig die Werbeplakate zu sehen bekam …

Der Dritte im Bunde des Freundestrios ist bereits erwähnter Frauenschwarm Bobby, der nicht völlig zu Unrecht während seines Wehrdiensts (Teil vier, „Hasenjagd") von Unteroffizier Ramirez (Josef Shiolach) den Spitznamen „Elvis Presley" verpasst bekommt. Mit der Treue nimmt er es nicht so genau. Außerdem knackt er Autos, um seine gerade aktuelle Freundin ausfahren zu können, und hat Sex, während seine beiden Gefährten unter dem Bett und im Schrank feststecken. In Teil fünf simuliert er außerdem das Ertrinken im Meer, um sich von der Aushilfsbademeisterin beatmen lassen zu können („Ich wette, die hat meine Zunge im Hals, bevor es dunkel wird"), und besteht eine Mutprobe an einem Abgrund während eines Motorradrennens in den Dünen. Als er mitbekommt, dass seine jüngere Schwester sich mit Benny trifft, verprügelt er ihn. In Teil sechs, „Ferienliebe", der auf einem Kreuzfahrtschiff spielt, taucht er einmalig in einem „Eis am Stiel"-Film nicht auf, da er Urlaub in Amerika macht. Der wahre Hintergrund seiner Abwesenheit war ein Streit von Darsteller Jonathan Segal, im Privatleben bekennender Homosexueller, mit Regisseur Dan Wolman.

Auf ihrer Jagd nach der holden Weiblichkeit sind die drei Jungs auch über das sich konstant durch die Reihe ziehende Schauen durch Gucklöcher in Umkleide- und Duschkabinen hinaus wahrlich keine Kinder von Traurigkeit: Sie befestigen Spiegel an ihren Schuhen, um dadurch den Slip von Mitschülerinnen und Lehrerinnen sehen zu können, schleichen ohne zu zahlen in ein Kino, fangen sich bei einer Prostituierten Filzläuse ein und klauen Leergut vom Hinterhof eines Lebensmittelgeschäfts, um es dort wieder abzugeben. Von den Schauspielern der alten Besetzung spielte 2001 in einer Neuverfilmung nur noch Zachi Noy mit, der sich frühzeitig dazu bekannt hatte, es als angenehm zu empfinden, über seine Rolle berühmt geworden zu sein – auch wenn er das Schicksal vieler Kollegen teilte, auf diese eine festgelegt zu werden.

Kein Artikel über „Eis am Stiel" wäre indes vollständig, wenn er die wichtige Rolle des Soundtracks ausblenden würde. Little Richards "Long Tall Sally" steht am Anfang der flotten Auftaktszene des ersten Werks, das nicht von ungefähr als Film über „Liebe, Freundschaft und peppige Musik" beworben wurde. In diesem Zusammenhang muss auch der Name Jack Fishman erwähnt werden. Der Filmkomponist zeichnete als „music supervisor" verantwortlich und bewies durch seine Auswahl nachdrücklich, dass es bei Musikempfehlungen um mehr als Computer-Arithmetik geht. Zahlreiche Rock'n'Roll-Klassiker von "Lollipop" über "Be Bop A Lula" bis "Let's Twist Again" verleihen den zugegebenermaßen intellektuell nicht gerade stimulierenden Plots Tempo und prägen diese vielleicht noch stärker als die Akteure. Dass es in den Filmen womöglich nicht um einzelne Charaktere, sondern um ein Lebensgefühl geht, könnten einstweilige Änderungen an den Namen der Hauptfiguren (außer Benny) beweisen. Musikalisch dürfen Stehblues-Begleitungen, oftmals einleuchtend mit weiblichen Vornamen versehen ("Hey Paula", "Tell Laura I Love Her"), natürlich auch nicht fehlen. Besonders charmant ist es, wenn ein Song genau so wie die aktuell Angebetene heißt ("Tammy", "Ginny Come Lately"). Trotzdem bleibt der Titel von Teil zwei eine Illusion. Eine „Feste Freundin" hätte die Fortführung der Reihe erschwert, zumal das Thema Beziehungen im Vergleich zu den Slapstickeinlagen immer weiter in den Hintergrund rückte. Außerdem wirken die Filme zunehmend so, als ob sie in den 80ern nicht nur gedreht worden wären, sondern auch dann spielen würden. Irgendwann wiederholt sich auch der dennoch stets gelungene Soundtrack, und so manche Strandszene wirkt eher wie ein überdrehter Eis-Werbespot. Einmal fällt sogar der im Lichte der 50er Jahre sinnfreie Name „E.T."

Die acht Teile sind digital remastert und in voller Länge auf einer DVD-Box erhältlich, die ersten beiden obendrein als Super8-Versionen. In älteren Versionen geschnittene Szenen, die nachträglich eingefügt worden sind, liegen allerdings nicht mit deutschem Ton vor. Komplettsammler müssten sich darüber hinaus eine VHS-Kassette besorgen: Von „Hasenjagd" existiert über Johnnys Militärdienst ein zweiter Teil (!), gewissermaßen „4b". Zachi Noy und Sybille Rauch, die 1981 übrigens auch in „Lass laufen, Kumpel!" der Ruhrpott-Sex-Klamauk-Reihe gemeinsam auftraten, stehen im Mittelpunkt des unter der Regie von Siggi Schissel gedrehten Films. Er ist in der besagten Box allerdings nicht enthalten.

Thorsten Pöttger

Ophelia Shtruhl in *Lemon Popsicle*

Dafna Armoni in *Going Steady*

Orna Dagan in *Hot Bubblegum*

Bea Fiedler in *Private Popsicle*

Bea Fiedler in *Baby Love*

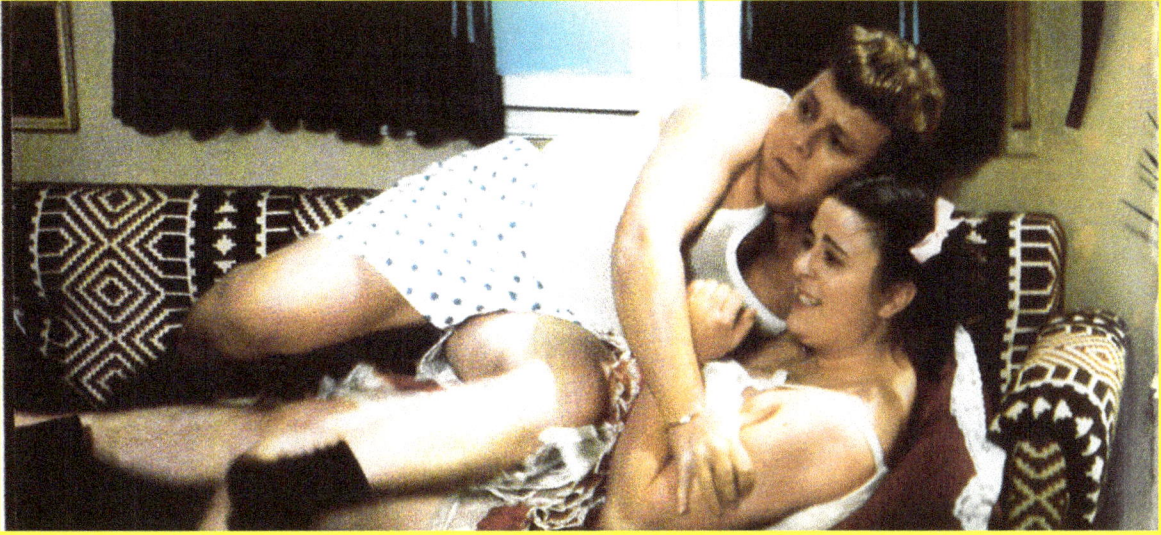
Alexandra Kaster in *Up Your Anchor*

Sibylle Rauch in *Young Love*

Eva Astor in *Young Love*

Sissi Pitz in *Summertime Blues*

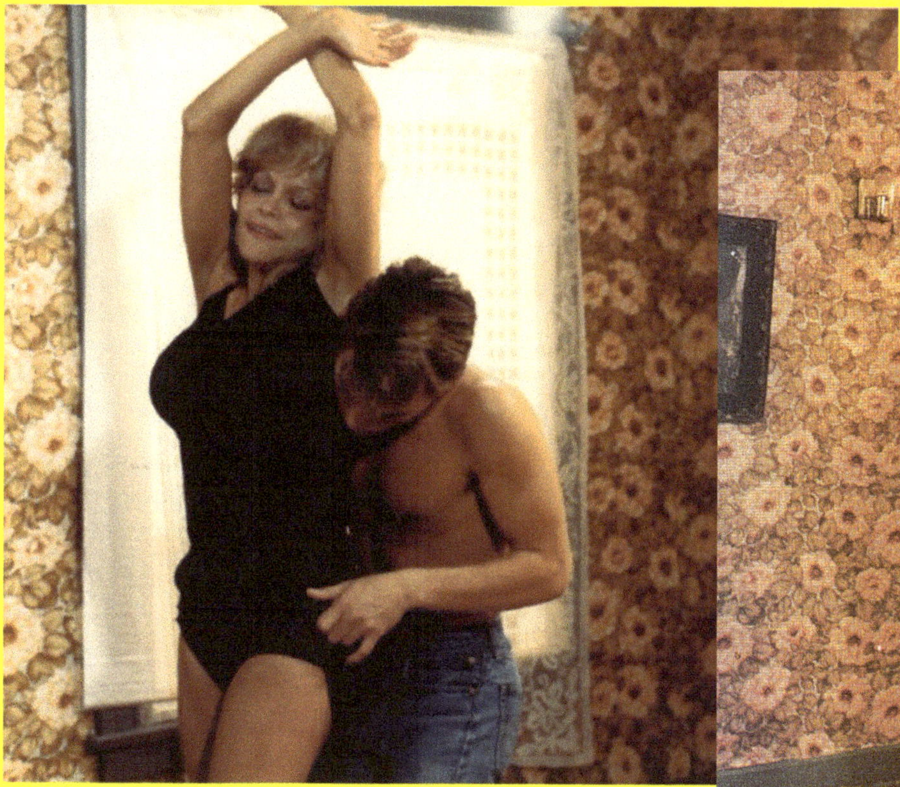

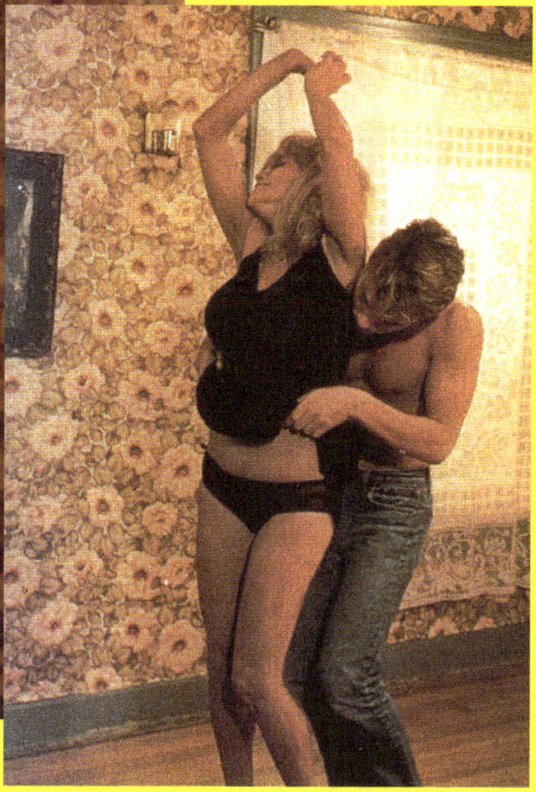

Louisa Moritz in *The Last American Virgin*

Die letzte AMERIKANISCHE JUNGFRAU

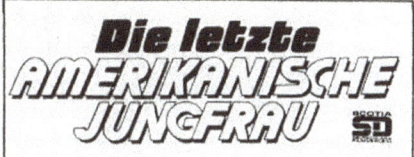

Nancy Brock in The *Last American Virgin*

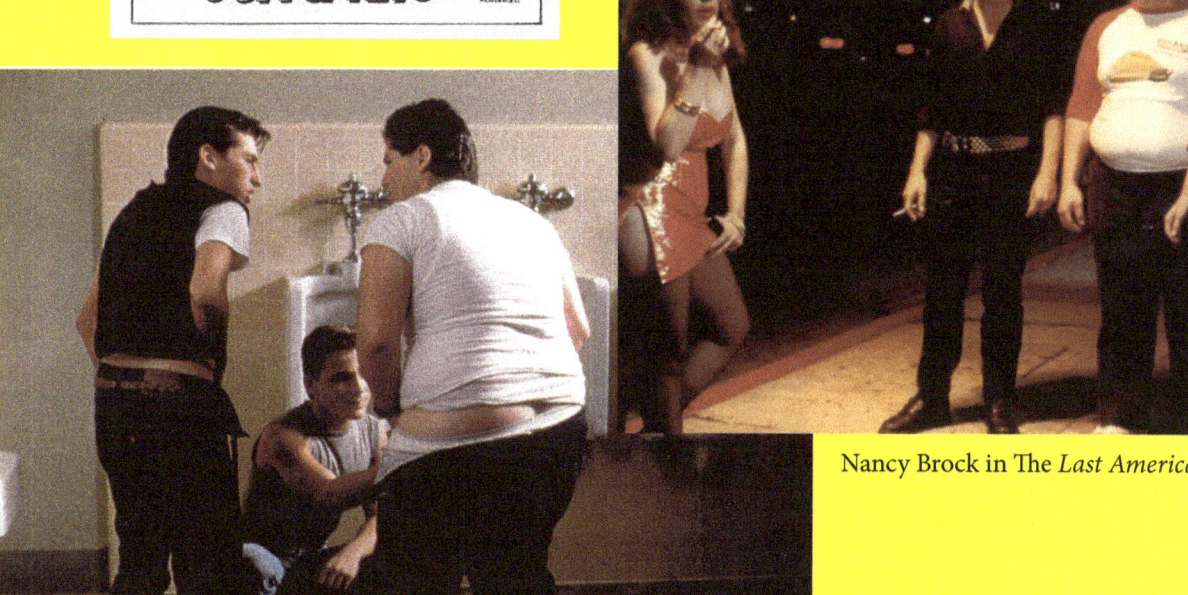

Home Movie Releases
Super 8mm

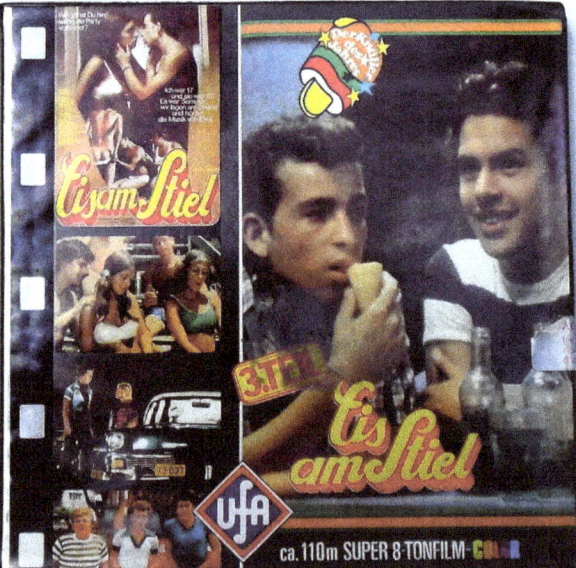

The first home movie releases of the *Lemon Popsicle* films were on the Super 8mm film format in Germany in 1979. Forty-five-minute edits of *Lemon Popsicle* and *Going Steady* were released in three parts each running about fifteen minutes. The following year, the same company, UFA, released the complete films on video tape. The strangest scene in the *Lemon Popsicle* series comes in *Up Your Anchor,* when the boys screen the Super 8mm version of *Lemon Popsicle* and watch themselves!

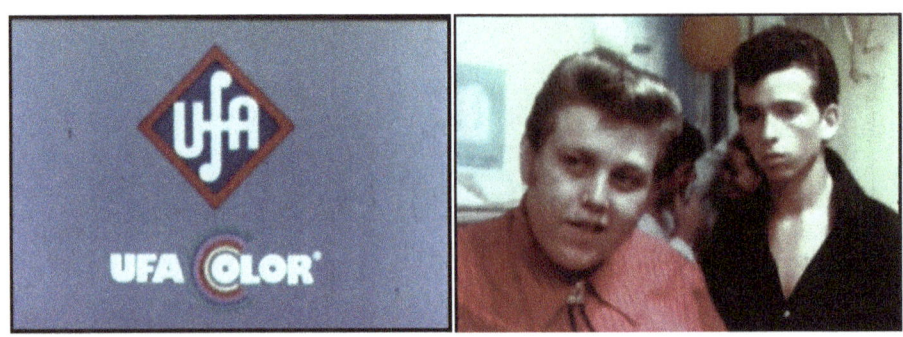

Video

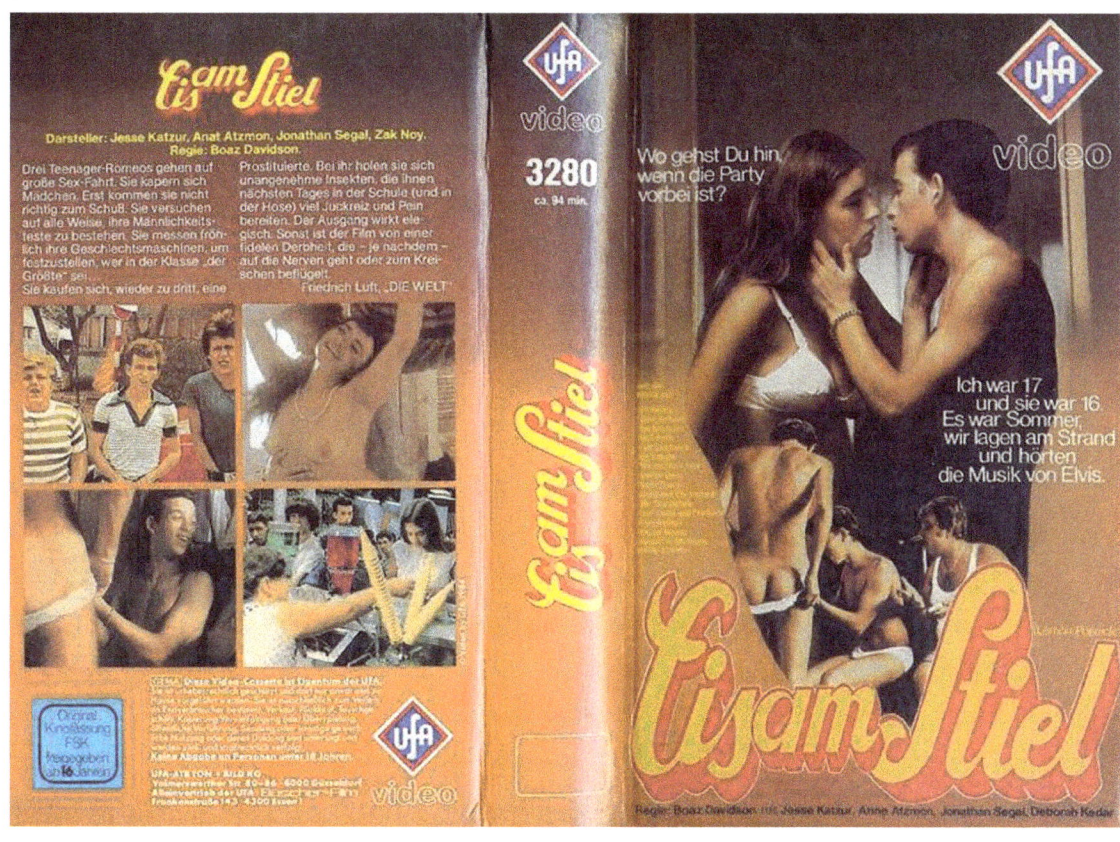

The first release of *Lemon Popsicle* on video tape was by UFA in Germany in 1980

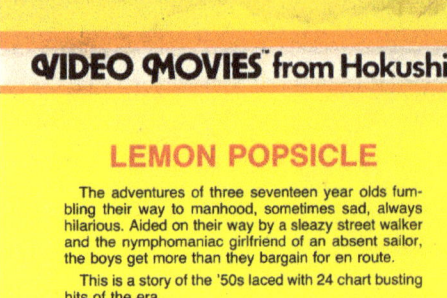
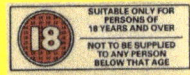

In the UK, *Lemon Popiscle* was released on VHS, Betamax and V2000 in February 1981.

Italian VHS for *Private Popsicle 2* with a more than bizarre title curiously written in English!

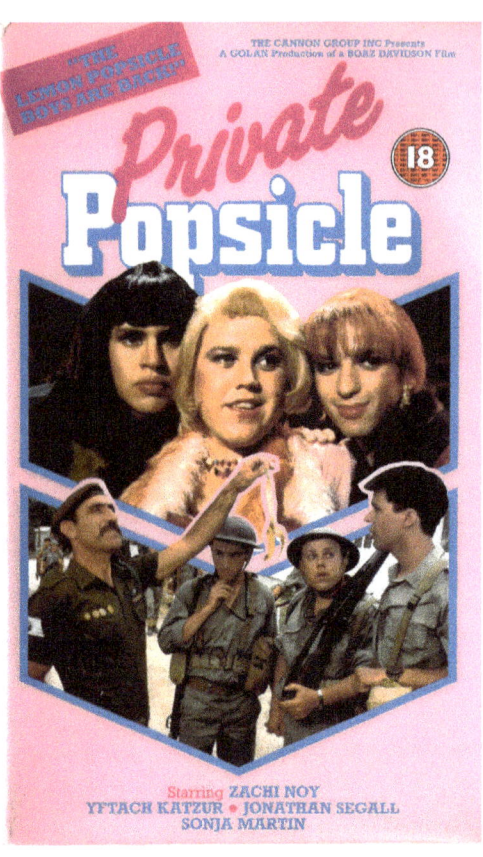

Out of school for the summer — and into mischief again — those three rascals, Benji, Bobby and Huey are spending their holiday concentrating on their two main obsessions — motorcycles and the fairer sex!
Benji is particularly smitten by Bobby's kid sister and his interest in her threatens to break up the boys' friendship. Benji thinks Gili is old enough, Bobby thinks she's too young and Huey has to step in as referee.
Benji's baby love will make this an unforgettable vacation — and the funniest "Popsicle" so far!

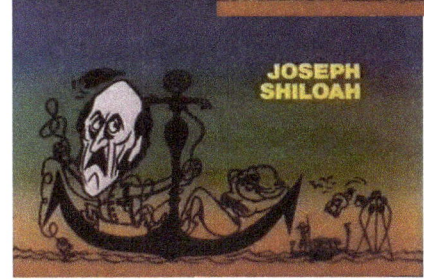

VHS grabs of caricatures in the title sequence of the English print.

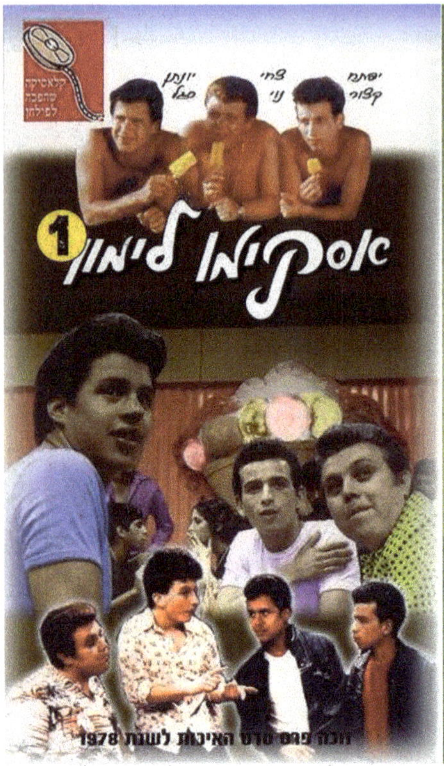

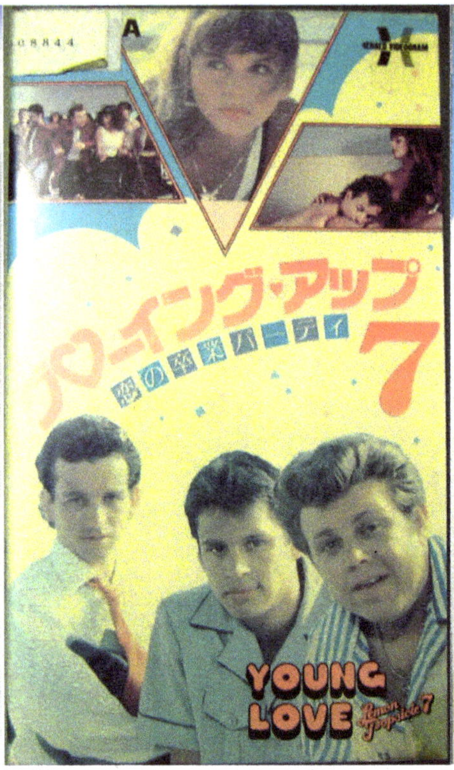

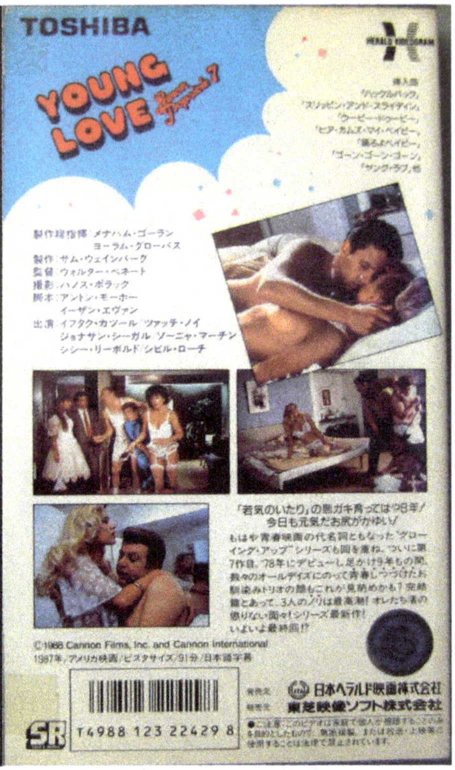

TV Screenings

The closest the films have come to playing on the British network TV channels is a VHS box of *Lemon Popsicle* appearing as set dressing in the first episode of *Game On* in 1995. *Lemon Popsicle* made its UK TV debut on the cable channel, Bravo TV, playing eight times between 4th May 2000 and 17th October 2000.

In Germany, the films are a staple on regional and national channels:

Komödien-Serie
Mit David Faustino
18.00 Elf 99
18.45 RTL aktuell
19.15 Explosiv – Das Magazin
19.45 Gute Zeiten, schlechte Zeiten
Mit Andreas Elsholz & Sandra Keller
20.15 Die Heimatmelodie
21.10 Sylter Geschichten
Start einer neuen deutschen Serie
22.15 Eis am Stiel I
Israel. Komödie (1977)
0.00 Kesse Teens - Die erste Liebe
Erotikfilm

21.50 Die Frau ohne Gedächtnis
US-Krimi (1976)
23.05 Crime Story

MTV
13.00 VJ Simone
16.00 Greatest Hits
17.00 Coca-Cola Report
17.15 At the Movies
17.30 News at Night
17.45 3 fom1
18.00 The Soul of MTV
18.30 Prime
20.00 Dial MTV
20.30 Most wanted
22.00 Greatest Hits
23.00 Coca-Cola Report
23.15 At the Movies

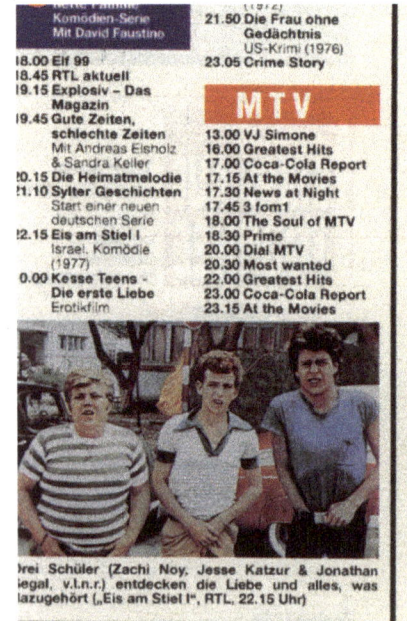

Drei Schüler (Zachi Noy, Jesse Katzur & Jonathan Segal, v.l.n.r.) entdecken die Liebe und alles, was dazugehört („Eis am Stiel I", RTL, 22.15 Uhr)

(Wdh.)
15.20 Remington Steele
16.10 Mr. Belvedere
16.35 Bezaubernde Jeannie
17.05 Trick 7
18.25 Herzbube mit zwei Damen
18.55 Unser lautes Heim
19.25 Roseanne
20.00 Nachrichten
20.15 Belizaire – Der Cajun
US-Western (1985)
Mit Armand Assante
22.20 Mancuso FBI
Mit Robert Loggia
23.15 Duell der Giganten
Chin. Actionfilm (1977)

23.50 Werbetrommel

MTV
13.00 VJ Simone
16.00 Greatest Hits
17.00 Coca-Cola Report
17.15 At the Movies
17.30 News at Night
17.45 3 fom1
18.00 The Pulse with Swatch
Designer-Mode
18.30 Prime
20.00 Dial MTV
20.30 Most wanted
22.00 Greatest Hits
23.00 Coca-Cola Report
23.15 At the Movies

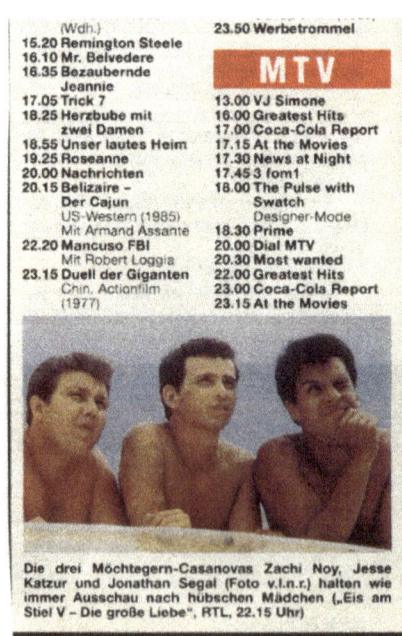

Die drei Möchtegern-Casanovas Zachi Noy, Jesse Katzur und Jonathan Segal (Foto v.l.n.r.) halten wie immer Ausschau nach hübschen Mädchen („Eis am Stiel V – Die große Liebe", RTL, 22.15 Uhr)

14.40 Love Boat (Serie)
15.30 Verliebt in eine Hexe
Familien-Serie
16.05 Rauchende Colts
Western-Serie
17.10 Nachbarn (Serie)
17.50 Ein Duke kommt selten allein
Action-Serie
19.05 Glücksrad
Quiz-Show
20.00 T. J. Hooker
Krimi-Serie
21.00 Kid Blue
Spielfilm
22.55 Erben des Fluchs
Krimi-Serie
23.45 Stunde der Filmemacher
Filmgeschichte(n)
0.00 Bettgeflüster bei Kanal 4
0.10 Tanz auf Kanal 4

14.05 Yesterday (Wdh.)
15.05 P.O.P. (Wdh.)
16.05 Start (Wdh.)
17.00 Cartoons
17.35 bim bam bino
Kinderprogramm
17.50 Die Schlümpfe
Zeichentrick
18.15 bim bam bino
18.20 Cartoons
19.15 Fashion Affairs
Familien-Serie
19.40 Ruck Zuck
Spielshow
20.15 30 Grad Minus
Franz. Spielfilm
22.25 Nachtstreife
Krimi-Serie
23.20 Heldentaten (Wdh.)
0.05 Cinemathek (Wdh.)
1.05 Zia
Konzert/Südafrik. Gruppe

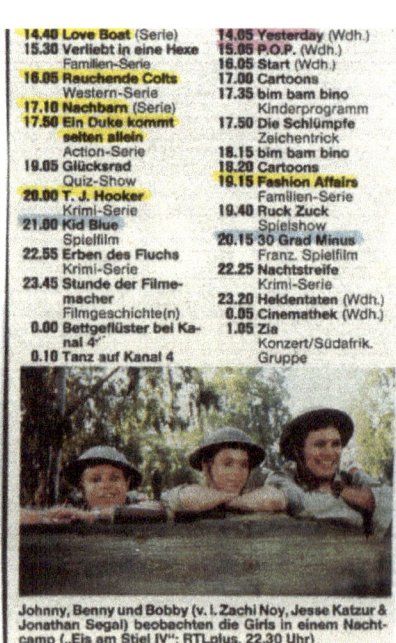

Johnny, Benny und Bobby (v. l. Zachi Noy, Jesse Katzur & Jonathan Segal) beobachten die Girls in einem Nachtcamp („Eis am Stiel IV"; RTLplus, 22.30 Uhr)

'Fumbles, Flirtations and Holidays. With teenage hormones going berserk, *Lemon Popsicle* Movie Night is taking the viewers back to the 1950s. Summer, sun, Rock 'n' Roll and scantily clad beauties on the beach of Tel Aviv. "A film about love and upbeat music", it said euphorically in the 1978 cinema trailers. RTL Nitro have a threesome available for all fans of the cult *Lemon Popsicle* series.'

DVD The first DVD release was in Germany. All eight films (with *Guru Jakob* as an extra) were released in mostly cut versions in a box-set on 4th September 2004. This release was quickly followed by better releases in Japan and Israel (August 2005). The Israeli release extras included an unsubtitled commentary by Yoram Globus and Eli Tabor, an eight-minute from-the-set documentary, and a newly filmed reunion of the stars visiting Zachi Noy and his basement filled with *Lemon Popsicle* memorabilia.

Noy: "In Russia, it is incredibly successful. Today in each house in Russia you will find, in one drawer, the Bible and in the second drawer, *Eskimo Limon*!"

Katzur: "What is the Russian title?"

Noy: "*Shvedna Rozinka*. It's like *Hot Bubblegum*. It looks like they took it from our third movie and translated it to Russian. Every immigrant from Russia who comes to Israel got his impression of Israel through *Eskimo Limon*. That's why they come here because they see beautiful girls and lots of joy."

Katzur: "We came to this, that we are increasing immigration to Israel. Israel received how many? More than a million Russian immigrants because of *Eskimo Limon* and Zachi Noy!"

Noy: "In Europe, they launched an eight-pack DVD in German called *Eis Am Stiel,* which means 'Popsicle on a Stick'. This pack is sold for 80 Euros, from which we don't see a nickel so far, but maybe we will get some in the future."

Sagall: "WOW! The temple of Zachi. WOW! He is a Star!

An English-dubbed version of *Going Steady* was released on DVD in the States on the Substance label in 2006. The first time the films were released with English dubbing was the Hungarian DVD releases supervised by Karsten Kwyas in 2007. Kwayas also supervised the 16x9 anamorphic mastering and the Dolby Digital 2.0 for the second release of the films on DVD in Germany. That edition included the Super 8mm film versions among the extras.

The first British releases on DVD reached the shops in December 2008 and was a box set by Blackhorse Entertainment containing the first seven films. Alas they were mastered in the then outdated 4:3 format and only in 1.0 mono. A second, improved but still unsatisfactory, British release came in September 2010 on the esteemed Arrow label. A company executive told me: "Arrow did issue the original series on DVD in frankly appalling editions a long while back (way before my time). They were sourced from tape masters complete with dropouts, warps and the rest - as though they'd gotten hold of ancient ex-rental copies and transferred those to disc! I suspect it'd be a case of waiting for quality masters to be made, much as we did with the US remake, *The Last American Virgin*, which did much better than expected on blu-ray. (And prompted us to also release *Porky's*, which then did much, much worse than expected!). But it's an interesting series, especially for the insights into Golan and Globus' early years."

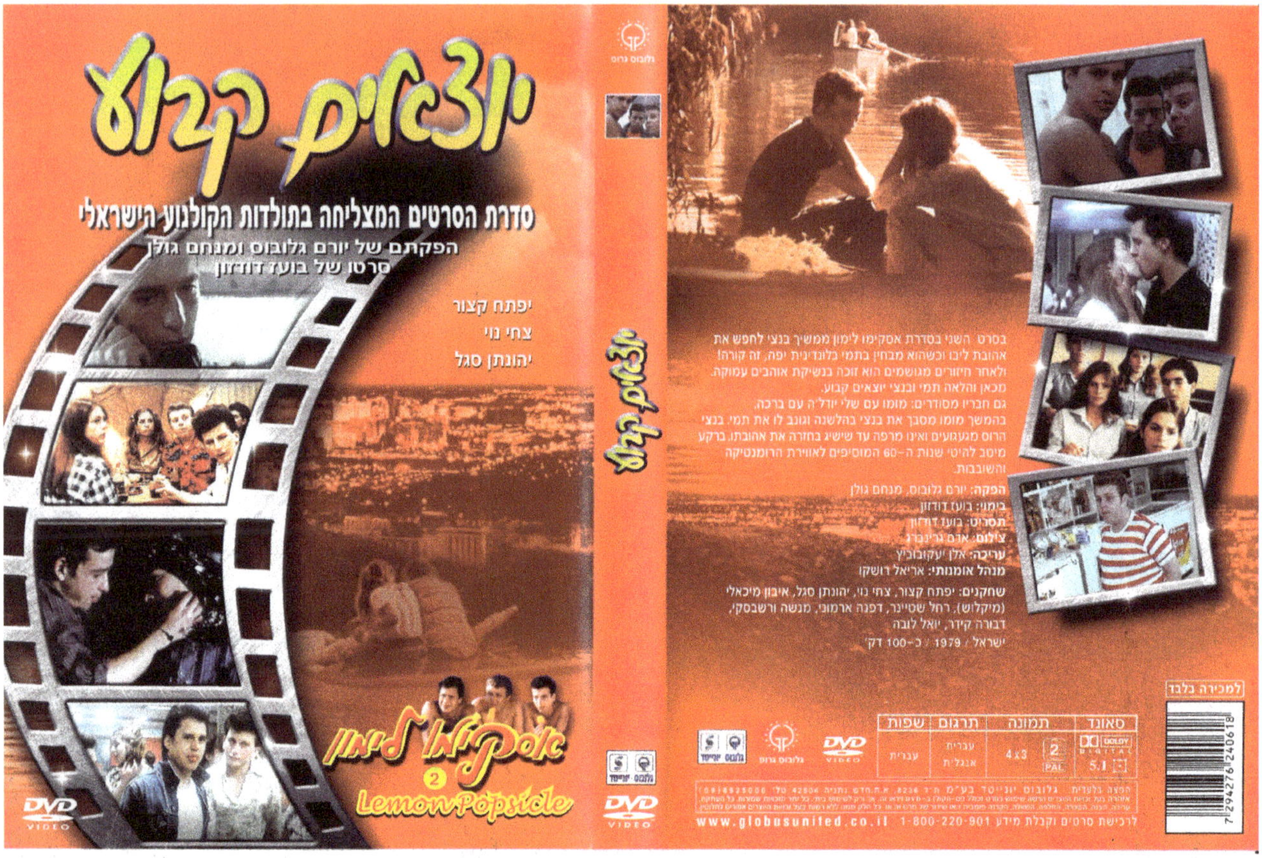

יוצאים קבוע
סדרת הסרטים המצליחה בתולדות הקולנוע הישראלי
הפקתם של יורם גלובוס ומנחם גולן
סרטו של בועז דודזון
יפתח קצור
צחי נוי
יהונתן סגל
אסקימו לימון 2
Lemon Popsicle
בסרט השני בסדרת אסקימו לימון ממשיך בנצי לחפש את אהובת ליבו וכשהוא מבחין בתמי בלונדינית יפה, זה קורה! ולאחר חיזורים מגושמים הוא זוכה בנשיקת אוהבים עמוקה. מכאן והלאה תמי ובנצי יוצאים קבוע.
גם חבריו מסודרים: מומו עם שלי יודל'ה עם ברכה.
בהמשך מומו מסבך את בנצי בהלשנה וגונב לו את תמי. בנצי הרוס מגעגועים ואינו מרפה עד שישיג בחזרה את אהובתו. ברקע מיטב להיטי שנות ה-60 המוסיפים לאווירת הרומנטיקה והשובבות.
הפקה: יורם גלובוס, מנחם גולן
בימוי: בועז דודזון
תסריט: בועז דודזון
צילום: אדם גרינברג
עריכה: אלן יעקובוביץ
מנהל אומנותי: אריאל רושקו
שחקנים: יפתח קצור, צחי נוי, יהונתן סגל, איבון מיכאלי (מיקלוש), רחל שטיינר, דפנה ארמוני, מנשה ורשבסקי, דבורה קידר, יואל לובה
ישראל / 1979 / כ-100 דק'
סאונד
תמונה
תרגום
שפות
עברית
אנגלית
עברית
4x3
5.1
למכירה בלבד
www.globusunited.co.il

BOAZ DAVIDSON FILMJE
FORRÓ RÁGÓGUMI
SZOKNYAVADÁSZOK
ANGYALBŐRBEN
LEMON POPSICLE – PRIVATE POPSICLE
ADS

Lemon Popsicle 5
Baby Love
18

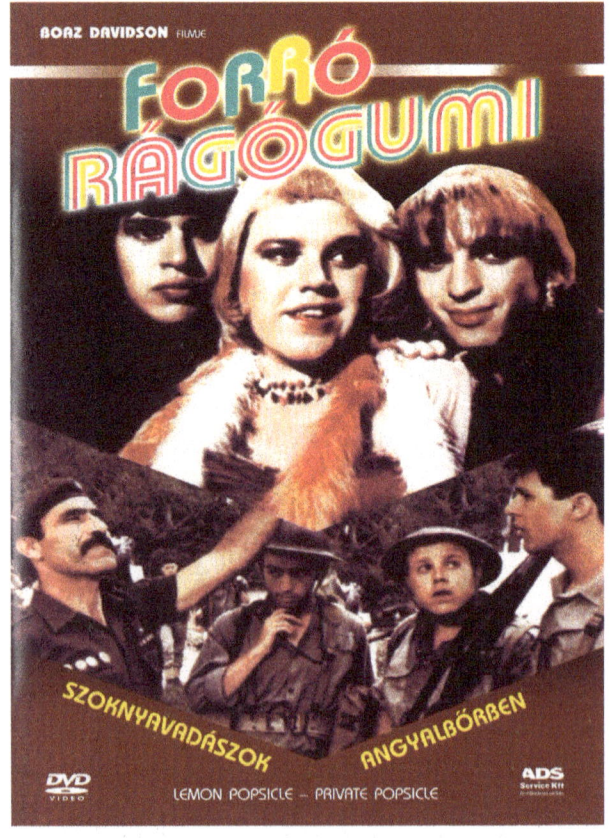

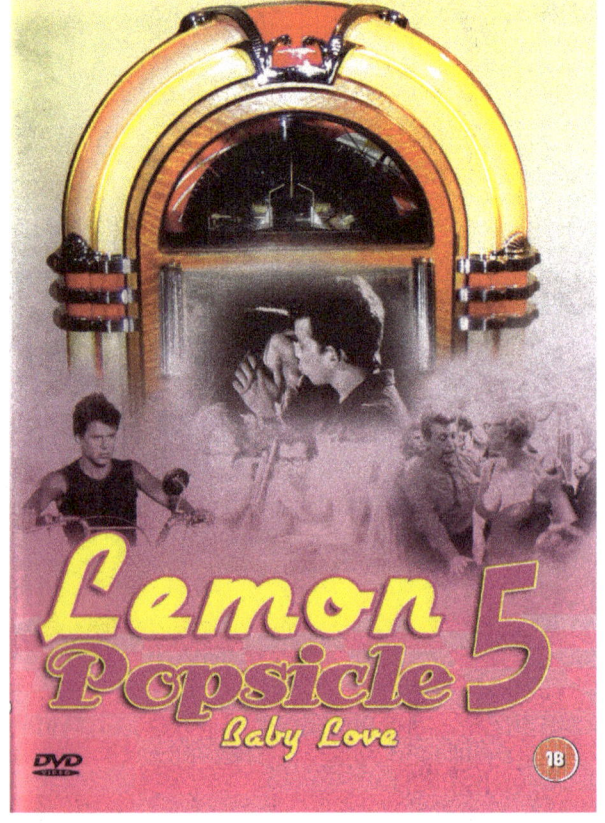

אהבה צעירה
סדרת הסרטים המצליחה בתולדות הקולנוע הישראלי
יפתח קצור
צחי נוי
יהונתן סגל
מצורף בונוס
הסרט השמיני בסדרה
"בלוז לקיץ"
אסקימו לימון
7
Lemon Popsicle
DVD

DIE GROSSE LIEBE
Eis am Stiel 5

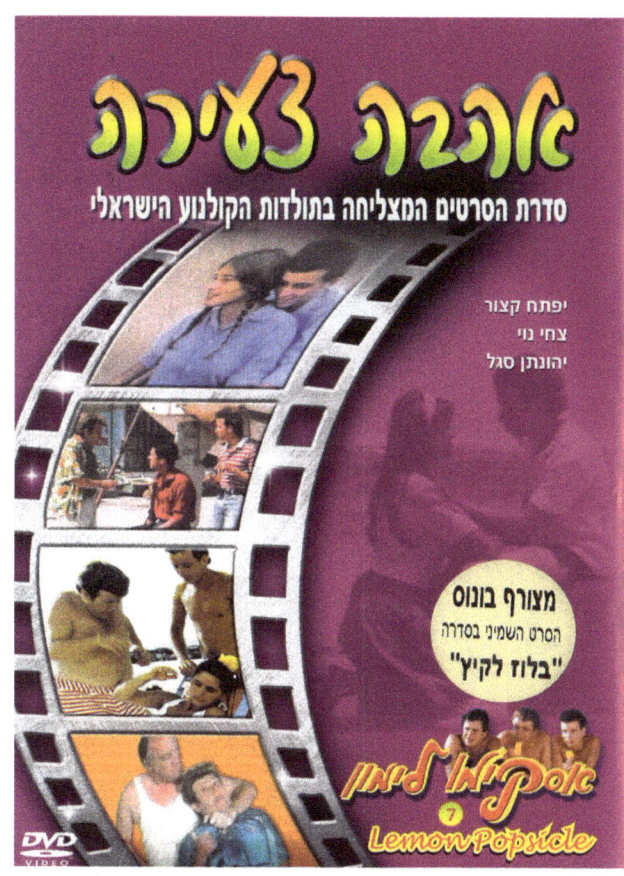

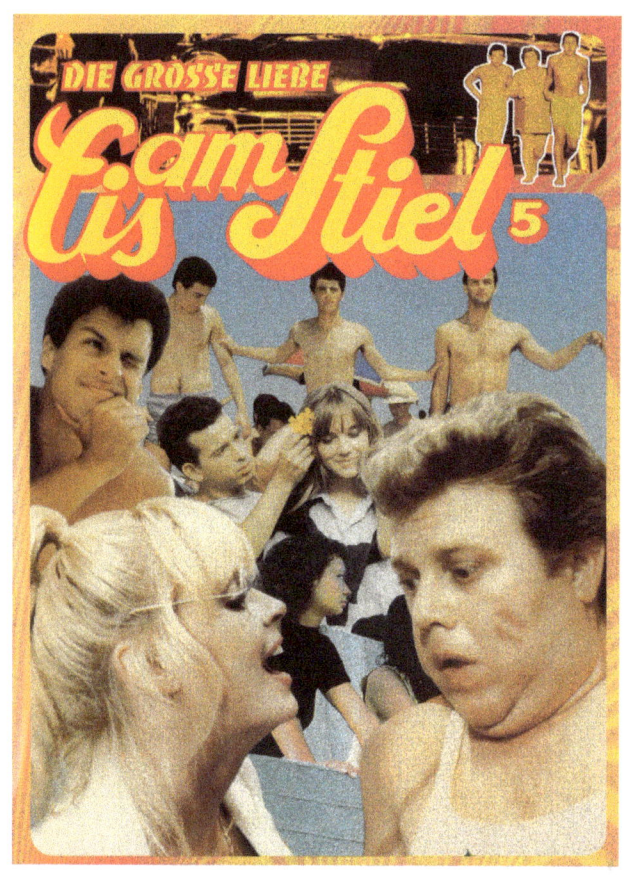

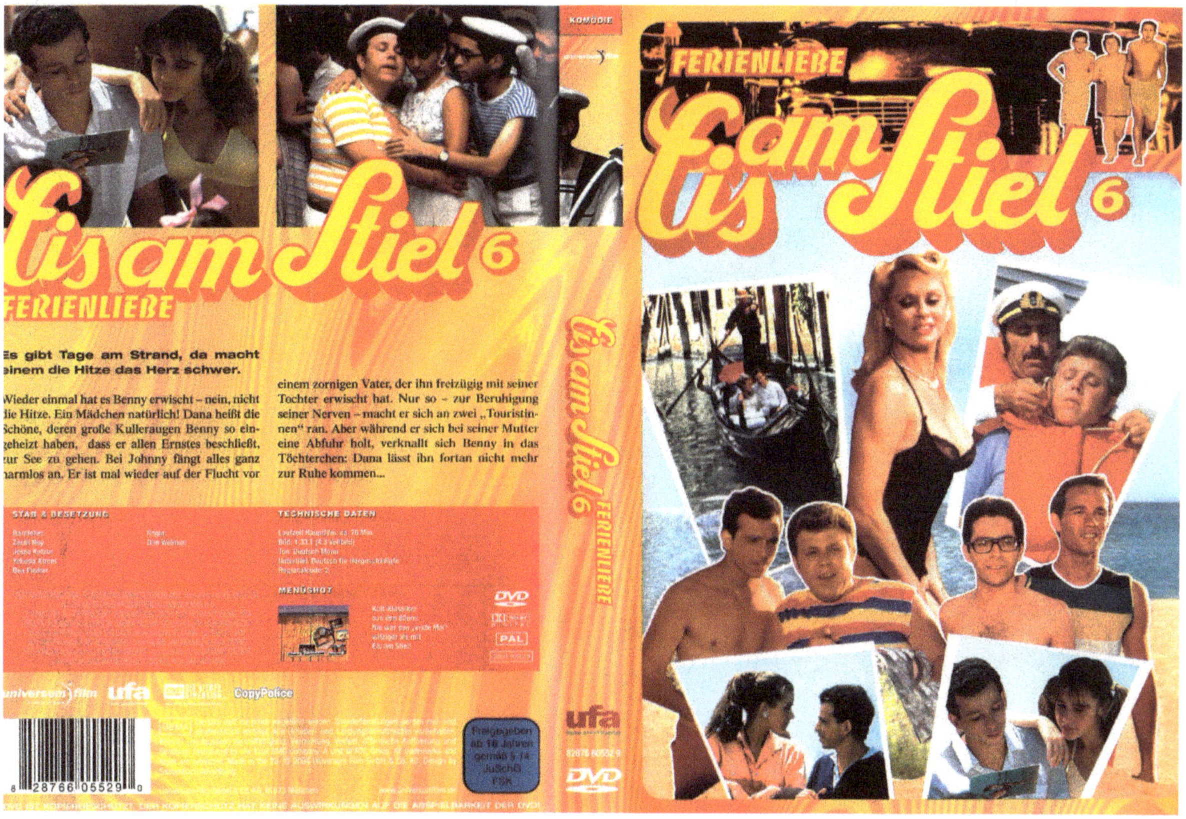
Eis am Stiel 6
FERIENLIEBE
Es gibt Tage am Strand, da macht einem die Hitze das Herz schwer.
Wieder einmal hat es Benny erwischt – nein, nicht die Hitze. Ein Mädchen natürlich! Dana heißt die Schöne, deren große Kulleraugen Benny so eingeheizt haben, dass er allen Ernstes beschließt, zur See zu gehen. Bei Johnny fängt alles ganz harmlos an. Er ist mal wieder auf der Flucht vor einem zornigen Vater, der ihn freizügig mit seiner Tochter erwischt hat. Nur so – zur Beruhigung seiner Nerven – macht er sich an zwei „Touristinnen" ran. Aber während er sich bei seiner Mutter eine Abfuhr holt, verknallt sich Benny in das Töchterchen: Dana lässt ihn fortan nicht mehr zur Ruhe kommen...
STAB & BESETZUNG
TECHNISCHE DATEN
MENÜSHOT
universum film
ufa
CopyPolice
KOMÖDIE
Eis am Stiel 6 FERIENLIEBE
DVD
PAL
ufa
DVD
FERIENLIEBE
Eis am Stiel 6

Spanish DVD

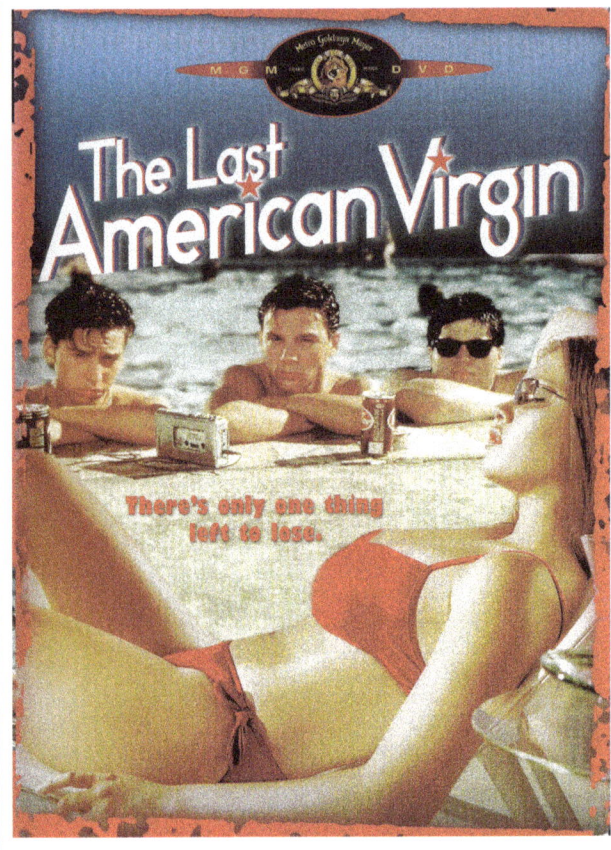

USA DVD

The first of the films to be released on Blu-ray

THE LEMON POPSICLE BOOK

© Roy Mitchell, Paul Sutton, 2016

Roy Mitchell and Paul Sutton are identified as the authors of this book.
The moral rights of the authors have been asserted.

Published by Buffalo Books
Cambridge, UK
camerajournal@yahoo.com

All rights reserved. No part of this publication may be reproduced,
stored in a retrieval system or transmitted in any form or by any means electronic,
including but not limited to photocopying, recording and print on demand,
without the prior written permission of the authors.

This book is sold subject to the condition that it shall not, by way of trade
or otherwise, be lent, re-sold, hired out or otherwise circulated without the publisher's
prior consent in any form of binding or cover other than that in which it is published.

ISBN: 978-0-9931770-6-4 (paperback)

Also by Paul Sutton:

Talking about Ken Russell
The Moving Picture Boy Gallery
The Moving Picture Girl Gallery
Six English Filmmakers
Lindsay Anderson, The Diaries
if.... A British Film Guide
Becoming Ken Russell
The Young and the Old
Understanding Gary Numan

Printed in the USA and England

www.ingramcontent.com/pod-product-compliance
Lightning Source LLC
Chambersburg PA
CBHW061925290426
44113CB00024B/2821